高职高专经济贸易类专业系列教材

外贸单证实务

主　编　姬文桂　林继玲

副主编　潘小燕　袁照稳

参　编　陈　慧　刘　琦　方慧英

　　　　李　娴　陈凯燕　徐筱然

机械工业出版社

本书以外贸流程为线索，内容涵盖外贸业务各环节所涉及单证的相关理论知识和填制方法，具体包括：国际贸易销售合同、信用证、商业发票、包装单据、保险单据、运输单据、原产地证书、报检与报关单据、汇票和其他单据等。本书有如下特色：①以同一个业务案例作为各项目的导入部分贯穿整本书，读者根据案例中的业务进展可以清楚了解整个外贸流程，同时提供案例涉及相关单证的填制范本，让读者能直观学习相关项目的知识技能；②重视实训，每个项目都配有大量实操训练，学生可边学边练；③内容新颖，所有单证范本及填制要点，已根据最新政策更新，与真实业务中的单证相符。

本书可作为高职高专商务英语、国际贸易、国际商务、报关与报检、国际货运代理、国际物流及其他经济类专业的教材，也可作为外贸企业的业务培训教材，还可作为从事相关专业的业务人员考取职业资格证书的参考用书。

图书在版编目（CIP）数据

外贸单证实务/姬文桂，林继玲主编．—北京：机械工业出版社，2019.2（2024.1重印）
高职高专经济贸易类专业系列教材
ISBN 978-7-111-61971-0

Ⅰ．①外… Ⅱ．①姬… ②林… Ⅲ．①进出口贸易—原始凭证—高等职业教育—教材 Ⅳ．①F740.44

中国版本图书馆 CIP 数据核字（2019）第 024434 号

机械工业出版社（北京市百万庄大街 22 号　邮政编码 100037）
策划编辑：孔文梅　　　　责任编辑：孔文梅　董宇佳
责任校对：黄兴伟　刘雅娜　封面设计：鞠　杨
责任印制：邓　博
北京盛通数码印刷有限公司印刷
2024 年 1 月第 1 版第 7 次印刷
184mm×260mm・10.25 印张・232 千字
标准书号：ISBN 978-7-111-61971-0
定价：35.00 元

电话服务	网络服务
客服电话：010-88361066	机 工 官 网：www.cmpbook.com
010-88379833	机 工 官 博：weibo.com/cmp1952
010-68326294	金 书 网：www.golden-book.com
封底无防伪标均为盗版	机工教育服务网：www.cmpedu.com

前言

近年来，随着我国对外开放力度的不断加大和国际贸易的不断发展，外贸人才的需求也越来越旺盛，而"外贸单证"这一课程因其实用性，一直以来都是国际贸易和商务英语专业的核心课程之一。对于高职高专院校而言，它是一门直接与岗位工作对接，帮助学生掌握外贸实操技能并考证上岗的专业技能课程。

目前，高等职业教育正处于改革的重要阶段，如何使课程建设与职业需要有效接轨，达到教育部对高职院校"促进专业与产业对接，课程内容与职业标准对接，教学过程与生产过程对接，学历证书与职业资格证书对接，职业教育与终身教育对接"的"五对接"要求，并在课程设计时充分考虑"教什么？教到什么程度？怎么教？什么时间教？在哪里教？"等问题十分关键。因为这些因素蕴含着课程理念、课程目标、课程内容、课程模式和课程的开发方式的设计，是我国高职教育改革的重点。我们编写本书正是以此为指导思想，尝试工学结合，以"学习内容就是工作任务，通过工作过程实现学习目的"的形式探索"外贸单证"课程新的教学模式——学习领域内容与工作领域内容保持一致；学习过程与工作过程保持一致；学习任务与工作任务保持一致。

本书以合作企业的外贸岗位和真实工作环节为背景，注重实际操作技能的培养和训练，要求学生在教师的指导下完成签订合同，审核信用证，填制商业发票、包装单据、保险单据、运输单据、原产地证书、报关报检单据、汇票、装船通知、受益人证明等项目工作；并通过课本练习和相关外贸软件，模拟实际工作环境与场景，最大限度地实现课堂与职业岗位的无缝对接。

具体来说，本书有以下特点：

（1）全覆盖 本书几乎包括外贸业务中所有单证及其填制流程。书中的单证完全取自实际业务，最大限度展现单证与业务的原貌，使整本书线索清晰，有明显的整体感；并以业务情景为引导，把理论讲解与业务操作相结合，实现了知识性和趣味性的有机结合。

（2）真实性 每个项目开头都以企业情景案例导入作为该项目理论知识与实操技能学习的背景依托，并以此案例业务流程贯穿全文，强调对现代国际贸易中经常使用的单证的讲解与填写训练，所述内容与国际贸易业务高度吻合。书中的单证来自现实的业务操作，且内容翔实、可操作性强，非常实用。

（3）实操性 本书理论叙述简明扼要，通俗易懂，强调学生的动手能力。单据都有填制要点指导与实例示范，简单易学；每个项目都安排了实操训练，有利于巩固所学内容。

（4）时效性　本书采用最新的单证填制规范，如"项目八　报检与报关单据"，就是以我国于2018年8月1日后实行的报关报检融合后新规范的报关单为蓝本进行填制。全书按我国各部门相关规定，选编全新题材和案例，有助于学生了解国际商务活动中的新术语、新规范和发展的新动态。

本书由姬文桂和林继玲安排策划、拟订大纲、主持编写，并负责全书的统稿与定稿。香港某公司市场部经理汤明明担任技术顾问，为本书提供实际案例与相关资料。参与本书编写、审核的教师均具有丰富的国际贸易知识和"外贸单证"课程的教学经验。具体分工如下：袁昭稳编写项目一及补充练习，姬文桂编写项目二及其他教辅资料，潘小燕编写项目三、项目四，林继玲编写项目五、项目七，刘琦编写项目六及综合实训四，袁昭稳与刘琦共同编写项目八，陈慧编写项目九，方慧英编写项目十，李娴编写综合实训一，陈凯燕编写综合实训二，徐筱然编写综合实训三。

本书在编写过程中参考了大量的资料与文献，所参阅的文献只能列出一部分，还有大量相关资料无法一一列出，在此，谨向所有使本书编者受益的作者们致以真诚的谢意。对其他相关人员也深表诚挚的谢意。特别感谢香港相关公司的鼎力支持与帮助。由于编者水平有限，书中难免有疏忽与不妥之处，恳请广大读者批评指正。

为方便教学，本书配备了电子课件等教学资源。凡选用本书作为教材的教师均可登录机械工业出版社教育服务网www.cmpedu.com免费下载。如有问题请致电010-88379375联系营销人员。也可以通过QQ进行联系，QQ：945379158。

编　者

目录

前　言

项目一　国际贸易销售合同 / 1
　　一、背景知识 / 2
　　二、认识销售合同 / 3
　　实操训练 / 10

项目二　信用证 / 13
　　一、背景知识 / 14
　　二、依据合同审核信用证 / 16
　　三、申请开立信用证 / 18
　　实操训练 / 23

项目三　商业发票 / 29
　　一、背景知识 / 30
　　二、认识发票 / 31
　　三、信用证中关于商业发票的条款举例 / 36
　　实操训练 / 38

项目四　包装单据 / 40
　　一、背景知识 / 41
　　二、认识包装单据 / 44
　　实操训练 / 47

项目五　保险单据 / 49
　　一、背景知识 / 50
　　二、认识投保单 / 54
　　三、认识保险单 / 58
　　实操训练 / 64

项目六　运输单据 / 69
　　一、背景知识 / 70
　　二、认识海上运输单据 / 72
　　三、认识航空货运单 / 82
　　实操训练 / 88

项目七　原产地证书 / 92
　　一、背景知识 / 93
　　二、认识一般原产地证书 / 97
　　三、认识普惠制原产地证书 / 102
　　实操训练 / 104

项目八　报检与报关单据 / 108
　　一、背景知识 / 109
　　二、认识报关单 / 110
　　实操训练 / 124

项目九　汇票 / 127
　　一、背景知识 / 128
　　二、认识汇票 / 130
　　实操训练 / 135

项目十　其他单据（装运通知书、受益人证明、
　　　　船公司证明等）/ 137
　　一、背景知识 / 138
　　二、认识其他单据 / 138
　　实操训练 / 144

附录 / 148
　　综合实训一　CIF 信用证项下整套单据
　　　　　　　的填制 / 148
　　综合实训二　CFR 信用证项下整套单据
　　　　　　　的填制 / 150
　　综合实训三　CIF 信用证项下整套单据
　　　　　　　的填制（全英文）/ 152
　　综合实训四　托收项下全套出口单据的
　　　　　　　填制 / 154

参考文献 / 158

项目一
Project I

国际贸易销售合同
Sales Contract

学习目标（Learning Aims）

- 了解合同成立的条件。
- 熟悉国际贸易销售合同的主要类型和相关法规。
- 掌握国际贸易销售合同主要条款的表述规范。

情景导入（Lead-in Situation）

我国科林国际贸易（香港）有限公司【Kelin International Trading (HK) Co., Ltd，以下简称科林国际贸易公司】与美国环球采购服务有限公司（Globe Sourcing Service Co., Ltd，以下简称环球采购公司）在经过多次交易磋商后对纯棉T恤衬衫的交易达成一致意见，初步确定了合同的各项主要条款。不久，环球采购公司业务经理约翰·W.里根亲自到访科林国际贸易公司，对该公司进行了实地考察，充分了解了该公司的生产经营能力以及产品的各项主要技术指标和加工工艺。科林国际贸易公司外贸业务员全程陪同参观，并对公司生产的纯棉T恤衬衫在用料、技术标准、生产流程等方面进行了详细讲解。约翰·W.里根先生对其产品非常满意，并表示愿意与科林国际贸易公司保持长久的合作关系。在互信互利及平等自愿的基础之上，双方就首次交易事项进行了确认，并签订了销售合同书。

一、背景知识（Background Knowledge）

（一）合同成立的时间（Time of Contract）

根据《联合国国际货物销售合同公约》的规定，"合同于按照该公约规定对发价的接受生效时订立"，而接受生效的时间又以接受通知到达发盘人或按交易习惯及发盘要求做出接受的行为为准。在现实经济活动中，有些合同成立的时间有特殊规定。《中华人民共和国合同法》第三十二条规定："当事人采用合同书形式订立合同的，自双方当事人签字或者盖章时合同成立。"

（二）合同成立的有效条件（Conditions for the Establishment of a Contract）

（1）当事人必须在自愿和真实的基础上达成协议。
（2）当事人应具有相应的民事权利能力和民事行为能力。
（3）合同必须具有对价和合法的约因。
（4）合同的标的和内容必须合法。
（5）合同的形式必须符合法律规定的要求。

（三）书面合同的形式（Forms of a Written Contract）

国际上对货物销售合同的形式没有特定的限制。进出口贸易的买卖双方可采用正式的合同书、确认书、协议，也可采用信件、备忘录、意向书、订单等形式。此外，"书面形式"还包括电报、电传等。

（四）合同的内容（Contents of a Contract）

国际贸易销售合同通常由约首、正文和约尾三部分组成。

1. 约首

① 合同名称。
② 合同编号。
③ 签约日期。
④ 签约地点。
⑤ 签约各方名称与地址。
⑥ 各方的签约意愿或合同序言。

2. 正文

正文又包括主要交易条件和一般交易条件两部分。
（1）主要交易条件：
① 货物描述：品质、规格型号、数量、单价、贸易术语、总价。
② 包装：包装类型、件数。

③ 运输：装运日期、运输方式、启运港与目的港。
④ 付款条件：付款方式、付款期限。
⑤ 保险条款：险种、保险额度的比例、采用的保险条款。
⑥ 检验条款：检验方法与地点。
（2）一般交易条件：
① 仲裁。
② 单据的要求。
③ 不可抗力。
3．约尾
① 语言及其效力。
② 合同份数。
③ 附件及其效力。
④ 生效日期与地点。
⑤ 双方当事人（法人代表或其授权人）的签字。

（五）合同的履行（Performance of a Contract）

我国绝大多数出口合同为 CIF 合同或 CFR 合同，并且一般采用信用证付款方式。在出口合同的履行过程中，包括备货、催证、审证、改证、租船订舱、报关、报检、保险、装船和制单结汇等多项环节。

二、认识销售合同（Understand the Sales Contract）

（一）销售合同样本（A Sample of Sales Contract）

销售合同（中英文对照）

Sales Contract

合同号 Contract No. ＿＿＿＿＿＿＿

日期 Date: ＿＿＿＿＿＿＿

签约地点 Signed at: ＿＿＿＿＿＿＿

卖方 Sellers: ＿＿＿＿＿＿＿＿＿＿＿＿＿＿＿＿＿ 买方 Buyers: ＿＿＿＿＿＿＿＿＿＿＿＿＿＿＿＿＿

电话：   电话：

Tel.: ＿＿＿＿＿＿＿＿＿＿＿＿＿＿＿＿＿＿＿＿ Tel.: ＿＿＿＿＿＿＿＿＿＿＿＿＿＿＿＿＿＿＿＿

传真：   传真：

Fax: ＿＿＿＿＿＿＿＿＿＿＿＿＿＿＿＿＿＿＿＿ Fax: ＿＿＿＿＿＿＿＿＿＿＿＿＿＿＿＿＿＿＿＿

经买卖双方确认根据下列条款订立本合同：

The undersigned Sellers and Buyers have confirmed this contract in accordance with the terms and conditions stipulated below:

1. 货号 Art. No.	2. 名称及规格 Descriptions of Goods	3. 数量 Quantity	4. 单价 Unit Price	5. 金额 Amount

6. 合计 Totally:

7. 总值（大写）：_____
Total Value (in words) : _____

8. 允许溢短_____%
_____% more or less in quantity and value allowed.

9. 成交价格术语：FOB/CFR/CIF/DDP 等
Terms: _____

10. 包装：_____
Packing: _____

11. 装运唛头：_____
Shipping Marks: _____

12. 运输起讫：由_____经_____到_____
Shipment _____ from _____ to _____

13. 转运：允许/不允许；分批装运：允许/不允许
Trans shipment: allowed / not allowed.
Partial shipments: allowed / not allowed.

14. 装运期：_____
Shipment Date: _____

15. 保险：由_____按发票金额110%投保_____险，另加保_____险至_____为止。
Insurance: To be effected by _____ for 110% of the invoice value covering _____ with additional _____ up to _____.

16. 付款条件：
Terms of Payment:

① 买方不迟于_____年____月____日前将100%的货款用即期汇票/电汇送抵卖方。
The buyers shall pay 100% of the sales proceeds through sight (demand) draft / by T/T remittance to the sellers not later than _____.

② 买方须于_____年____月____日前通过银行开出以卖方为受益人的不可撤销即期信用证，并注明在上述装运日期后____日在中国议讨有效，信用证须注明合同编号。
The buyers shall issue an irrevocable L/C at sight through bank in favour of the sellers prior to indicating L/C shall be valid in China through negotiation within _____ days after the shipment effected, and the L/C must mention the Contract Number.

③ 付款交单：买方应凭卖方开具给买方的见票后即须付款跟单汇票付款，付款时交单。
Documents against payment (D/P): The buyers shall duly make the payment against documentary draft made out to the buyers at sight by the sellers.

④ 承兑交单：买方应凭卖方开具给买方的见票后_____日承兑跟单汇票付款，承兑时交单。
Documents against acceptance (D/A): The buyers shall duly accept the documentary draft made out to the buyers at _____ days by the sellers.

17. 所需单据：卖方应将下列单据提交银行议付/托收。
Documents Required: The sellers shall present the following documents required for negotiation /collection to the banks.

整套正本清洁提单。
Full set of clean on Board Ocean Bills of Lading.

商业发票一式_____份。
Signed commercial invoice in _____ copies.

装箱单或重量单一式_____份。
Packing list / weight memo in _____ copies.

由_____签发的质量与数量证明书一式_____份。
Certificate of quantity and quality in _____ copies issued by _____.

保险单一式_____份。
Insurance policy in _____ copies.

由_____签发的产地证一式_____份。
Certificate of Origin in _____ copies issued by _____.

18. 装运通知：一旦装运完毕，卖方应即电告买方合同号、品名、已装载数量、发票总金额、毛重、运输工具名称及启运日期等。
Shipping Advice: The sellers shall immediately, upon the completion of the loading of the goods, advise the buyers of the Contract No., names of commodity, loaded quantity, invoice value, gross weight, name of vessel and shipment date by TLX/FAX.

19. 检验与索赔：
Inspection and Claims:

① 卖方在发货前由检验机构对货物的品质、规格和数量进行检验，并出具检验证明书。
The buyers shall have the qualities, specifications, quantities of the goods carefully inspected by the Inspection Authority, which shall issue Inspection Certificate before shipment.

② 货物到达目的地口岸后，买方可委托当地的商品检验机构对货物进行复检。如果发现货物有损坏、残缺或规格和数量与合同规定不符，买方须于货物到目的地口岸的_____日内凭检验机构出具的检验证明书向卖方索赔。
The buyers have right to have the goods inspected by the local Commodity Inspection Authority after the arrival of the goods at the port of destination. If the goods are found damaged / short / their specifications and quantities not in compliance with that specified in the contract, the buyers shall lodge claims against the sellers based on the Inspection Certificate issued by the Commodity Inspection Authority within _____ days after the goods arrival at the destination.

③ 如买方提供索赔，凡属品质异议须于货到目的地口岸之日起_____日内提出；凡属数量异议须于货到目的地口岸之日起_____日内提出。对所装货物所提任何异议应由保险公司、运输公司或邮递机构负责的，卖方不负任何责任。

The claims, if any regarding to the quality of the goods, shall be lodged within _____ days after arrival of the goods at the destination; if any regarding to the quantities of the goods, shall be lodged within _____ days after arrival of the goods at the destination. The sellers shall not take any responsibility if any claim concerning the shipping goods are up to the responsibility of Insurance Company / Transportation Company / Post Office.

20．不可抗力：如因不可抗力造成本合同部分或全部不能履约，卖方不负任何责任，但卖方应将上述发生的情况及时通知买方。

Force Majeure: The sellers shall not hold any responsibility for partial or total non-performance of this contract due to Force Majeure, but the sellers shall advise the buyers on time of such occurrence.

21．争议解决方式：任何因本合同而发生或与本合同有关的争议，应提交中国国际经济贸易仲裁委员会，按该会的仲裁规则进行仲裁。仲裁地点在中国深圳。仲裁裁决是终局的，对双方均有约束力。

Disputes Settlement: All disputes arising out of the contract or in connection with the contract, shall be submitted to the China International Economic and Trade Arbitration Commission for arbitration in accordance with its Rules of Arbitration in Shenzhen, China. The arbitral award is final and binding upon both parties.

22．法律适用：本合同之签订地或发生争议时货物所在地在中华人民共和国境内或被诉人为中国法人的，适用中华人民共和国法律，除此以外，适用《联合国国际货物销售合同公约》。

Law Application: It will be governed by the law of the People's Republic of China under the circumstances that the contract is signed or the goods while the disputes arising are in the People's Republic of China or the defendant is Chinese legal person, otherwise it is governed by United Nations Conference on Contracts for the International Sale of Goods.

23．文字：本合同采用中英文书写，两种文字具有同等法律效力。两种语言在解释上若有冲突或歧义，以中文解释为准。

Versions: This contract is made out in both Chinese and English of which version is equally effective. Conflicts between these two languages arising there from, if any, shall be subject to Chinese version.

24．附加条款（本合同上述条款与本附加条款有抵触时，以本附加条款为准）：

Additional Clauses (conflicts between contract clause here above and this additional clause, if any, it is subject to this additional clause)：

25．本合同共_____份，自双方代表签字（盖章）之日起生效。

This contract is in _____ copies, effective since being signed/sealed by both parties.

卖方代表人：_____　　　买方代表人：_____
Representative of the sellers: _____　　Representative of the buyers: _____
签字：_____　　　签字：_____
Authorized signature: _____　　Authorized signature: _____

（二）情景导入中的销售合同（Sales Contract of the Lead-in Situation）

SALES CONTRACT

No.: TXT264
Date: APR. 20, 2018
Signed at: SHENZHEN

Sellers: 科林国际贸易（香港）有限公司
KELIN INTERNATIONAL TRADING (HK) CO., LTD
Address: RM2403, BLOCK A2,YIHE PLAZA, NO. 413, GUANGZHOU, CHINA
Buyers: GLOBE SOURCING SERVICE CO., LTD
Address: 1407, 80TH STREET, S.W., NOVI, MICHIGAN, USA

The sellers agree to sell and the buyers agree to buy the under mentioned goods on the terms and conditions stated below.

Shipping Mark	Description of Goods	Quantity	Unit Price	Amount
	100% COTTON COLOUR WAVE T-SHIRT		CIF NEW YORK	
G.S.S	TM111	2,000 PCS	USD 11.00/PC	USD 22,000.00
TXT264	TM222	2,000 PCS	USD 10.00/PC	USD 20,000.00
NEW YORK	TM333	1,000 PCS	USD 9.50/PC	USD 9,500.00
C/No. 1-300	TM444	1,000 PCS	USD 8.50/PC	USD 8,500.00
	Total:	6,000 PCS		USD 60,000.00

1. With 5% more or less both in amount and quantity allowed at the sellers' option.
2. Packing: PACKED IN CARTONS OF 20 PCS EACH
3. Time of Shipment: LATEST DATE OF SHIPMENT 180830
4. Port of Loading: SHEKOU PORT, SHENZHEN
5. Port of Destination: NEW YORK
6. Insurance: To be covered by the sellers for 110% of full invoice value against <u>ALL RISKS AND WAR RISK AS PER PICC</u> up to <u>NEW YORK</u> only.
7. Payment:

By irrevocable L/C to be available by sight draft to reach the sellers before 6/30/2018 and to remain valid for negotiation in China until 15 days after the aforesaid time of shipment. The L/C must specify that transshipment and partial shipments are allowed.

8. Partial Shipments: Allowed.
9. Transshipment: Allowed.
10. Quality/Quantity Discrepancy and Claim:

In case of quality discrepancy, claim should be filed by the buyers within <u>60</u> days after the arrival of the goods at port of destination; while for quantity discrepancy, claim should be filed by the buyers within <u>30</u> days after the arrival of the goods at port of destination. It is understood that the sellers shall not be liable for any discrepancy of the goods shipped due to causes for which the Insurance Company, Shipped Company, Post Office or other transportation organizations are liable.

11. Force Majeure:

Either party shall not be held responsible for failure or delay to perform all or any part of this agreement due to flood, fire, earthquake, draught, war or any other events which could not be predicted, controlled, avoided or overcome by the relative party. However, the party affected by the event of Force Majeure shall inform the other parties of its occurrence in writing as soon as possible and thereafter send a certificate of the event issued by the relevant authorities to the other parties within 15 days after its occurrence.

12. Arbitration:

All disputes arising from the execution of this agreement shall be settled through friendly consultations. In case no settlement can be reached, the case in dispute shall then be submitted to the Foreign Trade Arbitration Commission of the China Council for the Promotion of International Trade for Arbitration in accordance with its Provisional Rules of Procedure. The decision made by this commission shall be regarded as final and binding upon both parties. Arbitration fees shall be borne by the losing party, unless otherwise awarded.

Sellers:
KELIN INTERNATIONAL
TRADING (HK) CO., LTD

李怡华

Buyers:
GLOBE SOURCING SERVICE CO., LTD

John. W. Reagan

（三）合同条款解析（Analysis of Contract Terms）

1．品名、品质条款

要明确、具体地列明商品的名称、规格、等级、标准、商标牌名、样品编号等。商品名称一般不可以用统称。质量指标规定要科学、合理。例如：

（1）Toy Bear Size 26" (exactly as Sample YN022).

（2）Milk Powder (Protein 60% Min, Fat 5% Max).

（3）Sheep Wool containing 20% cashmere, allowing 1% more or less.

2．数量条款

数量条款主要包括商品的具体数量及计量单位。例如：

（1）500M/T, with 5% more or less at the sellers' option.

（2）About/approximately 2,000 inches.

3．包装条款

合同中的包装条款一般包括包装材料、包装方式、每件包装中所含物品的数量或重量。例如：

（1）In cartons of 15kg net, each one wrapped with poly-bag.

（2）In iron drums, each 10 drums packed in one wooden case, each 500 wooden cases packed in one 40ft container.

4．价格条款

合同中的价格条款一般包括计量单位、单位价格、计价货币和贸易术语。例如：

（1）USD 500 per metric ton CIF New York.

（2）USD 1,000 per bale CFRC2% Hong Kong.

（3）JPY 10,000 per dozen FOB Shanghai less 3% discount.

5．装运条款

合同中的装运条款一般包括装运时间、装运地点、目的地、分批装运、转运等内容，有些合同还规定卖方应予以交付的单据和有关装运通知的条款。例如：

（1）Shipment: From China port to Manchester during Mar./Apr. in two equal lots.

（2）Shipment: From Shenzhen to Sydney on or before May 31st, 2018, with partial shipments and transshipment allowed.

6．保险条款

不同贸易术语下，保险条款的内容不同，在 FOB、CFR、FCA、CPT 术语下，保险条款只需列明保险责任由买方负责即可。例如：

Insurance: To be covered by the buyers.

在 CIF 和 CIP 术语下，保险条款应包括投保人、保险金额、投保险别及保险条款依据等内容。例如：

（1）Insurance: To be covered by the sellers for 110% of total invoice value against FPA and War Risk as per and subject to the relevant Ocean Marine Cargo Clauses of the People's Insurance Company of China.

（2）Insurance: To be covered by the sellers for 110% of total invoice value against ICC(A) and ICC War clause cargo as per and subject to the Institute Cargo Clause.

7．支付条款

（1）汇付条款。一般包括汇付时间、具体的汇付方法、汇付金额等。例如：

Payment: The buyers should pay the total value to the sellers in advance by T/T not later than Oct. 31, 2018.

（2）托收条款。一般包括交单的条件、付款或承兑责任以及付款期限等内容。例如：

Payment: The buyers shall pay against documentary draft drawn by the sellers at 15 days after the date of draft. The shipping documents are to be delivered against payment only.

（3）信用证条款。一般包括开证时间、开证银行、受益人、信用证类型、金额、到期日等内容。例如：

Payment: The buyers shall open through a bank acceptable to the sellers an irrevocable Letter of Credit payable by draft at sight to reach the sellers 45 days before the month of shipment, valid for negotiation in Guangzhou, China till the 15th day after the latest date of shipment.

实操训练（Skill Training）

一、将以下合同主要条款翻译为英文

1. 货号
2. 品名及规格
3. 数量及总值均有_____%的增减，由卖方决定。
4. 生产国和制造厂家
5. 唛头
6. 装运期限
7. 目的口岸
8. 保险：由卖方按发票金额110%投保至_____为止的_____险。
9. 装运条件
10. 装运口岸

二、简答题

1. 一份为法律所认可的合同应具备哪些条件？
2. 以 CIF 条件出口货物并使用信用证付款需经过哪些主要环节？哪些环节最为重要？

三、根据以下买卖双方的往来信函填写销售合同书

Mail 1:

Mar. 3, 2018

To: Huizhou Light Industrial Products Imp. & Exp. Corp.

Dear Mr. Wang,

Thank you very much for your hospitality in your booth at the Ambiente Fair 2018 in Frankfurt.

I am interested in candles Art. No. 501 in the packing of 25-pc paper boxes. The quantity will be one 20-ft container for the start.

Therefore you are kindly requested to give me your best price rather than USD 0.72 per box quoted at the fair, so that I can send you my order for prompt shipment.

Awaiting your reply with best regards.

John Hendry
Boston Trading Co. Ltd., USA

Mail 2:

Mar. 5, 2018

Dear Mr. Hendry,

It was a great pleasure to meet you at the Ambiente Fair 2018 and receive your inquiry for our candles.

In fact, the price I quoted at the fair is already the most favorable one. However, in order to save time and to start business, I'll further lower my price as follows:

CANDLES ART. NO. 501, USD 0.71/BOX FOB YANTIAN PORT, SHENZHEN.

I'm sure this will be acceptable to you. Let us start our business and we'll offer you our best service.

Looking forward to your early acceptance.

Thanks and best regards,
Wang Dayang
Huizhou Light Industrial Products Imp. & Exp. Corp.

Mail 3:

Mar. 6, 2018

Dear Mr. Wang,

Thank you for your e-mail and new price, which I expected to be lower but accept, noting that this is the first between us.

I would also like to order candles Art. No. 502 in 10-pc boxes at the price of USD 0.14/box. Please confirm. Therefore our order is as follows:

One 20-ft container of CANDLES ART. NO. 501, 50%; CANDLES ART NO. 502, 50% packed in paper boxes of 25-pc and 10-pc respectively, 50 boxes to a carton respectively.

Please inform us roughly how many cartons a 1×20' container can hold.

Please also infirm us of your payment terms and the earliest shipment date. I'm awaiting your good service, high quality and fine packing as you promised at the fair, to enable both of us to build a good cooperation to our mutual benefit.

Yours truly,
John Hendry

Mail 4:

Mar. 7, 2018

Dear Mr. Hendry,

Thank you for your new order, but we think your price for 10 pcs/box candles of USD 0.14 per box is too low. Our calculation points to USD 0.155 per box. But in order to start, we think we can accept USD 0.15/box. If you agree, I will fax you our sales contract for your signature.

Payment: By irrevocable Letter of Credit payable by draft at sight.

Delivery: Within 45 days after the covering L/C is received.

For your information, according to our calculation, a 20-ft container can hold 600 cartons of 10-pc boxes and 300 cartons of 25-pc boxes.

By the way, can you tell us the name of the port of destination for our reference?

Best wishes,
Wang Dayang

Mail 5:

Mar. 8, 2018

Dear Mr. Wang,

Hello my friend, I'm afraid I don't agree to USD 0.155 for 10-pc boxes. The best I can do is USD 0.145/box , for the start of our cooperation.

As I explained earlier, you should accept the above price, taking into consideration the higher cost of freight at my expense.

Payment and date of shipment are fine. Please accept our bid, so that we can proceed with the opening of the relative L/C.

By the way, we would want the goods to be shipped to Boston.

Best regards,
John Hendry

Mail 6:

Mar. 10, 2018

Dear Mr. Hendry,

As the cost of raw material is increasing sharply these days, we are facing big problems, I hope you can understand us.

However, in order to make the ball start rolling, we accept your price for candles in 10-pc boxes at USD 0.145/box. Please find the attached S/C No. D2018PA100, and sign and return one copy for our file.

Also enclosed is our banking information, please open the covering L/C as soon as possible and fax us a copy of it for our reference.

We are glad to have concluded this initial transaction with you. We hope this would mark the beginning of a long-standing and steady business relationship between us.

Yours,
Wang Dayang

项目二 Project II

信用证
Letter of Credit

学习目标（Learning Aims）

- 了解信用证的特点与形式。
- 熟悉信用证中的当事人、代码和基本内容。
- 能够依据合同审核相关的信用证。

情景导入（Lead-in Situation）

科林国际贸易公司与环球采购公司在经过多次交易磋商后对纯棉T恤衬衫的交易达成一致意见，于2018年4月20日签订了销售合同书（合同号：TXT264）。2018年5月20日，科林国际贸易公司收到中国银行通知的环球采购公司通过银行开出的信用证，公司业务部的业务员李怡华需要根据合同审核信用证，审核信用证需要严格按照合同的规定逐条核对，如果合同没有规定则需按相关规定与惯例加以修正。与此同时，业务员李怡华还需要学习如何为进口合同办理申请开立信用证的相关手续。

一、背景知识（Background Knowledge）

（一）认识信用证（Understand the Letter of Credit）

1. 信用证的定义与形式

信用证（Letter of Credit, L/C）是一种书面文件，是一家银行根据客户的要求和指示或以其自身的名义，向受益人开立的在一定期限内凭规定的单据支付一定金额的书面承诺。

信用证的形式可分为信开本和电开本。信开本（To Open by Airmail）是指开证银行采用印好的信函格式的信用证，开证后由航空邮寄通知行。电开本（To Open by Cable）是指开证行使用电报、电传、传真、SWIFT等各种电信方式将信用证条款传达给通知行。

SWIFT是环球银行金融电信协会（Society for Worldwide Interbank Financial Telecommunication）的英文简称。该组织采用会员制，会员共享协会数据交换平台等资源。会员银行利用SWIFT数据交换平台开立的信用证称为SWIFT信用证。它的特点是标准化、固定化、格式统一化，而且速度快、成本低，现已被世界各国的银行广泛使用。SWIFT信用证的开立格式代号为MT700和MT701，对SWIFT信用证的修改采用MT707标准格式传递。

2. 信用证的性质与特点

（1）信用证是一种银行信用。信用证是由开证银行以自己的信用做出付款的保证，开证银行承担第一付款责任，即只要受益人提交了符合信用证规定的单据，开证银行就必须付款。

（2）信用证是一种自足文件。信用证是依据销售合同开立的，但是一经开立，就成为独立于销售合同之外的另一种契约。信用证业务的一切关系人的权利和责任完全以信用证条款规定为准，不受销售合同的约束。

（3）信用证是一种纯单据业务。银行处理信用证业务只凭单据，而不管货物的状况如何。银行以受益人提交的单据是否与信用证条款严格相符为依据，决定是否付款。只要单据符合信用证的规定，即使货物没有如期运到目的港，银行也要付款；反之，只要受益人提交的单据与信用证规定不符，即使货物完好无损地到达目的港，银行也不会付款。

3. 信用证的基本当事人和内容

当前国际贸易中使用的信用证多为SWIFT信用证，所以本文以SWIFT信用证为例予以讲解。

（1）信用证的基本当事人。

① 开证申请人（Applicant）：申请人意指发出开立信用证申请的一方。

② 开证行（Issuing Bank）：开证行意指应申请人要求或代表其自身开立信用证的银行。

③ 受益人（Beneficiary）：受益人意指信用证中受益的一方。

④ 通知行（Advising Bank）：通知行意指应开证行要求通知信用证的银行。

⑤ 议付行（Negotiation Bank）：议付行意指根据开证行的授权买入或贴现受益人开立和提交的符合信用证规定的汇票及单据的银行。

⑥ 保兑行（Confirming Bank）：保兑行意指应开证行的授权或请求对信用证加具保兑的银行。

（2）信用证的基本内容可以归纳为六大类。

① 对信用证本身的说明：信用证的种类（Form of L/C）、信用证编号（L/C No.）、开证

日期（Issuing Date）、开证申请人（Applicant）、受益人（Beneficiary）、到期日与到期地点（Expire Date and Place）、开证银行（Issuing/Opening Bank）、通知银行（Advising/Notifying Bank）、信用证金额（L/C Amount）、单据提交期限（Documents Presentation Period）。

② 对货物的要求：名称（Name of Commodity）、规格（Specification）、数量（Quantity）、包装（Packing）、价格条件和单价（Trade Terms & Unit Price）。

③ 对运输的要求：装运港或启运地（Port of Loading or Shipment from）、卸货港或目的港（Port of Discharge or Destination）、装运期（Time of Shipment）、可否分批装运（Partial Shipment Allowed or Not Allowed）、可否转运（Transshipment Allowed or Not Allowed）、运输方式（Mode of Shipment）。

④ 对单据的要求：货物单据包括发票（Commercial Invoice）、装箱单（Packing List）、重量单（Weight List）、原产地证书（Certificate of Origin）、商检证明书（Inspection Certificate）、运输单据（Transport Documents）、保险单据（Insurance Documents）、其他单据。

⑤ 对汇票的要求：出票人（Drawer）、付款人（Drawee/Payer）、收款人（Payee）、付款期限（Tenor）、出票条款（Drawn Clauses）、出票日期（Date of Draft）。

⑥ 其他事项：附加条款或特别条款（Additional Conditions or Special Conditions）、开证行对议付行的指示（Instructions to Negotiation Bank）、背书议付金额条款和寄单方法（Endorsement Clauses & Method of Dispatching Documents）、开证银行付款保证条款（Engagement/Undertaking Clause）、惯例适用条款（Subject to UCP Clause）。

（二）SWIFT 信用证常用代码解读（Common Codes in SWIFT L/C）

项目类型	代码	栏位名称	说明
M	27	Sequence of Total	电文页次
M	40A	Form of Documentary Credit	跟单信用证类型
M	20	Documentary Credit Number	跟单信用证号码
M	40E	Applicable Rules	适用规则
M	31D	Date and Place of Expiry	信用证到期日与到期地点
O	51A	Applicant Bank	申请人银行
M	50	Applicant	开证申请人
M	59	Beneficiary	受益人
M	32B	Currency Code, Amount	币种代码、金额
O	39A	Percentage Credit Amount Tolerance	信用证金额增减比例
M	41A（D）	Available with ... by ...	指定……（银行）兑付，兑付方式为……
O	42C	Drafts at ...	汇票期限为……
O	42A（D）	Drawee	汇票付款人
O	43P	Partial Shipments	分批装运
O	43T	Transshipment	转运
O	44B	For Transport to ...	最终目的地为……
O	44E	Port of Loading / Airport of Departure	装货港或启运机场
O	44F	Port of Discharge / Airport of Destination	卸货港或目的地机场

(续)

项目类型	代码	栏位名称	说明
O	44C	Latest Date of Shipment	最晚装运日期
O	45A	Description of Goods and/or Services	货物及/或服务描述
O	46A	Documents Required	所需单据
O	47A	Additional Conditions	附加条款
O	71B	Charges	费用
O	48	Period for Presentation	交单期限
M	49	Confirmation Instructions	保兑指示
O	72	Sender to Receiver Information	银行间的通知

注:"M"指 Mandatory(必选),"O"指 Optional(可选)。

二、依据合同审核信用证(Examine L/C in Terms of the Contract)

(一)审证要点(Requirements)

审核信用证是银行和出口商共同承担的任务,其中银行主要负责鉴别信用证的真伪;而出口商则须将信用证条款与合同条款逐项逐句进行对照,审核信用证的内容与合同条款是否一致,若不一致,须要求开证申请人进行修改。

出口商审证要点包括:

(1)对照合同,审核信用证的性质,一般包括审核是否为"不可撤销"信用证,开证申请人、受益人姓名及地址是否正确,商品的名称、规格、包装、数量、金额(大小写)以及货币种类是否与合同相符,付款期限是否合理等。

(2)审核运输路线、分批装运和转运以及对运输工具的要求、装运期限的规定等是否符合我方的要求。

(3)审核信用证所要求单据的种类、份数及填制要求是否是我方能够办到的。

(4)关于银行费用的支付,一般应由开证申请人承担,但目前有些信用证规定开证行之外的费用由受益人承担,出口商应予以注意。

(5)找出信用证中的软条款。

(6)审核空白、边缘处加注的文字,这些字句是对信用证内容的重要补充或新的修改,必须认真对待。

(7)审核信用证有效期和到期地点。有效期和到期地点关系到出口商能否及时交单,所以有效期应与运输期限相协调,到期地点若在国外,应注意提前交单。

(二)情景导入中的信用证审核(Examine the L/C of the Lead-in Situation)

合同第 TXT264 号项下的信用证:

Letter of Credit

Sequence of Total   27:   1/1
Form of Doc. Credit   40A: IRREVOCABLE

Doc. Credit Number	20:	BL170197
Date of Issue	31C:	180629
Applicable Rules	40E:	UCP LATEST VERSION
Expiry	31D:	DATE 180622 PLACE USA
Applicant Bank	51D:	HSBC BANK (CHINA) CO., LTD
Applicant	50:	GLOBE SOURCING SERVICE CO., LTD
		1407, 80TH STREET, S.W., NOVI, MICHIGAN, USA
Beneficiary	59:	KELIN INTERNATIONAL TRADING (HK) CO., LTD
		RM2403, BLOCK A2, YIHE PLAZA, NO. 413, GUANGZHOU, CHINA
Amount	32B:	CURRENCY USD AMOUNT 6,000.00
Available with/by	41D:	ANY BANK BY NEGOTIATION
Drafts at …	42C:	15 DAYS AFTER SIGHT
Drawee	42D:	HSBC BANK (CHINA) CO., LTD
Partial Shipments	43P:	PROHIBITED
Transshipment	43T:	ALLOWED
Loading in Charge	44A:	SHEKOU PORT, SHENZHEN, CHINA
For Transport to …	44B:	LONDON, UK
Latest Date of Ship.	44C:	180420
Descript. of Goods	45A:	

100% COTTON COLOUR WAVE T-SHIRT CIF NEW YORK
6,000 PCS IN TOTAL PACKED IN 20-PC CARTONS
SHIPPING MARKS: G.S.S / TXT264 / NEW YORK / C/NO. 1-300

Documents Required 46A:

+ SIGNED COMMERCIAL INVOICE IN 5 COPIES SHOWING SEPARATELY FOB VALUE, FREIGHT CHARGE, INSURANCE PREMIUM, CIF VALUE AND COUNTRY OF ORIGIN.
+ FULL SET OF CLEAN ON BOARD OCEAN BILL OF LADING TO ORDER MARKED FREIGHT PREPAID PLUS TWO NON-NEGOTIABLE COPIES, NOTIFY: APPLICANT.
+ MARINE INSURANCE POLICY OR CERTIFICATE IN DUPLICATE, ENDORSED IN BLANK, FOR FULL INVOICE VALUE PLUS 10 PERCENT STATING CLAIM PAYABLE IN NEW YORK COVERING INSTITUTE CARGO CLAUSES (A) AND WAR RISKS.
+ PACKING LIST IN 5 COPIES.
+ CERTIFICATE OF ANALYSIS IN 5 COPIES.
+ BENEFICIARY'S CERTIFICATE CERTIFYING THAT ONE COPY EACH OF INVOICE, N/N B/L HAVE BEEN FAXED TO BUYER WITHIN 3 DAYS AFTER SHIPMENT.

Additional Cond.	47A:	

+ ALL DOCUMENTS MENTIONING THIS L/C NO.
+ BOTH AMOUNT AND QUANTITY PLUS OR MINUS 5 PCT ACCEPTABLE.
+ IF ANY DISCREPANCY, WE SHALL DEDUCT USD 50.00 BEING OUR FEE FROM THE PROCEEDS.
+ THE NAME, ADDRESS, TELEPHONE NO. OF SHIPPING AGENT MUST BE MENTIONED ON B/L.

Charges　　　　　　71B:
ALL BANKING CHARGES OUTSIDE USA INCLUDING COST OF WIRE AND REIMBURSEMENT CHARGE ARE FOR BENEFICIARY'S ACCOUNT.

Confirmation　　　　49: WITHOUT
Instructions to Bank 78:
+ UPON RECEIPT OF SHIPPING DOCUMENTS IN STRICT CONFORMITY WITH L/C TERMS, WE WILL COVER YOUR ACCOUNT AND LESS OUR COST OF WIRE IF ANY ACCORDING TO YOUR INSTRUCTION.
+ DRAFTS AND DOCUMENTS TO BE SENT TO US BY COURIER SERVICE MAILING.

经审核发现信用证有下列不符点：

On perusal, several discrepancies have been found as below.

1. The expiry date of the L/C should be on Sept. 15, 2018.
2. The place of expiry should be in China.
3. The amount should be USD60,000.00, not USD6,000.00.
4. The draft should be at sight instead of 15 days after sight.
5. Partial shipments should be allowed.
6. The destination port should be NEW YORK, USA.
7. The latest shipment is on or before August 30, 2018, not April 20, 2018.
8. The condition of insurance should be ALL RISKS AND WAR RISK AS PER PICC instead of Institute Cargo Clauses (A) and War Risks.

三、申请开立信用证（Application for Open L/C）

（一）申请开证的注意事项（Requirements Concerned）

（1）开证时间：进口商必须按照合同规定的时间办理信用证，如合同无规定，须本着保证出口商收到信用证后能够在合同规定的装运期限内准备好货物并完成装运的原则及时申请开证。

（2）**信用证的独立性**：信用证的条款应与合同的规定保持一致，但信用证是独立于合同及货物本身的自足性文件，因此合同的规定都应在信用证中明确列出。

（3）**特殊的规定或操作惯例**：例如，国外通知行由开证行指定，不能由进口方指定；我国银行开出的信用证一般不允许加保兑条款；一般情况下不开可转让信用证；信用证中不允许有电报索偿条款的规定等。

（二）申请开立信用证的程序（Procedures of Application for L/C）

（1）向拟申请开立信用证的银行递交合同的副本及所需附件。

（2）填写开证申请书。凡是开办有信用证业务的银行都有自己固定格式的开证申请书。进口人应向银行领取后，按照银行规定填写一式三份（一份供业务部开展贸易，一份供财务部支付结算，一份交开证行存底）。开证申请书的填写务必依据合同规定，条款明确，内容完整。

开证申请书印有正反两面，正面包括申请日期、申请人信息、总金额、合同编号、受益人信息、开证方式、信用证性质、单据条款、汇款条款、货物描述、运输条款、费用条款、特殊要求、使用规则等内容；背面内容由银行事先印好，主要是申请人对开证行的声明及承诺，以明确申请人的职责。

（3）缴付开证保证金和开证手续费。开证申请人除非事先取得开证行的授信额度，否则须按照规定向银行缴付开证保证金。除此之外，还需缴纳一定金额的开证手续费。

开证行在收到开证申请书后，一般会执行"三查一保"。"三查"是指对开证申请书和开证人声明、申请人资信状况、开证应提交的有效文件等进行审查。"一保"是指经审查合格后银行会要求申请人缴纳开证保证金，并按照开证申请书所填内容开立信用证。信用证开立后，银行会向通知行发出信用证，同时将信用证副本送交开证申请人。

（三）开证申请书的样本与填制要点（Sample and Instructions）

各银行开证申请书形式上有所差异，但内容基本相同，现以中国建设银行的开证申请书为样本。

开证申请书正面内容：

中国建设银行

China Construction Bank

APPLICATION FOR IRREVOCABLE DOCUMENTARY CREDIT

TO: CHINA CONSTRUCTION BANK
_____ BRANCH

L/C NO.
Date:

Subject to the ICC Uniform Customs and Practice for Documentary Credits (latest revision), and to the terms and conditions overleaf, please issue an irrevocable documentary credit with term stated below by (please mark "×" in ☐).

☐ Full teletransmission　　☐ Mail/Airmail

☐ Brief teletransmission followed by mail confirmation

Expiry Date and Place of

Advising Bank (if blank, any bank at your option)	Applicant (full name & address)	
Beneficiary (full name & address)	Amount (in figures and words)	
Shipment from _____ to _____ Latest date of shipment _____ Price term: ☐ FOB ☐ CFR ☐ CIF _____	Partial shipment ☐ allowed ☐ not allowed	Transshipment ☐ allowed ☐ not allowed

Credit available by ☐ negotiation ☐ acceptance ☐ sight payment ☐ deferred payment with _____.

Draft(s) drawn on issuing bank at _____ sight for _____ % of invoice value.

Documents required:
☐ Signed Commercial Invoice in _____ copies indicating L/C No. and Contract No.
☐ Signed Packing List in _____ copies.
☐ Full set of clean on board Bill(s) of Lading marked "☐ Freight Prepaid ☐ Freight Collect" made out to order of _____, notifying ☐ applicant ☐ _____.
☐ Clean Air Waybills showing "☐ Freight Prepaid ☐ Freight Collect" and consigned to _____, notifying ☐ applicant ☐ _____.
☐ Rail Waybills showing "Freight Prepaid" and consigned to _____.
☐ Insurance Policy/Certificate in duplicate bland endorsed for 110% of the invoice value showing claims payable at destination in currency of the draft, covering All Risks and War Risks and _____.
☐ Certificate of Origin in _____ copies issued by _____.
☐ Other documents required:

Description of Goods (brief description without excessive detail):

Additional instructions:
☐ All banking charges outside the Issuing Bank including reimbursing charges are for account of Beneficiary.
☐ Documents must be presented within _____ days after the date of issuance of the transport documents but within the validity of the credit.
☐ Both credit amount and shipment quantity _____ % more or less are allowed.
☐ Third party as shipper is not acceptable.
☐ Short Form / Blank Back B/L is not acceptable.
☐ Other terms and conditions (if any):

In case of queries, please contact _____.
Tel. No. _____   Fax No. _____
☐ To be continued on separate continuation sheet(s).

开证申请书背面内容：

信用证开证申请人承诺书

公司已依法办妥一切必要的进口手续，兹谨请贵行为我公司依照申请书所列条款开立不可撤销跟单信用证，并承诺如下：

一、在申请开证时我公司（请用"×"选择其一）：
☐ 使用贵行与我公司签订的编号为_____《贸易融资额度合同》项下的
　　☐ 信用证开证额度。　☐ 信托收据额度。
☐ 使用编号为_____《信用证开证合同》。（适用于单笔业务）
☐ 存入贵行开证保证金，开证保证金比例为开证金额（含溢装金额）的_____%，即开证保证金金额为（币种、大写）_____，并使用贵行与我公司签订的编号为

_____《贸易融资额度合同》项下的_____额度，币种、金额为（大写）_____。

☐ 存入贵行开证保证金，开证保证金比例为开证金额（含溢装金额）的100%。

二、同意贵行依照国际商会《跟单信用证统一惯例》（最新版本）等办理该笔信用证业务，并同意承担由此产生的一切责任。

三、信用证项下的人民币和外币结算均通过贵行办理。

四、根据贵行要求，及时提供有关销售合同等文件及资料。

五、我公司承诺对贵行所负债务履行偿付义务。本条所称债务包括但不限于信用证项下应付货款、有关手续费、电信费、杂费、因贵行发生信用证项下垫付我公司应付的逾期利息、违约金、赔偿金、国外受益人拒绝承担的有关银行费用及贵行实现债权的费用。

六、如信用证需修改，由公司向贵行提出书面信用证修改申请。我公司保证支付因信用证修改而产生的一切费用（包括国外受益人拒绝承担的有关银行费用）。

七、在贵行信用证单据通知书规定的期限内，书面通知贵行办理对外付款/承兑/确定迟期付款/拒付手续，我公司愿承担由此引起的一切责任和后果。

八、我公司如因单据有不符之处而拟请贵行拒绝付款/承兑/确认迟期付款时，将在贵行单据通知规定的期限内，向贵行提出书面拒付请求及理由，依次列明所有不符点，同时将贵行交给我公司的资料全部退回贵行。对单据存在的不符点，贵行有独立的最终认定权和处理权，贵行有权确定是否对外付款/承兑/确认迟期付款。

九、如我公司申请开立的为即期信用证，且贵行认为单证无不符点，我公司承诺在贵行发出信用证单据通知书后三个银行工作日内，向贵行付清所有款项及有关费用。

如我公司申请开立的为远期信用证，则我公司在付款到期日前，向贵行付清所有款项及有关费用。

十、对外付款时，贵行有权从我公司在贵行开立的保证金账户直接划收或从我公司在中国建设银行系统开立的其他账户划收。如我公司未付清应付款项，则贵行有权行使担保权或采取其他措施实现债权。

十一、我公司发生名称、法定代表人（负责人）、住所、经营范围、注册资金变更等事项，将及时通知贵行。

十二、我公司发生承包、租赁、股份制改革、联营、合并、兼并、分立、合资、申请停业整顿、申请解散、申请破产等足以影响贵行债权实现的情形，将提前书面通知贵行，征得贵行同意，并按贵行要求落实债务的清偿及担保。

十三、我公司发生停业、歇业、被注销登记、被吊销营业执照、法定代表人或负责人从事违法活动、涉及重大诉讼活动、生产经营出现严重困难、财务状况恶化等情形，足以影响贵行债权实现的，均应立即书面通知贵行，并按贵行要求落实债务的清偿及担保。

十四、不与任何第三方签署有损于贵行权益的合同。

十五、由于开立信用证所基于的基础合同发生纠纷或由于第三方原因造成贵行损失的，我公司同意承担赔偿责任。

十六、贵行对任何文电、信函或单据传递中发生延误、遗失所造成的后果，或对于任何电信传递过程中发生的延误、残缺或其他差错，概不负责。

十七、信用证开立申请书应当用英文填写的部分及信用修改申请书一律用英文填写。如用中文填写而引起的歧义，贵行概不负责。

十八、因信用证开立申请书、信用证修改申请书字迹不清或词义含混而引起的一切后果均由我公司负责。

十九、贵行已应我公司要求做了相应的条款说明，我公司已全面、准确地理解本申请书的各项条款。我公司特做出上述承诺，并严格遵守。

二十、是否接受本公司的开证申请，由贵行根据有关规定办理。

二十一、本承诺书与正面信用证开立申请书为一份完整文本，我公司在正面开证申请书上的签字盖章对本承诺书同样有效力。

1．申请开证日期（Date）

申请开证日期填写在申请书的右上角。

2．开立方式（Issue by）

信用证的开立方式有信开（Mail/Airmail）、电开全文（Full Teletransmission）、简电后随寄电报证书（Brief Teletransmission Followed by Mail Confirmation）等。

3．信用证编号（L/C No.）

信用证编号由开证行填写。

4．信用证到期日与到期地点（Expiry Date and Place of）

信用证到期日与到期地点由申请人填写。

5．受益人（Beneficiary）

此栏必须填写全称及详细地址，还要注明联系电话、传真，便于有关当事人之间的联系。

6．通知行（Advising Bank）

通知行由开证行填写。

7．开证申请人（Applicant）

此栏必须填写全称及详细地址，还要注明联系电话、传真，便于有关当事人之间的联系。

8．信用证金额（Amount）

信用证金额必须用数字和文字两种形式表示，并且要表明币种。信用证金额是开证行付款责任的最高限额，必须根据合同的规定明确表示清楚，如果有一定比率的上下浮动幅度，也应表示清楚。

9．装运条款：从……至……（Shipment from ... to ...）

根据合同规定填写装运地（港）、目的地（港）及最晚装运日期，如有转运地（港）也应写清楚。

10．分批与转运（Partial Shipment & Transshipment）

根据合同规定选择"允许"或"不允许"，在选择的项目方框中打"×"。

11．价格术语（Trade Term）

此栏有 FOB、CFR、CIF 及"其他条件"四个备选项目，根据合同成交的贸易术语在该项前的方框中打"×"。如若为其他条件，需在选项后面注明。

12．付款方式（Credit Available by）

信用证有四种付款方式，包括议付、承兑、即期支付和延期支付，应根据合同规定在选定的付款方式项目方框中打"×"。

13. **汇票要求**（Draft(s) Drawn on...）

按合同规定填写信用证项下应支付发票金额的百分比。如合同规定所有货款都以信用证方式支付，须填写信用证项下汇票金额是发票金额的 100%；如合同规定该笔货款由信用证和托收两种方式支付，各支付 50%，则应填写信用证项下汇票金额是发票金额的 50%，依此类推。另外，还应填写汇票的支付期限，如即期、远期。若是远期汇票，还要填写具体的天数，如 30 天、60 天、90 天等。最后是填写付款人，根据《UCP600》规定，信用证项下汇票的付款人应是开证行或指定付款行。

14. **所需单据**（Documents Required）

所需单据的最后一条是"其他单据"，申请人一般可以在此条之前所列的条款中选定所需要的单据，如若前款中没有，则需在"其他单据"中另外列出。所需单据不但要填写单据名称，还要明确份数、内容、出单人等相关规定。

15. **货物描述**（Description of Goods）

此栏填写货物名称、规格、数量、包装、单价、唛头等，注意与合同保持一致。

16. **附加条款**（Additional Instructions）

从已列出的附加条款中选定所需选项并在方框中打"×"，如若所列内容与实际情况不符，可按合同规定在最后一条"其他条款"后按顺序填写完整。

17. **申请人信息**（Contact）

此处填写开证申请人的联系方式等信息，按实际填写。

18. **其他内容**（Others）

其他内容一般附在信用证开证申请书背面，申请人需阅读后签字盖章。另外，申请人需在开证申请书下方填写开户银行、账户号码、执行人、联系电话等内容并签字盖章。

实操训练（Skill Training）

一、从以下信用证中找出后面所列项目的内容，用英文填写

SWIFT 信用证

MT700 ISSUANCE OF DOCUMENTARY CREDIT

27	SEQ OF TOTAL	1/1
40A	FORM OF DC	IRREVOCABLE
20	DC NO	LIC570/126962
31C	DATE OF ISSUE	18 FEB 2018
40E	APPLICABLE RULES	UCP LATEST VERSION
31D	EXPIRY DATE AND PLACE	
	DATE OF EXPIRY	20 APR 2018
	PLACE OF EXPIRY	CHINA
50	APPLICANT	M.N.M.-COMERCIO INTERNACIONAL LDA
		PARQ.IND.SEIXAL LT 32-34
		FOROS-CATRAPONA
		2840 SEIXAL

59	BENEFICIARY	YEARISON IMPORT AND EXPORT CORPORATION LIMITED ROOM109-110 KOWLOON HONG KONG
32B	DC AMT	USD 10,277.80
39A	PCT CR AMT TOLERANCE	05/05
41D	AVAILABLE WITH/BY	BANCO ESPIRITO SANTO SA 1200 LISBON PORTUGAL BY PAYMENT
43P	PARTIAL SHIPMENTS	PROHIBITED
43T	TRANSSHIPMENT	ALLOWED
44A	LOADING/DISPATCH AT/FM	FUZHOU
44B	FOR TRANSPORTATION TO	LISBON
44C	LATEST DATE OF SHIPMENT	10 APR 2018

45A DISCRIPTIONS OF GOODS
  + 2,000 SETS OF RATTAN BASKETS, PACKED IN 680 CTNS AS PER PROFORMA INVOICE NO. YRS403 DD APR 02, 2018 FOB FUZHOU PORT
    A TOLERANCE OF MORE OR LESS 5 PCT ON QUANTITIES, ALLOWED

46A DOCUMENTS REQUIRED
  + COMMERCIAL INVOICE DULY SIGNED (ORIGINAL AND 4 COPIES)
  + FULL SET CLEAN ON BOARD MARINE BILLS OF LADING CONSIGNED TO THE ORDER OF MNM-COMERCIO INTERNACIONAL LDA, NOTIFYING THE CO. SANTO'S ENTERPRISE/ROTTERDAM-SQE 830109', MARKED FREIGHT COLLECT AND ISSUED BY EVERGREEN LINES.
  + WEIGHT NOTE.
  + PACKING LIST.
  + CERTIFICATE OF ORIGIN GSP FORM A.

47A ADDITIONAL CONDITIONS
    A HANDLING CHARGE OF USD 65.00 IS DUE ON ALL DOCUMENTS NEGOTIATED WITH DISCREPANCIES. THIS FEE PLUS TELEX/SWIFT CHARGES, IF ANY SHALL BE DEDUCTED FROM THE PROCEEDS. ADDITIONS, CORRECTIONS, ERASURES, AMENDMENTS MUST BE DULY STAMPED AND INITIALLED BY THE PARTY/ AUTHORITY ISSUING THE DOCUMENT IN QUESTION.
  + ALL DOCUMENTS MUST MENTION OUR L/C REFERENCE.
    ALL DOCUMENTS MUST BE SENT TO:
    BANCO ESPIRITO SANTO SA
    SERVICO OPERACOES DOCUMENTARIAS
    RUA CASTILHO, NR.26-4

		L250-069 LISBON
71B	DETAILS OF CHARGES	ALL BANKING CHARGES OUTSIDE PORTUGAL ARE FOR BENEFICIARY ACCOUNT.
48	PERIOD FOR PRESENTATION	WITHIN 10 DAYS AFTER ISSUANCE OF SHIPPING DOCUMENTS BUT WITHIN L/C VALIDITY.
78	INFO TO PRESENTING BK	UPON RECEIPT OF DOCUMENTS DULY IN ORDER AT OUR BANK WE WILL COVER ACCORDING TO YOUR INSTRUCTIONS.
57D	ADVISE THRU FULL N/A	HANG SENG BANK FUZHOU BR.
72	BK TO BK INFO	PLS. ACKNOWLEDGE RECEIPT OF L/C GIVING YR REF. NR AS WELL AS OURS.
TRAILER		(MAC: F2DE2C32)　(CHK: 4874DIC4263)

从上述信用证中找出以下内容（用英文写出）：

1．开证申请人：
2．受益人：
3．信用证编号：
4．开证日期：
5．信用证到期日与到期地点：
6．装运港：
7．目的港：
8．最晚装运日期：
9．分批装运与转运的要求：
10．商品数量及名称：
11．要求单据（只需列出单据名称）：
12．交单期限（如 L/C 无规定，则按 UCP 惯例办理）：
13．信用证金额：
14．信用证数量和金额增减百分比：
15．信用证有无保兑：
16．单据每个不符点扣费金额：
17．形式发票/合同编号与日期：
18．贸易术语（价格条件）：
19．开证行：
20．银行费用的支付方式：

二、翻译下列信用证的条款

信用证条款：

……

44C: LATEST DATE OF SHIPMENT: 180210

45A: DESCRIPTION OF GOODS AND/OR SERVICES:

    1,600PCS BABYWEAR

    AS PER ORDER NO.MY1301 AND S/C NO.MT13008

    CFR HAMBURG

    PACKED IN CARTON Of 20PCS EACH

46A: DOCUMENTS REQUIRED:

+ SIGNED COMMERCIAL INVOICES IN TRIPLICATE INDICATING LC NO. AND CONTRACT NO.
+ FULL SET (3/3) OF CLEAN ON BOARD OCEAN BILL OF LADING MADE OUT TO APPLICANT AND BLANK ENDORSED MARKED "FREIGHT TO COLLECT" NOTIFYING THE APPLICANT.
+ SIGNED PACKING LIST IN TRIPLICATE SHOWING THE FOLLOWING DETAILS: TOTAL NUMBER OF PACKAGES SHIPPED; CONTENT(S) OF PACKAGE(S); GROSS WEIGHT, NET WEIGHT AND MEASUREMENT.
+ CERTIFICATE OF ORIGIN ISSUED AND SIGNED OR AUTHENTICATED BY A LOCAL CHAMBER OF COMMERCE LOCATED IN THE EXPORTING COUNTRY.
+ INSURANCE POLICY/CERTIFICATE IN DUPLICATE ENDORSED IN BLANK FOR 120% INVOICE VALUE, COVERING ALL RISKS OF CIC OF PICC.

71B: CHARGES: ALL CHARGES AND COMMISSIONS ARE FOR ACCOUNT OF BENEFICIARY INCLUDING REIMBURSING CHARGES.

……

三、审证

根据下列合同条款及审证要求，审查国外来证。

销售合同
Sales Contract

卖方：HENAN BEST INTERNATIONAL TRADING CO., LTD

    33 EAST NONGYE ROAD, ZHENGZHOU CHINA

买方：HENRY FROST CHEMICAL CO.

    854 CALIFORNIA ST. SAN FRANCISCO, CA94104 USA

合同号：SJ09086

日期：JUNE 24, 2018

The undersigned Seller and Buyer agreed to close the following transactions according to the terms and conditions stipulated below:

商品名称及规格 Commodity & Specifications	数量 Quantity	CIF SAN FRANCISCO	
		单价 Unit Price	金额 Amount
SPHERICAL ALUMINUM POWDER			
1. E20T02	1,000KG	USD 15.60	USD 15,600.00
2. E20T03	1,000KG	USD 15.40	USD 15,400.00
3. E20T04	1,000KG	USD 15.20	USD 15,200.00
TOTAL	3,000KG		USD 46,200.00

TOTAL AMOUNT: SAY US DOLLARS FORTY SIX THOUSAND TWO HUNDRED ONLY

装运期： DURING SEPTEMBER 2018
包装： PACKED IN SEALED IRON DRUM, 180-200KG/DRUM
装运口岸及目的地：FROM TIANJIN TO SAN FRANCISCO
运输方式： BY SEA
转运及分批： ALLOWED
付款方式： BY IRREVOCABLE SIGHT L/C ISSUED BY THE ISSUING BANK APPROVED BY THE SELLER TO REACH THE SELLER ON OR BEFORE JULY 31, 2018.
保险： INSURANCE TO BE EFFECTED BY THE SELLER FOR 110% OF THE INVOICE VALUE COVERING ALL RISKS AND WAR RISKS AS PER CIC.
……

信用证
Letter of Credit

Sequence of Total	27:	1/1
Form of Doc. Credit	40A:	IRREVOCABLE
Doc. Credit Number	20:	ULS23076
Date of Issue	31C:	180730
Applicable Rules	40E:	UCP LATEST VERSION
Expiry	31D:	DATE 181031 PLACE CHINA
Applicant	50:	HENRY FROST CHEMICAL CO. 854 CALIFORNIA ST. SAN FRANCISCO CA94104 USA
Issuing Bank	52A:	BANK OF CHINA LOS ANGELES BRANCH
Beneficiary	59:	HENAN BEST INTERNATIONAL TRADING CO., LTD
Amount	32B:	CURRENCY USD 4,620.00
Available with/by	41D:	ANY BANK IN CHINA BY NEGOTIATION
Drafts at …	42C:	DRAFTS AT 15 DAYS AFTER SIGHT FOR FULL INVOICE VALUE
Drawee	42D:	BANK OF CHINA LOS ANGELES BRANCH
Partial Shipments	43P:	ALLOWED
Transshipment	43T:	PROHIBITED
Loading on Board	44A:	LIANYUNGANG PORT
For Transportation to …	44B:	SAN FRANCISCO
Latest Date of Shipment	44C:	SEPT. 30, 2018
Description of Goods	45A:	3,000KGS OF SPHERICAL ALUMINUM POWDER AS PER SJ09088 DATED JUNE 24, 2018 CIF LIANYUNGANG
Documents Required	46A:	1. SIGNED COMMERCIAL INVOICE IN 3 COPIES

		INDICATING L/C NO.
		2. CERTIFICATE OF ORIGIN IN 3 COPIES.
		3. PACKING LIST IN TRIPLICATE.
		4. 2/3 SET OF CLEAN ON BOARD OCEAN BILLS OF LADING MADE OUT TO ORDER AND BLANK ENDORSED. MARKED "FREIGHT PREPAID" AND NOTIFY APPLICANT, INDICATING CREDIT NUMBER.
		5. INSURANCE POLICY OR CERTIFICATE IN DUPLICATE ENDORSED IN BLANK FOR 120 PCT OF INVOICE VALUE INCLUDING INSTITUTE CARGO CLAUSES (ALL RISKS), INSTITUTE WAR CLAUSES, INSTITUTE STRIKES, RIOTS AND CIVIL COMMOTIONS CLAUSES.
Additional Conditions	47A:	BENEFICIARY'S CERTIFICATE REQUIRED STATING THAT ONE ORIGINAL B/L AND ONE SET OF NON-NEGOTIABLE COPIES OF SHIPPING DOCUMENTS HAVE BEEN SENT DIRECTLY TO APPLICANT AFTER SHIPMENT.
Period for Presentation	48:	DOCUMENTS MUST BE PRESENTED WITHIN 5 DAYS AFTER THE DATE OF SHIPMENT BUT WITHIN THE VALIDITY OF THE CREDIT.
Confirmation Instructions	49:	WITHOUT

四、案例分析

（1）我国进口商 A 公司与英国出口商 B 公司签订合同进口木材，采用信用证方式结算。A 公司在开证申请书上注明，90%的发票金额凭申请书中所列的全套单据付款，另外规定："10 pct of invoice value shall be payable against the performance guarantee by first class bank."开证行根据开证申请书使用 SWIFT 开出信用证。开证行在收到 B 公司的单据后进行了审核，确定单证相符，并在规定的期限内对外付款。A 公司付款赎单后，提出两个不符点：①履约保函未按照合同规定的格式开立；②保函由 BANK A 开立，而 BANK A 不是第一流的银行。A 公司因此认为开证行不应付款，要求开证行退回从其账上扣除的款项。

请问：A 公司所指出的不符点成立吗？为什么？

（2）我国进口商 ABC 公司与美国出口商 D 公司签订合同进口木材，采用信用证方式结算。ABC 公司在开证申请书上注明禁止转运，并且要求提交的运输单据种类为海运提单。开证行根据开证申请书使用 SWIFT 开出信用证。D 公司提交的海运提单包含了海运全程运输，并且提单上注明以下语句："Container shipment transshipment will take place."开证行审单以后确定单据相符，并对外付了款。申请人 ABC 公司收到单据后指出开证行未尽详细审单职责，不应对外付款，因为单据有不符点，理由是提单上显示了转运语句。

请问：ABC 公司所提出的不符点成立吗？为什么？

项目三
Project III

商业发票
Commercial Invoice

学习目标（Learning Aims）

- 熟悉商业发票的概念和作用。
- 掌握填制商业发票的相关规定与要求以及发票的类型。
- 能根据合同与相关要求熟练填制商业发票。

情景导入（Lead-in Situation）

科林国际贸易公司在收到环球采购公司的第 TXT264 号合同项下的信用证后，开始安排货物生产。备齐货物之后，业务员李怡华需要填制发票，以便办理后续的相关手续。

一、背景知识（Background Knowledge）

（一）商业发票的定义（Definition of Commercial Invoice）

商业发票（Commercial Invoice），贸易活动中通常简称发票（Invoice），是出口方向进口方开列的发货价目清单，是买卖双方记账的依据，也是进出口报关交税的总说明。商业发票必须注明买卖双方，并清楚列明买卖双方的日期、销售条款、装运数量、重量和/或体积、包装类型、货物的完整说明、单价和总值、保险费和运输费等。商业发票是海关为核定进口货物的真实价值、评定关税和其他税款所需要的凭证，是清关的必要文件之一，是全套单据的核心。

（二）商业发票的作用及相关规则（Functions of Commercial Invoice and Related Rules）

1. 商业发票的作用

（1）商业发票是交易的合法证明文件，是卖方向买方发送货物的凭证。
（2）商业发票是买卖双方收付货款和记账的凭证。
（3）商业发票是买卖双方办理报关、清关、纳税的凭证。
（4）商业发票是卖方填制货运单据的核心单据。
（5）在不使用汇票的情况下，商业发票可以代替汇票起付款凭证的作用。

2. 商业发票的相关规则

《跟单信用证统一惯例（UCP 600）》第十八条"商业发票"中规定如下：

a. A commercial invoice:

a. 商业发票：

i. Must appear to have been issued by the beneficiary (except as provided in article 38).

i. 必须在表面上看来系由受益人出具（第三十八条另有规定者除外）。

ii. Must be made out in the name of the applicant [except as provided in sub-article 38(g)].

ii. 必须做成以申请人的名称为抬头[第三十八条（g）款另有规定者除外]。

iii. Must be made out in the same currency as the credit.

iii. 必须将发票币别做成与信用证相同币种。

iv. need not be signed.

iv. 无须签字。

b. A nominated bank acting on its nomination, a confirming bank, if any, or the issuing bank may accept a commercial invoice issued for an amount in excess of the amount permitted by the credit, and its decision will be binding upon all parties, provided the bank in question has not honoured or negotiated for an amount in excess of that permitted by the credit.

b. 按照指定行事的被指定银行、保兑行（如有）或开证行可以接受金额超过信用证所允许金额的商业发票，倘若有关银行已兑付或已议付的金额没有超过信用证所允许的金额，则该银行的决定对各有关方均具有约束力。

c. The description of the goods, services or performance in a commercial invoice must correspond with that appearing in the credit.

c. 商业发票中货物、服务或行为的描述必须与信用证中显示的内容相符。

（三）其他常见的发票类型（Other Common Types of Invoices）

1. 海关发票

海关发票（Customs Invoice）是某些国家规定在进口货物时，必须提供其海关规定的一种固定格式和内容的发票。海关发票的作用包括：①供进口国海关核定货物的原产地，以采取不同的国别政策；②供进口商向海关办理进口报关、纳税等手续；③供进口国海关掌握进口商品在出口国市场的价格情况，以确定是否低价倾销，以便征收反倾销税；④供进口国海关作为统计的依据。因此，对进口商来说，海关发票是一种很重要的单据。目前，要求提供海关发票的国家主要有美国、加拿大和新西兰等。

2. 银行发票

银行发票（Banker's Invoice）是出口商为办理议付和结汇，以适应议付行和开证行需要而提供的发票，通常格式较简略。

3. 领事发票

领事发票（Consular Invoice）又称签证发票，是按某些国家法令规定，出口商对其国家输入货物时必须取得进口国在出口国或其邻近地区的领事签证的、作为装运单据的一部分和货物进口报关的前提条件之一的特殊发票。

4. 形式发票

形式发票（Proforma Invoice，P/I）也称预开发票或估价发票，是进口商为了向其本国当局申请进口许可证或请求核批外汇，在未成交之前，要求出口商按照拟成交的商品名称、单价、规格等条件开立的一份参考性发票。

二、认识发票（Understand the Invoices）

（一）商业发票的样本与填制要点（Sample and Instructions for Commercial Invoice）

(2) Issuer		商业发票 (1) COMMERCIAL INVOICE		
(3) To		(4) Invoice No.		(5) Invoice Date
(7) Transport Details		(6a) S/C No.		
		(6b) L/C No.		
(8) Marks and Numbers	(9) Number and Kind of Packages Description of Goods	(10) Quantity	(11) Unit Price	(12) Amount
	(13a) Total			
(13b) Total (in word):				
(14)				(15) Signature and Seal

商业发票无统一格式，一般由出口商自行设计，但内容必须符合信用证和合同的要求，基本内容及制单要点如下（参见样本）：

1．**单据名称**（Name of Document）

发票上应标明"Invoice"或"Commercial Invoice"字样。在信用证项下，单据名称应与信用证中的规定一致。

2．**出票人**（Issuer）

填写开具发票的公司（即出口商）的名称和地址。在信用证项下，出票人的名称和地址应与信用证受益人（Beneficiary）的名称和地址保持一致。

3．**受票人**（To）

俗称抬头，一般情况下填写进口商的名称和地址。在信用证项下，受票人的名称和地址应与信用证开证申请人（Applicant）的名称和地址一致。以托收方式支付货款时，应填写合同买方的名称和地址。

4．**发票编号**（Invoice No.）

发票编号一般由出口商按公司统一规律自行编制。

5．**发票日期**（Invoice Date）

发票日期一般是在信用证开证日期之后、信用证有效期之前。该日期不能早于合同的签订日期，又不能晚于提单的日期。

6．**合同编号及信用证编号**（S/C No. & L/C No.）

根据实际的合同与信用证的编号填写。

7．**运输信息**（Transport Details）

填写此单货物的运输路线及运输方式，如"From … to … by Sea/Air"。如有转运，注明转运地名称。例如："From Huangpu to New York on July 1, 2018 by Vessel."（所有货物于2018年7月1日通过海运，从广州黄埔港运往纽约港。）

8．**唛头**（Marks and Numbers）

若在合同或信用证中规定了唛头，按规定填写；若是散装货物填写"In bulk"，若为裸装货则注明"Naked"；若无唛头，应注明"N/M"字样。

9．**货物描述**（Number and Kind of Packages，Description of Goods）

这是发票的核心内容，一般情况下，必须详细注明货物的名称、规格、数量及包装类型等。采用信用证支付时，发票的货物描述必须与信用证中的描述一致。若信用证中的描述非常简单，可按合同要求列明货物的具体内容。

10．**数量**（Quantity）

按合同或信用证标明的装运数量填写，同时还必须标明数量单位，如"KG""CTNS"等。例如"10,000PCS"（注意单位的单复数）。注意该数量和计量单位既要与信用证或合同保持一致，也要与货物的实际装运数量一致。凡信用证数量前有"约""大概"或类似的词语，交货时允许数量有10%的增减幅度。

11．**单价**（Unit Price）

对应不同货物标明相应单价，注明货币单位及数量单位；完整的单价包括计价币种、金额、计量单位和价格术语。价格术语（贸易术语）一般写在此栏的最上方。

12. 总值（Amount）

每种商品的数量乘以单价得出的单项货物总值。

13. 发票的总金额（Total）

(13a)Total 是指发票各栏目的合计，用阿拉伯数字写出。(13b)Total (in words)要求用文字书写发票的总金额。例如：小写金额"USD 90,245.00"对应写为："Say US dollars ninety thousand two hundred and forty five only."除非信用证上另有规定，否则发票总值不能超过信用证金额。若信用证没有相关规定，则发票金额应与合同保持一致。

14. 补充信息及声明文字（也称为自由处置区）

如果信用证中要求在发票上加注各种费用金额、特定号码、有关证明等，一般将这些内容填写在此空白处。

15. 签字盖章（Signature and Seal）

根据《UCP 600》的规定，发票可不签字盖章。若信用证要求"Signed Invoice"，出口商则需要在发票上签字或加盖图章；若要求"Manually Signed Invoice"，则该发票必须手签。如果发票上有加注证明的字句（如"We certify that …"），此类发票也必须签字盖章。

（二）情景导入中的发票（Invoice of the Lead-in Situation）

科林国际贸易（香港）有限公司
KELIN INTERNATIONAL TRADING (HK) CO., LTD
COMMERCIAL INVOICE

INVOICE NO.:	PI170601
INVOICE DATE:	July 18, 2018
S/C NO.:	TXT264
S/C DATE:	APR. 20, 2018

TO: GLOBE SOURCING SERVICE CO., LTD
1407, 80th Street, S.W., Novi, Michigan, USA

FROM: SHEKOU PORT, SHENZHEN **TO:** NEW YORK **BY:** VESSEL

L/C NO.: BL170197   **ISSUE DATE:** June 29, 2018

Marks and Numbers	Description of Goods Number and Kind of Package	Quantity	Unit Price	Amount
			CIF New York	
G.S.S TXT264 NEW YORK C/No. 1-300	100% COTTON COLOUR WAVE T-SHIRT TM111 TM222 TM333 TM444 PACKED IN CARTONS OF 20 PCS EACH	 2,000 PCS 2,000 PCS 1,000 PCS 1,000 PCS 	 USD 11.00/PC USD 10.00/PC USD 9.50/PC USD 8.50/PC 	 USD 22,000.00 USD 20,000.00 USD 9,500.00 USD 8,500.00
	Total:	**6,000 PCS**		**USD 60,000.00**

SAY TOTAL: US DOLLARS SIXTY THOUSAND ONLY
FREIGHT: USD800.00
INSURANCE: USD330.00
FOB PRICE: USD58,870.00
COUNTRY OF ORIGIN: CHINA

Kelin International Trading (HK) Co., Ltd
(SEAL)
SIGNATURE: 李怡华

（三）海关发票的样本与填制要点（Sample and Instructions for Customs Invoice）

海关发票由出口商填写，其格式由进口国具体规定。此类发票包含的主要项目有货物的生产国别、货物名称、数量、唛头、出口地市价及出口售价等。

海关发票的格式和名称虽各不一样，但大致内容基本一致，需要注意的是每个国家的海关发票都有其固定格式，必须按规定填制，用错格式将构成单证不符。下面以美国海关发票为例，介绍其主要栏目及填制要点。

美国海关发票样本：

DEPARTMENT OF THE TREASURY
UNITED STATES CUSTOMS SERVICE   SPECIAL CUSTOMS INVOICE   Form Approved
19U.S.C.1481.1482.1484. (Use separate invoice for purchased and non-purchased goods.)   O.M.B. No. 48-RO342

(1) SELLER	(2) DOCUMENT NO. *	(3) INVOICE NO. AND DATE *
	(4) REFERENCES *	
(5) CONSIGNEE	(6) BUYER (if other than consignee)	
	(7) ORIGIN OF GOODS	
(8) NOTIFY PARTY *	(9) TERMS OF SALE, PAYMENT, AND DISCOUNT	
(10) ADDITIONAL TRANSPORTATION INFORMATION *	(11) CURRENCY USED	(12) EXCH. RATE (if fixed or agreed)	(13) DATE ORDER ACCEPTED

(14) MARKS AND NUMBERS ON SHIPPING PACKAGES	(15) NUMBER OF PACKAGES	(16) FULL DESCRIPTION OF GOODS	(17) QUANTITY	UNIT PRICE		(20) INVOICE TOTALS
				(18) HOME MARKET	(19) INVOICE	

(21) ☐ If the production of these goods involved furnishing goods or services to the seller (e.g., assisted such as dies, molds, tools, engineering work) and the value is not included in the invoice price, check box (21) and explain below.

(22) PACKING COSTS

(27) DECLARATION OF SELLER/SHIPPER (OR AGENT)

(A) ☐ I declare: If there are any rebates, drawbacks or bounties allowed upon the exportation of goods, I have checked box (A) and itemized separately below.	(B) ☐ If the goods were not sold or agreed to be sold, I have checked box (B) and have indicated in column (19) the price I would be willing to receive.	(23) OCEAN OR INTERNATIONAL FREIGHT
		(24) DOMESTIC FREIGHT CHARGES
I further declare that there is no other invoice differing from this one (unless otherwise described below) and that all statements contained in this invoice and declaration are true and correct.	(C) SIGNATURE OF SELLER/ SHIPPER (OR AGENT):	(25) INSURANCE COSTS
		(26) OTHER COSTS (specify below)

(28). THIS SPACE FOR CONTINUING ANSWERS

THIS FORM OF INVOICE REQUIRED GENERALLY IF RATE OF DUTY BASED UPON OR REGULATED BY VALUE OF GOODS AND PURCHASE PRICE OR VALUE OF SHIPMENT EXCEEDS USD500. OTHERWISE USE COMMERCIAL INVOICE.

1．卖方（Seller）
填写出口商的名称和地址。

2．单据编号（Document No.）
通常为发票编号，可不填。

3．发票编号和日期（Invoice No. and Date）
填写该商业发票编号和出单日期，可不填。

4．有关资料（References）
填写信用证编号、合同编号等，可不填。

5．收货人（Consignee）
填写美国境内收货人的名称和地址。如提单未提供收货人名称，应填开证申请人或信用证规定的实际收货人。托收或汇款项下填写合同的买方。

6．买方（Buyer）
如果买方不是收货人（Consignee）则此栏填买方，如果买方与收货人为同一人则此栏填"Same as Consignee"。

7．货物原产地（Origin of Goods）
应填"CHINA"。

8．通知方（Notify Party）
填写提单通知方，亦可不填。

9．价格条件、支付条款和折扣（Terms of Sale, Payment, and Discount）
价格条件根据商业发票填写。支付条款填付款的方式，如"L/C""Collection"或"Remittance by T/T"等。折扣有则填，如"Discount 1%"；没有则填"No discount"，或不填。

10．货物运输的补充说明（Additional Transportation Information）
填启运港、目的港、船名、开航日、转船或途经港口等。

11．使用货币（Currency Used）
填写发票使用的货币，如"USD"。

12．汇率（Exchange Rate）
使用美元以外的货币时应填写当时的汇率，如使用美元则不填。

13．接受订单日期（Date Order Accepted）
通常填订单日期，没有订单则不填。

14．唛头和箱号（Marks and Numbers on Shipping Packages）
根据商业发票上的唛头和箱号填写。

15．包装件数（Number of Packages）
根据商业发票上的包装件数填写。

16．货物的详细说明（Full Description of Goods）
根据商业发票上的货物描述填写。

17．数量（Quantity）
根据商业发票上的数量填写。

18．国内市场价格（Home Market Unit Price）
应填人民币价，此单价应按低于FOB折成人民币值的4%左右填写，表示有4%的出口利润。但如信用证无特殊要求，此栏可以不填。

19．**发票价格**（Invoice Unit Price）

根据商业发票所列价格逐项填写。

20．**发票总金额**（Invoice Totals）

根据商业发票上的总金额填写。

21．如果货物的生产涉及压型、模具、工具、工程设计等，且这些成本未包括在发票价值之内，则在本栏方格内注"√"标记，并在下面（28）栏说明。

If the production of these goods involved furnishing goods or services to the seller (e.g., assisted such as dies, molds, tools, engineering work) and the value is not included in the invoice price, check box (21) and explain below.

22．**包装费用**（Packing Costs）

23．**海洋或国际运费**（Ocean or International Freight）

24．**国内运费**（Domestic Freight Charges）

25．**保险费**（Insurance Costs）

26．**其他费用**（Other Costs）

（22）～（26）栏均应按实际填写。注意各项费用合计应与货款总金额协调一致。

27．**卖方/托运人（或其代理人）声明**[Declaration of Seller/Shipper (or Agent)]

本栏分以下三 项内容：

（A）如货物出口享受回扣、退税或补助津贴，则在本栏方格内注"√"标记，并在下面（28）栏内分别列明。

If there are any rebates，drawbacks or bounties allowed upon the exportation of goods, I have checked box (A) and itemized separately below.

（B）如货物未售出或同意售出，则在本栏方格内注"√"标记，并在（19）栏注明愿意接受的价格。

If the goods were not sold or agreed to be sold, I have checked box (B) and have indicated in column (19) the price I would be willing to receive.

（C）本人进一步声明，没有与此不同的其他发票（除非下文另有说明），且此发票内的一切声明和申报都是真实和正确的。

I further declare that there is no other invoice differing from this one (unless otherwise described below) and that all the statements contained in this invoice and declaration are true and correct.

卖方/托运人或其代理人签字[Signature of Seller/Shipper (or Agent)]：要手签，不能盖章。

28．**需要继续说明的问题**（This Space for Continuing Answers）

三、信用证中关于商业发票的条款举例（Examples of Related Terms for Commercial Invoice in the L/C）

（1）Signed commercial invoice, one original and two copies.

已签署的商业发票，一正二副。

（2）Signed commercial invoice in 6 copies.

已签署的商业发票一式六份。

（3）Beneficiary's manually signed commercial invoice in four folds.
受益人手签的商业发票一式四份。

（4）Signed commercial invoice in 3 copies price CIF Bangkok showing FOB value, freight charges and insurance premium separately.
已签署的商业发票一式三份，CIF 曼谷价，分别显示 FOB 价、运费和保险费。

（5）Signed commercial invoice in duplicate showing a deduction of USD 200.00 being commission.
已签署的商业发票一式两份，显示扣除 200 美元作为佣金。

（6）Manually signed invoice in five folds certifying that goods are as per Contract No. ABC567 of 03.10, 2018 quoting L/C No.
手签发票一式五份，须证明货物符合 2018 年 3 月 10 日订立的 ABC567 号合同，注明信用证号码。

（7）Signed commercial invoice combined with certificate of origin and value in triplicate as required for imports into Nigeria.
已签署的商业发票，连同产地证明和货物价值声明，一式三份为输入尼日利亚所需。

（8）Signed commercial invoice in quintuplicate, certifying merchandise to be of Chinese origin.
已签署的商业发票一式五份，注明产品的原产地为中国。

（9）5% discount should be deducted from total amount of the commercial invoice.
商业发票的总金额须扣除 5%折扣。

（10）Signed commercial invoice in five folds certifying that goods are as per Contract No. 12345 of 03.11, 2018 quoting L/C No. and BTN/HS No. and showing original invoice and a copy to accompany original set of documents.
已签署的发票一式五份，须证明货物符合 2018 年 3 月 11 日订立的 12345 号合同，注明信用证号码和布鲁塞尔税则分类号码，并显示正本发票和一份副本随附原套单证。

（11）Commercial invoice in triplicate showing separately FOB value, freight charges, insurance premium, CIF value and country of origin.
商业发票一式三份，分别显示 FOB 价、运费、保险费、CIF 价和原产国。

（12）Commercial invoice in quadruplicate indicating the following:
① Each item is labeled "Made in China".
② One set of non-negotiable shipping documents has been airmailed in advance to the buyer.
商业发票一式四份，并表明以下内容：
① 每件商品标明"中国制造"。
② 一套副本装运提单已被预先航空邮寄给买方。

（13）Developing Country Clause:
(A) The last process in the manufacture of the goods described below was performed in China.
(B) Not less than 50% of their factory work costs is represented by the sum of the materials, manufacturing wages and factory overhead expenses performed in China.
商业发票上须备注关于发展中国家的声明：

（A）以下货物的最后工序都是在中国完成的。
（B）不少于 50%的工厂成本由在中国产生的原材料、加工薪酬和间接制造费用的总和表示。

实操训练（Skill Training）

一、单选题

1. 一般情况下，商业发票的金额应与（　　）一致。
   A. 合同金额　　　B. 信用证金额　　　C. 保险金额　　　D. 实际发货金额
2. 发票上的货物数量应与信用证一致，如信用证在数量前使用"约""大约"字眼时，应理解为（　　）。
   A. 货物数量有不超过 5%的增减幅度
   B. 货物数量有不超过 10%的增减幅度
   C. 货物数量有不超过 3%的增减幅度
   D. 货物数量不得增减
3. 海关发票是由（　　）制定的一种特殊发票格式。
   A. 出口方　　　B. 进口方　　　C. 出口国海关　　　D. 进口国海关
4. 下列哪点不是商业发票的作用（　　）。
   A. 是进出口报关完税必不可少的单据　　B. 是全套单据的核心
   C. 是结算货款的依据　　D. 是物权凭证
5. 发票的日期在结汇单据中应（　　）。
   A. 早于汇票的签发日期　　B. 早于提单的签发日期
   C. 早于保险单的签发日期　　D. 是最早签发的单据
6. 根据《UCP 600》的规定，商业发票中货物的描述（　　）。
   A. 可以使用统称，不得与信用证中有关货物的描述有抵触
   B. 可以使用统称，并可与信用证中有关货物的描述有所不同
   C. 必须完全符合信用证中的描述
   D. 必须与合同的描述完全一致
7. 某批货物经中国香港转船后运往加拿大，海关发票"Country of Transshipment"栏应填报为（　　）。
   A. W/T at Hong Kong　　　B. China
   C. N/A　　　D. W/T from Hong Kong
8. 商业发票的抬头人一般是（　　）。
   A. 受益人　　　B. 开证申请人　　　C. 开证银行　　　D. 卖方
9. （　　）是结汇单证中最重要的单据，能让有关当事人了解一笔交易的全貌，且其他单据的填制都应以其为依据。
   A. 装箱单　　　B. 发票　　　C. 原产地证书　　　D. 提单
10. 海关发票的抬头人一般是（　　）。
    A. 开证申请人　　　B. 受益人　　　C. 进口国海关　　　D. 进口地的收货人

二、根据以下信用证信息填制商业发票

Issuing Bank: TOKYO BANK LTD., TOKYO

L/C No. : 6248

Date of Issue: 180816

Application: SAKA INTERNATIONAL FOOD CO. 26 TORIMI-CHO NISHI-PU, NAGOYA 546, JAPAN

Beneficiary: NINGBO NATIVE PRODUCTS CO. NO. 115 DONGFENG ROAD, NINGBO, CHINA

Loading in Charge: NINGBO, CHINA

For Transportation to: NAGOYA, JAPAN

Description of Goods: 20M/T FRESH BAMBOO SHOOTS AT CIF NAGOYA USD1080.00 PER M/T AND 30M/T FRESH ASPARAGUS AT CIF NAGOYA USD1600.00 PER M/T AS PER CONTRACT NO. NP94051

Documents Required: +COMMERCIAL INVOICE IN TRIPLICATE AND CERTIFY THAT THE GOODS ARE OF CHINESE ORIGIN.

Shipping Marks: NO MARKS

制作发票的日期：2018年8月16日；发票编号：BP8500555。

三、案例分析

甲公司（卖方）与乙公司（买方）签订了买卖合同，合同约定"验货后10天内付款300万元"。卖方按时交了货，买方也进行了验收，验收合格。然而买方不肯支付货款，理由是要求卖方先开具正式发票，但卖方表示拒绝并认为应该是先付款后开发票，进而双方发生争执。请问究竟是应该卖方先开发票还是应该买方先给钱？

项目四
Project IV

包装单据
Packing Documents

学习目标（Learning Aims）

- 了解包装单据和运输标志的基本概念、作用和要求。
- 掌握货物运输中的不同标志及其用途。
- 掌握填制包装单据的基本内容和填制技巧。

情景导入（Lead-in Situation）

科林国际贸易公司完成第 TXT264 号合同项下货物的生产并通过相关部门的验货后，业务员李怡华与买方环球采购公司相关业务员沟通，依据买方对货物外包装和内包装的要求开始装箱入柜。按照信用证的规定，最晚装运日期为 8 月 30 日，即要求科林公司负责人在 8 月 30 日之前办理完相关手续，并准备好货物出运的相关文件。因此李怡华在完成了发票的填制后，还要在规定时间内根据出货单填制装箱单等包装单据。

一、背景知识（Background Knowledge）

（一）包装的种类（Categories of Packing）

出口包装一般有大包装、小包装和中性包装之分。

大包装指外包装，主要用于保护商品，避免运输、储存、装卸过程中的丢失或损坏。

小包装也指内包装或销售包装，主要起到改善商品形象、提高商品价值，有利于促销的作用。

中性包装（Neutral Packing）是指商品内外均未标明生产国别、地名和厂商的名称，也不标明商标或牌号的包装。主要是为了适应国外市场的特殊要求，如转口销售，有可能交易对象不是最终的买家，而只是一个中间商，所以要使用中性包装。或者为了打破某些进口国家的关税和非关税壁垒，并适应交易的特殊需要，它是出口国家厂商加强对外竞销和扩大出口的一种手段。常用的中性包装有两种：一是无牌中性包装，这种包装既无生产国别、地名、厂名，也无商标牌号，主要用于一些尚待进一步加工的半制成品，其主要目的是降低成本；二是有牌中性包装，这种包装不注明商品生产国别、地名、厂名，但要注明买方指定商标或牌号，同时也加注国外商号名称或表示其商号的标记。

（二）包装单据的定义（Definition of Packing Document）

包装单据（Packing Document）是指一切记载或描述商品包装情况的单据，是商业发票的附属单据，也是货运单据中的一项重要单据。

国际贸易中的货物，除了小部分属于散装货物或裸装货物外，绝大多数都需要包装。因此在通常情况下，包装单据是必不可少的文件之一。进口地海关验货、公证行检验、进口商核对货物时，都以包装单据为依据来了解包装内的具体内容，以便其对货物进行接收和销售。

（三）包装单据的作用及相关条款（Functions of Packing Document and Related Terms）

1．包装单据的作用

（1）包装单据是出口商填制商业发票及其他单据时计量和计价的基础资料。

（2）包装单据是进口商清点数量或重量以及销售货物的依据。

（3）包装单据是海关查验货物的凭证。

（4）包装单据是公证或商检机构查验货物的参考资料。

2．信用证中有关包装单据的条款举例

（1）Packing list in duplicate.
装箱单一式两份。

（2）Signed packing list, one original and one copy.
签字装箱单，一正一副。

（3）Signed packing list in quadruplicate showing gross weight, net weight, measurement, colour, size and quantity breakdown for each package.

签字装箱单一式四份,并注明每包货物的毛重、净重、体积、颜色、尺寸和数量。
(4) Packing list in triplicate issued by beneficiary indicating quantity, gross and net weight of each package/container.
由受益人出具的装箱单一式三份,指出每一包裹或集装箱的毛重和净重。

(四)包装单据的种类(Kinds of Packing Documents)

1. 装箱单

装箱单(Packing List)又称包装单,明确阐明装箱货物的名称、规格、唛头、箱号、件数、毛/净重等内容。其主要作用是对商业发票内容的补充以及作为海关、进出口商等验货的凭据。装箱单除了需要按照装箱的情况详细列明商品包装的具体情况(如货号、色号、尺寸搭配、毛/净重以及包装的尺码)以外,其他项目内容的填写与发票相同。

2. 重量单

重量单(Weight List)是包装单据的一种,对于按照装货重量成交的货物,重量单是出口商在装运时必须向进口商提供的一种证明文件。它重点说明商品每箱毛重、净重的情况,供买方安排运输、存仓时参考。

3. 尺码单

尺码单(Measurement List)是一种偏重于说明每件货物的包装尺码和总尺码的包装单据。如果货物不是统一尺码,应逐一列出每件的尺码。

除了上述常见的包装单据外,还有以下包装单据:
① 规格单(Specification List)。
② 包装声明(Packing Declaration)。
③ 包装说明(Packing Specification)。
④ 包装提要(Packing Summary)。
⑤ 重量证书(Weight Certificate)。
⑥ 花色搭配单(Assortment List)。
⑦ 磅码单(Weight Memo)。

(五)包装的标志和用途(Packing Marks and Functions)

包装标志是为了便于货物交接,防止错发错运,便于识别、运输、仓储以及海关等有关部门进行查验等工作,便于收货人提取货物,而在进出口货物的外包装上标明的记号。通常箱类包装的包装标志应粘贴在包装件的端面或侧面。包装标志可分为运输标志、指示性标志和警告性标志。

1. 运输标志

运输标志(Shipping Marks)俗称"唛头",是贸易合同、发货单据中有关标志事项的基本部分。它一般由简单的几何图形以及字母、数字等组成。其主要内容包括:①收货人代号;②发货人代号或合同号;③目的地名称;④件数、批号。此外,有的运输标志还包括原产地、重量和体积等内容。运输标志的内容繁简不一,由买卖双方根据商品特点和具体要求商定。

2. 指示性标志

指示性标志(Indicative Marks)是指按商品的特点,对于易碎或需防湿、防颠倒等商品,在包装上用醒目图形或文字标明货物需小心轻放、防潮湿、此端向上等。

指示标志用来指示运输、装卸、保管人员在作业时需要注意到的事项，以保证货物的安全。这种标志主要表示货物的性质及其堆放、开启、吊运等的方法。

根据 GB/T 191—2008《包装储运图示标志》规定，在有特殊要求的货物外包装上应直接印刷、粘贴、拴挂、钉附或喷涂相应的图示标志，如易碎物品、向上、怕晒、怕雨、重心点、禁止翻滚、由此吊起等（见图 4-1）。

图 4-1 指示性标志

3. 警告性标志

警告性标志（Warning Marks）又称危险品标志，是指在特殊物品（如爆炸品、易燃物品、腐蚀品和氧化剂等）的外包装上表明其危险性质的文字或图形说明（见图 4-2）。

图 4-2 警告性标志

二、认识包装单据（Understand the Packing Documents）

（一）装箱单的样本与填制要点（Sample and Instructions for Packing List）

(4) Issuer				装箱单 (1) PACKING LIST		
(5) To				(2) Invoice No.		(3) Date
(15) From			To			
(6) Marks & Numbers	(7) Description of Goods	(8) Quantity	(9) Package	(10) G.W.	(11) N.W.	(12) Meas.
	(13) Total					

(14) SAY TOTAL:

(16) Signature and Seal

1．单据名称（Name of Document）

填写装箱单、重量单和尺码单的中英文字样。如果是信用证项下，则按照信用证中的英文名称填写。

2．发票编号（Invoice No.）

填写商业发票编号。包装单据可以有单独的编号，但因为商业发票是核心单据，一般都用商业发票的编号作为包装单据的编号。

3．出单日期（Date）

出单日期可以按发票日期填写。包装单据的制作一般在发票之后，所以也可以晚于发票日期，但是不能晚于提单日期。

4．出单人（Issuer）

填写出口商的名称和地址。

5．受单人（To）

即抬头人，填写进口商的名称和地址，要求与开证申请人或合同买方一致。

6．唛头（Marks & Numbers）

唛头应与发票、提单等单据的唛头一致。

7．货物描述（Description of Goods）

填写商品的名称、规格和型号等。包装单据的货物描述应与发票和信用证内容一致，如有总称应先注明总称，再逐项列明货名。

8．数量（Quantity）

如果每种规格产品的数量不同，应将不同规格的产品数量分别表示出来，再给出合计数。

9．包装件数（Package）

填写每种货物的外包装件数。如有 8 件产品（8 PCS）以每箱 4 件打包为 2 个纸箱（2 Cartons），则"Quantity"处填"8 PCS"，"Package"处填"2 Cartons"。此外，合计栏处要注明外包装的总件数。

10．毛重（单件/合计）[Gross Weight (per package / total)]

如果货物有多种规格，每种规格的毛重不同，则应分别列出毛重。如果货物的单件不是定量包装，如粮谷类麻袋包装的商品，一般只能填写每袋大约的重量。比如，第一袋货物是 90 千克，第二袋是 89.7 千克，第三袋是 90.4 千克……每一袋的重量不可能完全一致。这种情况下的商品尽可能不出具包装单据，如果要出具，则必须整批货物每袋都过磅、编号，并做记录。如果有一万袋，则必须过磅一万次，然后在包装单上列出一万个数。这种包装单据又称为"磅码单"，非常麻烦。

11．净重（单件/合计）[Net Weight (per package / total)]

填写每个包装件的净重，同时合计栏处要注明总净重。

12．体积（单件/合计）[Measurement (per package / total)]

填写每个包装件的体积及合计体积。

13．数量（Total）

用阿拉伯数字填写本单货物外包装件数。

14．总数量（Say Total）

用大写英文填写本单货物外包装件数。

15．运输详情（From / To）

填写启运港和目的港的名称，如：启运港是深圳，目的港是日本东京，则填写"From SHENZHEN to TOKYO"。

16．签字盖章（Signature and Seal）

如果信用证要求签署（Signed），则出口商必须在此栏加盖公司图章并署名。

（二）装箱单实例（Models of Packing List）

1. 情景导入中的装箱单

科林国际贸易（香港）有限公司

KELIN INTERNATIONAL TRADING (HK) CO., LTD

PACKING LIST

TO: GLOBE SOURCING SERVICE CO., LTD
1407, 80th Street, S.W., Novi, Michigan, USA

INVOICE NO.: PI170601
INVOICE DATE: July 18, 2018
S/C NO.: TXT264
S/C DATE: APR. 20, 2018

FROM: SHEKOU PORT, SHENZHEN **TO:** NEW YORK **BY:** VESSEL

Marks and Numbers	Description of Goods	Quantity	Package	G.W.	N.W.	Meas.
G.S.S TXT264 NEW YORK C/No. 1-300	100% COTTON COLOUR WAVE T-SHIRT TM111 TM222 TM333 TM444 PACKED IN CARTONS OF 20 PCS EACH	2,000 PCS 2,000 PCS 1,000 PCS 1,000 PCS	100 Cartons 100 Cartons 50 Cartons 50 Cartons	550 KGS 550 KGS 275 KGS 275 KGS	500 KGS 500 KGS 250 KGS 250 KGS	2.82 CBM 2.82 CBM 1.41 CBM 1.41 CBM
	Total:	6,000 PCS	300 Cartons	1,650 KGS	1,500 KGS	8.46 CBM

SAY TOTAL: THREE HUNDRED CARTONS ONLY

KELIN International Trading (HK) Co., Ltd
(SEAL)
SIGNATURE: 李怡华

2. 贸易实务中的装箱单

图4-3为贸易实务中的装箱单样例。

图4-3 装箱单样例

实操训练（Skill Training）

一、单选题

1. 下列单证不属于包装单据的是（　　）。
   A．重量单　　　　　　　　　　B．尺码单
   C．装货单　　　　　　　　　　D．装箱单
2. 包装单据一般不应显示货物的（　　），因为进口商把商品转售时只要交付包装单据和货物，不愿泄露其购买成本。
   A．品名、总金额　　　　　　　B．单价、总金额
   C．包装件数、品名　　　　　　D．品名、单价
3. 表示唛码标记的英文缩写是（　　）。
   A．N/B　　　　　　　　　　　B．N/M
   C．N/N　　　　　　　　　　　D．B/L
4. 直接接触商品并随商品进入零售网点与消费者见面的包装称为（　　）。
   A．运输包装　　　　　　　　　B．中性包装
   C．定牌包装　　　　　　　　　D．销售包装
5. 信用证中规定"Packing list in five copies."，则受益人提交的装箱单的份数应为（　　）。
   A．五份副本　　　　　　　　　B．一份正本和四份副本
   C．不需要提交正本　　　　　　D．五份正本和五份副本
6. 合同中如果未注明商品重量是按毛重还是按净重计算时，则习惯上应按（　　）计算。
   A．毛重　　　　　　　　　　　B．净重
   C．以毛作净　　　　　　　　　D．公量
7. 定牌中性包装是指（　　）。
   A．有商标、牌名，无产地、厂名　　B．无商标、牌名，无产地、厂名
   C．有商标、牌名，有产地、厂名　　D．无商标、牌名，有产地、厂名
8. 货物外包装上印有一把火，这种标志属于（　　）。
   A．运输标志　　　　　　　　　B．唛头
   C．指示性标志　　　　　　　　D．警告性标志
9. 货物的外包装上印刷有一只酒杯，这种标志属于（　　）。
   A．危险性标志　　　　　　　　B．指示性标志
   C．警告性标志　　　　　　　　D．易燃性标志
10. 箱类包装的包装标志应粘贴在包装件的（　　）。
    A．端面或侧面　　　　　　　　B．包装明显处
    C．四个侧面　　　　　　　　　D．上面

二、根据以下材料填制装箱单

Issuing Bank: HSBC BANK (CHINA) CO., LTD
L/C No.: CMD 20808
Applicant: HONG KONG ABC COMPANY
NO.18 BUILDING BROADSTONE STREET, HONG KONG, CHINA
Beneficiary: NINGBO SHANYA IMP & EXP CO.
NO. 12 ZHISHAN ROAD, NINGBO, CHINA
Covering: FROZEN SOYABEANS 10M/T CIF HONG KONG USD 920.00 PER M/T
FROM NINGBO TO HONG KONG
Packing: IN SEAWORTHY CARTONS
SIZE IS 30CM×30CM×40CM/CTN
Net Weight: 20KGS PER CARTON
Gross Weight: 21KGS PER CARTON
Invoice No.: SY22
Invoice Date: APR. 15, 2018
Contract No.: SYA2018663

项目五
Project V

保险单据
Insurance Documents

学习目标（Learning Aims）

- 了解国际上通行的货物运输相关法规与条款。
- 熟悉国际货物运输保险的范畴和保险单据的类别。
- 能够熟练填制投保单。
- 能够填制和审核保险单。

情景导入（Lead-in Situation）

因双方贸易以 CIF 方式开展，出口商科林国际贸易公司在收到货代公司已将 6 000 件纯棉 T 恤衬衫安全送达深圳蛇口港口的通知后，立即安排业务员李怡华填制投保单，向中国人民财产保险股份有限公司（PICC Property & Casualty Co., Ltd，以下简称中国人保财险公司）申请投保。中国人保财险公司审核后确认承保，并于当天签发了保险单。

一、背景知识（Background Knowledge）

国际贸易过程中，货物经过装卸、运输、存储等环节，难免会因自然灾害、意外事故或其他外来风险（如战争、政治因素等）而破损、丢失，甚至会导致交易失败。为了在货物受损时能够得到赔偿，买卖双方应在装运前为货物办理好运输保险。

货物运输保险是以运输途中的货物作为保险标的，保险人对被保险货物遭遇的承保责任范围内的损失负赔偿责任的保险。

（一）国际货物运输保险条款及险别（Clauses and Coverages of International Cargo Transportation Insurance）

在国际货物运输保险中，常用的保险条款包括"中国保险条款"和"协会货物条款"。我国进出口贸易一般采用中国保险条款，如外商有特殊要求，也会采用国际保险市场上通用的协会货物条款。

1. 中国保险条款

中国保险条款（China Insurance Clauses，CIC）由中国人保财险公司根据国际保险市场操作惯例并结合我国贸易实际情况制订，中国人民银行及中国保险监督委员会审批颁布。CIC 保险条款按运输方式分为海洋、陆上、航空和邮包运输保险条款四大类，具体包括以下八种条款：

（1）海洋运输货物保险条款（包括平安险、水渍险和一切险）。
（2）海洋运输冷藏货物保险条款。
（3）海洋运输散装桐油保险条款。
（4）陆上运输货物保险条款（包括陆运险和陆运一切险）。
（5）陆上运输冷藏货物保险条款。
（6）航空运输货物保险条款（包括航空运输险和航空运输一切险）。
（7）邮包保险条款（包括邮包险和邮包一切险）。
（8）活牲畜、家禽的海洋、陆上、航空运输保险条款。

海洋运输货物保险条款所包含的险别可分为基本险和附加险，具体如图 5-1 所示。

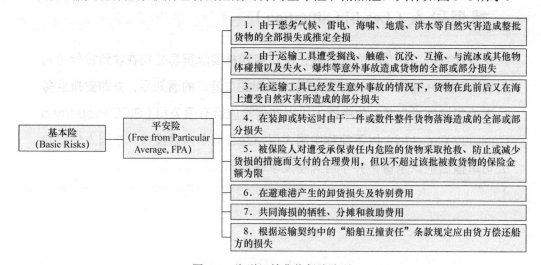

图 5-1　海洋运输货物保险险别

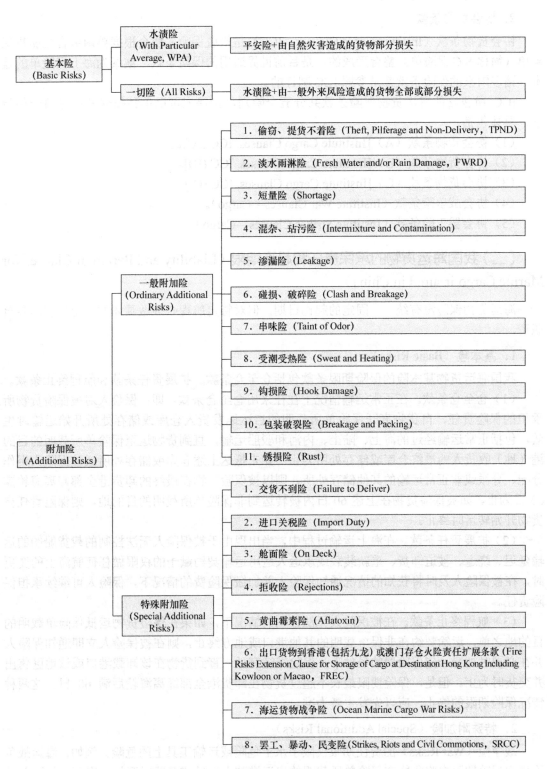

图 5-1 海洋运输货物保险险别（续）

2．协会货物条款

协会货物条款（Institute Cargo Clauses，ICC）是伦敦保险人协会根据英国劳合社船货保险单（简称 S.G.保险单）整合形成的，是目前世界通用的保险条款，被奉为海上保险单的蓝本，诸多国家的保险条款都是参照 ICC 制订的。

ICC 所包含的海运货物保险条款共分五个险别，投保人可以单独投保其中任何一种险别，具体包括：

（1）协会货物条款（A）[Institute Cargo Clauses, ICC (A)]。
（2）协会货物条款（B）[Institute Cargo Clauses, ICC (B)]。
（3）协会货物条款（C）[Institute Cargo Clauses, ICC (C)]。
（4）协会战争险条款（Institute War Clauses—Cargo）。
（5）协会罢工险条款（Institute Strikes Clauses—Cargo）。

（二）我国海运货物的承保责任和起讫期限（Liability and Period of Clauses for Marine Cargo insured in China）

海运货物保险没有统一、固定的起讫日期，但对特定航程必须做具体的规定以明确各自职责。

1．基本险（Basic Risks）

我国海运货物基本险的保险期限条款包括仓至仓条款、扩展责任条款和航程终止条款。

（1）仓至仓条款。在正常运输情况下往往采用仓至仓条款，即：保险人对被保险货物所承担的保险责任，自货物离开保险单所载明的启运地发货人仓库或储存处所开始运输时生效，包括正常运输经过的海上、陆上、内河和驳船运输，直到货物运至保险单所载明的目的港（地）收货人的最终仓库或储存处所为止。如未抵达上述仓库或储存处所或被保险人用作分配、分派或非正常运输的其他储存处所，则以被保险货物在最终的卸货港全部卸离海轮满 60 日为止。如被保险货物在上述 60 日内被转运到非保险单所载明的目的地，则保险责任自货物开始转运时终止。

（2）扩展责任条款。在海上运输过程中，当出现由于被保险人无法控制的载货船舶的运输延迟、绕道、被迫卸货、重新装载或承运人运用运输契约赋予的权限做任何航海上的变更时，在被保险人及时将获知的情况通知保险人并加缴保险费的情况下，保险人可继续承担保险责任。

（3）航程终止条款。在被保险人无法控制的情况下，如果在保险货物运抵保险单载明的目的地之前，运输契约在非保单载明的其他港口或地方终止，则在被保险人立即通知保险人并在必要时加缴一定保险费的条件下，保险继续有效，直到货物在该卸载港口或该地区售出并交货时为止。但是，保险期限最长不超过货物在卸货港全部卸离海轮后满 60 日。这两种情况保险期限的终止，应以先发生者为准。

2．特殊附加险（Special Additional Risks）

战争险（War Risks）的责任期限仅限于水上危险或运输工具上的危险。例如，海运战争险规定保险期限自将货物在保险单所载明的启运港装上海轮或驳船时开始，直到在保险单所载明的目的港将货物卸离海轮或驳船为止，如果货物不卸离海轮或驳船，则保险责任最长延至货物到目的港之当日午夜起满 15 日为止。如在中途港转船，则不论货物在当地卸载与否，保险责任以海轮到达该港或卸货地点的当日午夜起满 15 日为止，待再装上续运的海轮时，保险人仍继续负责。

（三）货运保险的操作流程（Application Procedures for Cargo Insurance）

首先需根据贸易合同所采用的贸易术语确定，买卖双方之间应由谁办理保险事宜。在出口贸易中，如果以 CIF 或 CIP 术语成交，则由卖方负责办理投保；如果以 FOB、FCA、CFR、CPT 术语成交，则由买方负责办理投保，但卖方须在货物装船后立即通知买方，以便其顺利办理投保。负责办理投保的一方应按合同约定的保险金额、险别和适用条款向保险公司投保，投保的一般程序如下。

1．选择投保险别

选择险别时要考虑的因素包括风险与损失的关系、包装、航行路线和停靠港口等。

2．确定保险金额

保险金额是被保险人对保险标的的实际投保金额，是保险人承担责任限额的标准和计收保险费的基础。国际货物买卖中，凡按 CIF 或 CIP 条件达成的合同一般均规定保险金额，而且其数值通常是在发票金额的基础上增加一定的百分率，即"投保加成率"。若合同未规定，则按《UCP 600》规定办理，即卖方有义务按 CIF 或 CIP 价格的总值另加 10%作为保险金额。计算公式为

$$保险金额 = CIF（CIP）价 \times （1+投保加成率）$$

3．填写国际运输保险投保单

投保单是投保人向承保人提出投保的书面申请。

4．支付保险费，取得保险单

保险费计算公式为

$$保险费 = 保险金额 \times 保险费率$$

例如，某 CIF 合同价值为 12 000 美元，投保一切险与战争险，保险费率分别为 0.6%和 0.4%，请问保险金额和保险费各为多少？

$$保险金额 = 12\,000 \times 110\% = 13\,200 \text{ 美元}$$
$$保险费 = 13\,200 \times （0.6\%+0.4\%） = 132 \text{ 美元}$$

5．保险索赔

进出口货物在保险责任有效期内发生属于保险责任范围内的损失，被保险人按照保险单的有关规定向保险公司提出赔偿要求，即为保险索赔。

（四）保险单据的种类（Types of Insurance Documents）

保险单据是保险公司在接受投保人投保后出具的，证明保险人与被保险人之间订有保险合同的文件。它是合格的保险合同的证明，也是投保人索赔和保险公司理赔的主要依据，是一种潜在的利益凭证。保险单据可分为以下几种类型。

1. 保险单

保险单（Insurance Policy）是最正式的保险单据形式，俗称"大保单"。保险单正面印有海上保险的基本事项，背面列明一般保险条款的全文，以规定当事人双方的权利和义务。在 CIF 或 CIP 合同中，出口商结汇时必须提交相关保险单据。

2. 保险凭证

保险凭证（Insurance Certificate）俗称"小保单"，只有正面的基本内容，背面没有印制保险条款。保险凭证虽格式简单，但作用与保险单完全相同。

3. 联合凭证

联合凭证（Combined Certificate）又称承保证明（Risk Note），是我国保险公司特别使用的、较保险凭证更为简化的保险单据。联合凭证是发票和保险单相结合的一种凭证，是最简单的保险单据。保险公司在出口商业发票上注明保险编号、承保险别、保险金额、装载船名、开航日期等，并正式签章作为已经承保的证据，至于其他项目均按发票上所列明者为准。联合凭证具有与保险单相同的效力，但不能背书转让。

4. 预约保险单/保险声明书

预约保险单（Open Policy / Open Cover）项下货物一经启运，即自动按预约保险单所列条件承保；但被保险人在获悉每批货物启运时，应立即以保险声明书（Insurance Declaration）的形式将该批货物的名称、数量、保险金额、船名、起讫港口、航次、开航日期等通知保险公司，银行可将保险声明书作为一项单据予以接受。《UCP600》规定：可以接受保险单代替预约保险项下的保险证明书或声明书（An insurance policy is acceptable in lieu of an insurance certificate or a declaration under an open cover）。

5. 暂保单

暂保单（Cover Note）又称临时保险书，是保险公司在保险单或保险凭证签发之前发出的临时单证。暂保单的内容比较简单，仅表明投保人已经办理了保险手续，并等待保险公司处理和签发正式保单。暂保单不是订立保险合同的必经程序，但是具有和正式保单同等的法律效力，不过有效期一般不超过 30 日。当正式保单生效后，暂保单自动失效。如保险公司最后考虑不出立保险单时，可以终止暂保单的效力，但必须提前通知投保人。《UCP600》规定：暂保单将不被接受（Cover notes will not be accepted）。

6. 保险批单

保险批单（Endorsement）是保险公司在保险单出立后，应投保人的要求出具的对保险内容进行补充或变更的一种凭证。批单一经签发即成为保险单的组成部分，具有补充、变更原保险单内容的作用。实务操作中，批单应粘贴在保险单上，并加盖骑缝章，批单的效力优于保险单。

二、认识投保单（Understand the Application for Insurance）

投保单是由投保人向承保人办理投保申请时填制、签署并递交的单证。在 CIF/CIP 的价格条件下，投保手续由卖方办理；而在 CFR / CPT / FOB / FCA 的价格条件下，投保手续由买方办理。

（一）投保单样本（A Sample of Application for Insurance）

中国人民财产保险股份有限公司
PICC PROPERTY AND CASUALTY COMPANY LIMITED

货物运输险投保单
APPLICATION FOR CARGO TRANSPORTATION INSURANCE

（1）投保单号
Application No.

注意：请您在保险人明确说明本投保单及适用保险条款后，如实填写本投保单，您所填写的材料将构成签订保险合同的要约，成为保险人核保并签发保险单的依据。除双方另有约定外，保险人签发保险单且投保人向保险人缴清保险费后，保险人开始按约定的险种承保货物运输保险。

（2）投保人 Applicant			
（3）被保险人 Insured			电话 Tel.
（4）合同号 Contract No.	（5）信用证号 L/C No.		（6）发票号 Invoice No.
（7）标记 Marks & Nos.	（8）包装及数量 Package & Quantity	（9）保险货物项目 Goods	（10）发票金额 Invoice Value 投保加成 Plus about ____% 保险金额 Amount Insured 费率 Rate（%） 保险费 Premium
（11）装载运输工具 Per Conveyance:		（12）提单号 B/L No.	
（13）启运日期： Date of Commencement:		（14）赔款偿付地点 Claims Payable at:	
（15）航行路线　自　　　　　经　　　　　到达（目的地） 　　　Route:　　From　　　　Via　　　　To（Destination）			
（16）包装方式：1. 散装　2. 纸箱　3. 瓶装　4. 木箱　5. 编织袋　6. 真空袋　7. 桶装　8. 裸装　9. 苫布 　　　　10. 其他方式：____			
（17）运输方式：1. 集装箱　2. 冷藏箱　3. 拼箱　4. 整船　5. 舱面　6. 其他方式：____			
（18）货物项目：1. 精密仪器　是□　否□　2. 旧货物　是□　否□　船龄：____年建			
（19）投保险别 Conditions:	投保人可根据投保意向选择投保险别及条款，并画√确认，但保险人承保的险及适用条款以保险人最终确定并在保险单上列明的险种、条款为准。		
进出口海洋运输：	□ 一切险　　　　□ 水渍险　　　　□ 平安险　　　（PICC《海洋运输货物保险条款》） □ ICC (A)　　　 □ ICC (B)　　　 □ ICC (C)　　　（伦敦协会货物条款）		
进出口航空运输：	□ 航空运输险　　□ 航空运输一切险　　　　　　　（PICC《航空运输货物保险条款》）		
进出口陆上运输：	□ 陆运险　　　　□ 陆运一切险　　　　　　　　　（PICC《陆上运输货物保险条款》）		
特殊附加险：	□ 战争险　　　　□ 罢工险　　　　　　　　　　　（□ PICC 条款　　□ 伦敦协会货物条款）		
国内水陆运输：	□ 基本险　　　　□ 综合险　　　　　　　　　　　（《国内水路、陆路货物运输保险条款》）		
国内航空运输：	□ 航空运输险　　□ 航空运输一切险　　　　　　　（PICC《航空运输货物保险条款》）		
其他承保条件：			
（20）特别约定 Special Conditions:			

投保人声明：
1. 本人填写本投保单之前，保险人已经就本投保单及适用的保险条款的内容，尤其是关于保险人免除责任的条款及投保人和被保险人义务条款向本人做了明确说明，本人对该保险条款及保险条件已完全了解，并同意接受保险条款的约束。
2. 本投保单所填各项内容均属事实，同意以本投保单作为保险人签发保险单的依据。
3. 保险合同自保险单签发之日起成立。

（21）投保人签字（盖章）　　　　　　　　　　　　　　　　　　（22）日期
　　 Applicant's Signature（and Seal）：　　　　　　　　　　　　　Date:

（二）投保单填制要点（Instructions for Application for Insurance）

1．投保单号（Application No.）

此栏由保险公司填写。

2．投保人（Applicant）

此栏填写投保申请人的名称。

3．被保险人（Insured）

此栏填写被保险人的名称。采用托收方式付款时，填写出口商的名称。采用信用证付款时，如无特别规定，一般填写信用证的受益人名称；如有特别规定，则按信用证的规定填写。若 L/C 规定"Insurance Policy made out to the order of ×××Bank"，则此栏应填为"To the order of ×××Bank"，否则就会构成单证不符。

4．合同号（Contract No.）

此栏填写本次投保标的的买卖合同的编号。

5．信用证号（L/C No.）

此栏填写本次交易中买方开来的信用证的编号。如采用托收方式支付，则此栏空白不填。

6．发票号（Invoice No.）

此栏填写本次投保标的的商业发票的编号。

7．标记（Marks & Nos.）

此栏填写装运唛头，与发票、提单上的相同栏目内容一致。此栏也可填写"As per Invoice No.×××"。

8．包装及数量（Package & Quatity）

此栏填写最大包装件数，与发票、装箱单、提单上相同栏目内容一致。散装货物填写"In Bulk"。如果货物价格以重量计价，除表示件数外，还应注明毛重或净重。

9．保险货物项目（Goods）

按发票品名填写，若发票品名繁多也可使用统称。

10．保险金额及保险费

（1）发票金额（Invoice Value）：此栏填写发票的实际金额，这是计算保险金额的基础。

（2）投保加成（Plus about __%）：此栏填写投保加成率。如果信用证或合同有规定，则按规定填写；如果没有规定，则一般加成 10%。

（3）保险金额（Amount Insured）：此栏按照合同或信用证的规定填写，如无明确规定，应按货款的 CIF 或 CIP 价的 110%填写。保险金额小数点后的尾数应进位取整，不能采用四舍五入法，如：2 905.04 美元要进一位，取 2 906 美元，而不能采用四舍五入法取值 2 905 美元。

（4）费率[Rate(%)]和保险费（Premium）：通常填写"As arranged"或"Paid"。

11．装载运输工具（Per Conveyance）

此栏填写运输工具的名称，如是海运填写船名；如是空运，填写航班名称。如果中途转船，各程运输的船名都应填写在该栏。例如，第一程船名是"Victory"，第二程船名是"East Wind"，则此栏应填写"Victory / East Wind"。

12．提单号（B/L No.）

此栏填写本保险单项下货物海运提单的编号，根据提单的实际情况填写。

13．启运日期（Date of Commencement）

此栏填写本保险单项下货物运输单据的签发日期，或填写"As per B/L No.×××"。

14．赔款偿付地点（Claims Payable at）

此栏填写保险赔款的偿付地点和偿付的货币名称，根据合同或信用证规定的保险条款填写。若信用证未做规定，或是以托收方式支付货款，则此栏填写目的港（地），赔付货币填与投保金额相同的货币。

15．航行路线（Route）

在 From 后面填写装运港（地）名称，在 To 后面填写目的港（地）名称，如有转运还须在 Via 后面填写转运港（地）名称。例如"From Dalian, China via Pusan to Tokyo, Japan"。若海运至目的港，保险承保至内陆城市，则应在目的港后注明。例如"From Shanghai to Liverpool and Thence to Birmingham"。

16．包装方式

按实际外包装选择。

17．运输方式

按实际选择。

18．货物项目

按实际选择。

19．投保险别（Conditions）

此栏根据信用证或合同规定的保险条款填写，并注明保险所依据的保险条款名称，例如"Covering All Risks and War Risks as per Ocean Marine Cargo Clause of PICC."。

20．特别约定（Special Conditions）

此栏填写信用证或合同对保险单据的特别要求，若没有则此栏留空。

21．投保人签字（盖章）[Applicant's Signature (and Seal)]

此栏填写投保人全称、地址和电话，由经办人签名，并加盖投保人的公章。

22．日期（Date）

此栏填写投保的日期。

三、认识保险单（Understand the Insurance Policy）

保险单是依据投保人填写的投保单的内容，由保险公司填制、签署并交付投保人的单据。其内容与投保单基本相同。

（一）保险单样本（A Sample of Insurance Policy）

中国人民财产保险股份有限公司
PICC PROPERTY AND CASUALTY COMPANY LIMITED

保险单号
Policy No.

货物运输保险单
CARGO TRANSPORTATION INSURANCE POLICY

（1）发票号　　　　　　　　　　　　　　提单号
　　　Invoice No.　　　　　　　　　　　 B/L No.
　　　合同号　　　　　　　　　　　　　　信用证号
　　　Contract No.　　　　　　　　　　　L/C No.
（2）被保险人
　　　Insured: _____

中国人民财产保险股份有限公司（以下简称本公司）根据被保险人的要求，以被保险人向本公司缴付约定的保险费为对价，按照本保险单列明条款承保下述货物运输保险，特订立本保险单。
This policy of insurance witnesses that PICC Property and Casualty Company Limited (hereinafter called "the company"), at the request of the insured and in consideration of the agreed premium paid to the company by the insured, undertakes to insure the undermentioned goods in transportation subject to the conditions of this policy as per the clauses printed overleaf.

（3）标记 Marks & Nos.	（4）包装及数量 Package & Quantity	（5）保险货物项目 Goods	（6）保险金额 Amount Insured

（7）承保险别
　　　Conditions:
（8）总保险金额
　　　Total Amount Insured: _____
（9）保费　　　　　　　　　　　（10）装载运输工具
　　　Premium: _____　　　　　　　Per Conveyance: _____
（11）启运日期
　　　Date of Commencement: _____
（12）启运自　　　　　　经　　　　　　　　至
　　　From: _____　Via: _____　To: _____

所保货物如发生本保险单项下可能引起索赔的损失，应立即通知本公司或下述代理人查勘。如有索赔，应向本公司提交正本保险单（本保险单共有2份正本）及有关文件。如一份正本已用于索赔，其余正本则自动失效。
In the event of loss or damage which may result in a claim under this policy, immediate notice must be given to the company or agent as mentioned hereunder. Claims, if any, one of the original policies which has been issued in 2 original(s) together with the relevant documents shall be surrendered to the company. If one of the original policies has been accomplished, the others to be void.

　　　　　　　　　　　　　　　　　　中国人民财产保险股份有限公司（签章）
（13）赔款偿付地点　　　　　　　　保险人
　　　Claim Payable at: _____　Underwriter: _____
（14）签单日期
　　　Issuing Date: _____

（二）保险单填制要点（Instructions for Insurance Policy）

1．发票号/提单号/合同号/信用证号（Invoice No. / B/L No. / Contract No. / L/C No.）

分别填写本批货物的发票编号、提单编号、合同编号和信用证编号。

2．被保险人（Insured）

此栏填写被保险人的名称。采用托收方式付款时，填写出口商的名称。采用信用证付款时，如无特别规定，一般填写信用证的受益人名称；如有特别规定，则按信用证的规定填写。若 L/C 规定"Insurance Policy made out to the order of ×××Bank"，则此栏应填为"To the order of ×××Bank"，否则就会构成单证不符。

3．标记（Marks & Nos.）

与发票中的唛头一致。

4．包装及数量（Package & Quantity）

按装箱单的总量如实填写，如"100CTNS/2,000DOZ"。

5．保险货物项目（Goods）

填写本批货物的英文名称。

6．保险金额（Amount Insured）

保险金额 = 发票总金额×（1+投保加成率）

如果计算得出的保险金额的小数点后有数字，无论多少都进一位成整数。例如：299 986.1 应进为 299 987。

7．承保险别（Conditions）

按合同或信用证中保险规定填写。

8．总保险金额（Total Amount Insured）

用文字（大写）书写总金额。

9．保费（Premium）

一般不列出，填写"As arranged"。

10．装载运输工具（Per Conveyance）

填写本批货物的船名与航次。

11．启运日期（Date of Commencement）

按实际填写。

12．启运自/经/至（From / Via / To）

填写具体港口名称，如"From Guangzhou to New York"。

13．赔款偿付地点（Claim Payable at）

填写具体的地点。一般为方便买方索赔，此栏填写保险公司在买方所在地的办事机构或代理公司所在地。

14．签单日期（Issuing Date）

此栏为保险公司签发本保险单的日期。

（三）保险单据实例（Models of Insurance Documents）

1. 情景导入中的保险单据

（1）投保单

中国人民财产保险股份有限公司
PICC PROPERTY AND CASUALTY COMPANY LIMITED

货物运输险投保单
APPLICATION FOR CARGO TRANSPORTATION INSURANCE

投保单号
Application No. **HZ562311**

注意：请您在保险人明确说明本投保单及适用保险条款后，如实填写本投保单，您所填写的材料将构成签订保险合同的要约，成为保险人核保并签发保险单的依据。除双方另有约定外，保险人签发保险单且投保人向保险人缴清保险费后，保险人开始按约定的险种承保货物运输保险。

投保人 Applicant	KELIN INTERNATIONAL TRADING (HK) CO., LTD			
被保险人 Insured	KELIN INTERNATIONAL TRADING (HK) CO., LTD		电话 Tel.	157×××3456
合同号 Contract No.	TXT264	信用证号 L/C No.	BL170197	发票号 Invoice No.	PI170601
标记 Marks & Nos.	包装及数量 Package & Quantity	保险货物项目 Goods	发票金额 Invoice Value	
G.S.S TXT264 NEW YORK C/No. 1-300	PACKED IN CARTONS OF 20 PCS EACH TM111 2,000 PCS TM222 2,000 PCS TM333 1,000 PCS TM444 1,000 PCS	100% COTTON COLOUR WAVE T-SHIRT	加成 Plus about ___10___ % 保险金额 Amount Insured 费率 Rate（%） 保险费 Premium	

装载运输工具 Per Conveyance: S.S. EAST WIND V. 23	提单号 B/L No. GD57861609
启运日期 Date of Commencement: AS PER B/L NO.	赔款偿付地点： Claims Payable at: NEW YORK
航行路线 自 Route: From SHEKOU PORT, SHENZHEN	经 Via 到达（目的地） To (destination) NEW YORK

包装方式：1. 散装 ☑2. 纸箱 3. 瓶装 4. 木箱 5. 编织袋 6. 真空袋 7. 桶装 8. 裸装 9. 苫布 10. 其他方式：____
运输方式：☑1. 集装箱 2. 冷藏箱 3. 拼箱 4. 整船 5. 舱面 6. 其他方式：____
货物项目：1. 精密仪器 是☐ 否☑ 2. 旧货物 是☐ 否☑ 船 龄：_____年建

投保险别： Conditions	投保人可根据投保意向选择投保险别及条款，并画√确认，但保险人承保的险别及适用条款以保险人最终确定并在保险单上列明的险种、条款为准。		
进出口海洋运输：	☑ 一切险 ☐ 水渍险 ☐ 平安险 ☐ ICC (A) ☐ ICC (B) ☐ ICC (C)		(PICC《海洋运输货物保险条款》) （伦敦协会货物条款）
进出口航空运输：	☐ 航空运输险 ☐ 航空运输一切险		(PICC《航空运输货物保险条款》)
进出口陆上运输：	☐ 陆运险 ☐ 陆运一切险		(PICC《陆上运输货物保险条款》)
特殊附加险：	☑ 战争险 ☐ 罢工险		(☐ PICC条款 ☐ 伦敦协会货物条款)
国内水陆运输：	☐ 基本险 ☐ 综合险		(《国内水路、陆路货物运输保险条款》)
国内航空运输：	☐ 航空运输险 ☐ 航空运输一切险		(PICC《航空运输货物保险条款》)
其他承保条件：			

特别约定
Special Conditions：

投保人声明：
1. 本人填写本投保单之前，保险人已经就本投保单及适用的保险条款的内容，尤其是关于保险人免除责任的条款及投保人和被保险人义务条款向本人做了明确说明，本人对该保险条款及保险条件已完全了解，并同意接受保险条款的约束。
2. 本投保单所填各项内容均属事实，同意以本投保单作为保险人签发保险单的依据。
3. 保险合同自保险单签发之日起成立。

投保人签字（盖章）   日期
Applicant's Signature (and Seal): KELIN INTERNATIONAL TRADING (HK) CO., LTD   Date: 2018年6月20日

(2) 保险单

中国人民财产保险股份有限公司
PICC PROPERTY AND CASUALTY COMPANY LIMITED

保险单号
Policy No. **GD440786003**

货物运输保险单
CARGO TRANSPORTATION INSURANCE POLICY

发票号　　　　　　　　　　　　　　　　　提单号
Invoice No. PI170601　　　　　　　　　　B/L No. GD57861609
合同号　　　　　　　　　　　　　　　　　信用证号
Contract No. TXT264　　　　　　　　　　 L/C No. BL170197
被保险人
Insured: KELIN INTERNATIONAL TRADING (HK) CO., LTD

中国人民财产保险股份有限公司（以下简称本公司）根据被保险人的要求，以被保险人向本公司缴付约定的保险费为对价，按照本保险单列明条款承保下述货物运输保险，特订立本保险单。
This policy of insurance witnesses that PICC Property and Casualty Company Limited (hereinafter called "the company"), at the request of the insured and in consideration of the agreed premium paid to the company by the insured, undertakes to insure the undermentioned goods in transportation subject to the conditions of this policy as per the clauses printed overleaf.

标记 Marks & Nos.	包装及数量 Package & Quantity	保险货物项目 Goods	保险金额 Amount Insured
G.S.S TXT264 NEW YORK C/No. 1-300	300 CTNS（6,000 PCS）	100% COTTON COLOUR WAVE T-SHIRT	USD 66,000.00

承保险别
Conditions:
ALL RISKS & WAR RISKS AS PER PICC
UP TO NEW YORK
总保险金额
Total amount insured: SAY US DOLLARS SIXTY-SIX THOUSAND ONLY
保费　　　　　　　　　　　　　　　　　　装载运输工具
Premium: AS ARRANGED　　　　　　　　 Per Conveyance: S.S EAST WIND V.023
启运日期
Date of Commencement: AS PER B/L NO.
启运自　　　　　　　　　　　　经　　　　　　　　　　　至
From: SHEKOU PORT, SHENZHEN　　Via:＿＿＿＿＿＿＿　To: NEW YORK

所保货物如发生本保险单项下可能引起索赔的损失，应立即通知本公司或下述代理人查勘。如有索赔，应向本公司提交正本保险单（本保险单共有 2 份正本）及有关文件。如一份正本已用于索赔，其余正本则自动失效。
In the event of loss or damage which may result in a claim under this policy, immediate notice must be given to the company or agent as mentioned hereunder. Claims, if any, one of the original policies which has been issued in 2 original(s) together with the relevant documents shall be surrendered to the company. If one of the original policies has been accomplished, the others to be void.

中国人民财产保险股份有限公司（签章）

赔款偿付地点　　　　　　　　　　　　　　保险人
Claim payable at: NEW YORK IN USD　　　Underwriter: ＿＿＿＿＿＿
日期
Date: 2018/07/21

2. 贸易实务中的保险单

图 5-2（正面）、图 5-3（反面）为贸易实务中的保险单样例。

PICC 中国人民财产保险股份有限公司
PICC PROPERTY AND CASUALTY COMPANY LIMITED

总公司设于北京　　　一九四九年创立　　　保险单号(POLICY NO.) PYIE201844195000███████
Head Office Beijing　　Established in 1949

货物运输保险 保险单 CARGO TRANSPORTATION INSURANCE POLICY

发票号(INVOICE NO.)：　　　　　　　　　提单号(B/L NO.) LLLDL██████
合同号(CONTRACT NO.)：　　　　　　　　信用证号(L/C NO.)：
被保险人(THE INSURED)：DI██████

中国人民财产保险股份有限公司(以下简称本公司)根据被保险人要求，以被保险人向本公司缴付约定的保险费为对价，按照本保险单列明条款承保下述货物运输保险，特订立本保险单。

THIS POLICY OF INSURANCE WITNESSES THAT PICC PROPERTY AND CASUALTY COMPANY LIMITED (HEREINAFTER CALLED "THE COMPANY") AT THE REQUEST OF THE INSURED AND IN CONSIDERATION OF THE AGREED PREMIUM PAID TO THE COMPANY BY THE INSURED, UNDERTAKES TO INSURE THE UNDERMENTIONED GOODS IN TRANSPORTATION SUBJECT TO THE CONDITIONS OF THIS POLICY AS PER THE CLAUSES PRINTED OVERLEAF.

标记(MARKS & NOS.)	包装及数量(PACKAGE & QUANTITY)	保险货物项目(GOODS)	保险金额(AMOUNT INSURED)
DILANIA LLC DESC:SHADOW BOX ITEM NO.: C/NO:OF	125 CTNS	MDF PHOTO FRAME WITH GLASS BUBBLE BAG STYROFOAM INSERT WHITE BOX MASTER CARTON HS CODE:4414009090	USD 6669.63

总保险金额(TOTAL AMOUNT INSURED)： USD SIX THOUSAND SIX HUNDRED AND SIXTY NINE AND SIXTY THREE CENTS ONLY

保费(PREMIUM)： AS ARRANGED　　　　启运日期(DATE OF COMMENCEMENT)： October 13, 2018
装载运输工具(PER CONVEYANCE)： CMA CGM THALASSA/143TXE
自(FROM)： SHEN ZHEN/CHINA
经(VIA)：
至(TO)： DALLAS/TX
承保险别(CONDITIONS)：
COVERING ALL RISKS AS PER OCEAN MARINE CARGO CLAUSES OF THE PICC PROPERTY AND CASUALTY COMPANY LIMITED. 2. INCLUDING STRIKES RISKS AS PER INSTITUTE STRIKES CLAUSES (CARGO)
1. The vessels for transportation must be qualified. PICC is not responsilbe for the loss when using the unqualified vessels or those vessels with over 25 years old.
2. For nuded cargo, second-used goods or ore, can only be supplied with FPA (free from particular average), overland transportation insurance, aero insurance and ICC C clause.
1. EXCESS FOR EACH AND EVERY LOSS: USD500 or 5% of the total loss, which is higher.
2. EXCESS FOR EACH AND EVERY LOSS: for fragile products，paper articles and wine products: USD800 or 5% of the total loss, which is higher.

所保货物如发生保险单项下可能引起索赔的损失，应立即通知本公司或下述代理人查勘。如有索赔，应向本公司提交正本保险单（本保险单共有 2 份正本）及有关文件。如一份正本已用于索赔，其余正本自动失效。

IN THE EVENT OF LOSS OR DAMAGE WHICH MAY RESULT IN A CLAIM UNDER THIS POLICY IMMEDIATE NOTICE MUST BE GIVEN TO THE COMPANY OR AGENT AS MENTIONED. CLAIMS, IF ANY, ONE OF THE ORIGINAL POLICIES WHICH HAS BEEN ISSUED IN 2 ORIGINAL(S) TOGETHER WITH THE RELEVANT DOCUMENTS SHALL BE SURRENDERED TO THE COMPANY. IF ONE OF THE ORIGINAL POLICIES HAS BEEN ACCOMPLISHED, THE OTHERS TO BE VOID.

VeriClaim Inc. ADD: Route 1- Box 256 Ben Wheeler Texas 75754 USA TEL: 001-903-8527516 TELEX: CABLE: FAX: 001-903-8527517 POST CODE: EMAIL:

保险服务请联系：
CONTACT INFORMATION OF INSURANCE SERVICE：
中国人民财产保险股份有限公司东莞分公司 PICC Property and Casualty Company Limited DONGGUAN Branch
电话(TEL)： 0769-95███
传真(FAX)： 0769-22███████
EMAIL：
地址(ADD)： 广东省东莞市东城区东部大道9号人保大厦

赔款偿付地点 (CLAIM PAYABLE AT) DALLAS/TX IN USD
签单日期(ISSUING DATE) 2018-10-13

保险人：
UNDERWRITER

图 5-2　保险单（正面）样例

中国人民财产保险股份有限公司
PICC PROPERTY AND CASUALTY COMPANY LIMITED

货物运输保险 保险单 CARGO TRANSPORTATION INSURANCE POLICY

PICC PROPERTY AND CASUALTY COMPANY LIMITED OCEAN MARINE CARGO CLAUSES(2009) I. Scope of Cover This insurance is classified into the following three Conditions-Free from Particular Average (F.P.A.), With Average (W.A.)and All Risks. Where the goods insured hereunder sustain loss or damage, the Insurer shall undertake to indemnify herefore according to the Insured Condition specified in the Policy and the Provisions of these Clauses: nbsp; 1. Free From Particular Average (F.P.A.)This insurance covers: (1) Total or Constructive Total Loss of the whole consignment hereby insured caused in the course of transit by natural calamities—heavy weather, lightning, tsunami,earthquake and flood. In case a constructive total loss is claimed for, the Insured shall abandon to the Company the damaged goods and all his rights and title pertaining thereto.The goods on eachlighter to or from the seagoing vessel shall be deemed a separate risk. "Constructive Total Loss" refers to the loss where an actual total loss appears to be unavoidable or the cost to beincurred in recovering or reconditioning the goods together with the forwarding cost to the destination named in the Policy would exceed their value on arrival. (2) Total or Partial Loss caused by accidents—the carrying conveyance being grounded, stranded, sunk or in collisionwith floating ice or other objects as fire or explosion. (3) Partial loss of the insured goods attributable to heavy weather, lightning and/or tsunami, where the conveyancehas been grounded, stranded, sunk or burnt, irrespective of whether the event or events took place before or after such accidents. (4) Partial or total loss consequent on falling of entire package or packages into sea during loading, transhipmentor discharge. (5) Reasonable cost incurred by the Insured in salvaging the goods or averting or minimizing a loss recoverable under the Policy, provided that such cost shall not exceed the sum insured of the consignment so saved . (6) Losses attributable to discharge of the insured goods at a port of distress following a sea peril as well as specialcharges arising from loading, warehousing and forwarding of the goods at an intermediate port of call or refuge. (7) Sacrifice in and Contribution to General Average and Salvage Charges. (8) Such proportion of losses sustained by the ship-owners as is to be reimbursed by the Cargo Owner under the Contractof Affreightment "Both to Blame Collision" Clause. 2. With Average (W.A.) Aside from the risks covered under F.P.A. condition as above, this insurance also covers partial losses of the insured goods caused by heavy weather, lightning, tsunami, earthquake and/or flood. 3. All Risks Aside from the risks covered under the F.P.A. and W.A. conditions as above, this insurance also covers all risks of loss of or damage to the insured goods whether partial or total, arising from external causes in the course of transit. II. ExclusionsThis insurance does not cover: 1、Loss or damage caused by the intentional act or fault of the Insured. 2、Loss or damage falling under the liability of the consignor. 3、Loss or damage arising from the inferior quality or& shortage of the insured goods prior to the attachment of this insurance. 4、Loss or damage arising from normal loss, inherent vice or nature of the insured goods, loss of market and/or delay in transit and any expenses arising therefrom. 5、Risks and liabilities covered and excluded by the Ocean Marine Cargo War Risks Clauses and Strike, Riot and Civil Commotion Clauses of this Company. III. Commencement and Termination of Cover 1、Warehouse to Warehouse Clause: This insurance attaches from the time the goods hereby insured leave the warehouse or place of storage named in the Policy for the commencement of the transit and continues in force in the ordinary course of transit including sea,land and inland waterway transits and transit in lighter until the insured goods are delivered to the consignee's fina warehouse or place of storage at the destination named in the Policy or to any other place used by the Insured for allocation or distribution of the goods or for storage other than in the ordinary course of transit. This insurance shall, however, belimited to sixty (60) days after completion of discharge of the insured goods from the seagoing vessel at the final portof discharge before they reach the above mentioned warehouse or place of storage. If prior to the expiry of the above mentioned sixty (60) days, the insured goods are to be forwarded to a destination other than that named in the Policy,this insurance shall terminate at the commencement of such transit. 2、If owing to delay, deviation, forced discharge, reshipment or transhipment beyond the control of the Insured or any change or termination of the voyage arising from the exercise of a liberty granted to the ship-owners under the contract of affreightment, the insured goods arrive at a port or place other than that named in the Policy, subject to immediate notice being given to the Company by the Insured and an additional premium being paid, if required, this insurance shall remain in force and shall terminate as hereunder: (1)If the insured goods are sold at port or place not named in the Policy, this insurance shall terminate on deliveryof the goods sold, but in no event shall this insurance extend beyond sixty (60) days after completion of discharge of theinsured goods from the carrying vessel at such port or place. (2)If the insured goods are to be forwarded to the final destination named in the Policy or any other destination,this insurance shall terminate in accordance with Section 1 above. IV. Duty of the Insured It is the duty of the Insured to attend to all matters as specified hereunder:nbsp; 1、The Insured shall take delivery of the insured goods in good time upon their arrival at the port of destination named in the Policy. In the event of any damage to the goods, the Insured shall immediately apply for survey to the surveyand /or settling agent stipulated in the Policy. If the insured goods are found short in entire package or packages orto show apparent traces of damage, the Insured shall obtain from the carrier, bailee or other relevant authorities(Customsand Port Authorities etc.) certificate of loss or damage and /or shortlanded memo.Should the carrier, bailee or the other relevant authorities be responsible for such shortage or damage, the Insured shall lodge a claim with them in writing and,if necessary, obtain their confirmation of an extension of the time limit of validity of such claim.If the Insured fails to fulfill the aforesaid obligations, the Insurer shall not be liable for the indemnity to the loss or damage attributableto such failure. 2、The Insured shall, and the Insurer may also, take reasonable measures immediately in salvaging the goods or preventing or minimizing a loss or damage thereto. The measures so taken by the Insured or by the Insurer shall not be considered respectively, as a waiver of abandonment hereunder, or as an acceptance thereof. The Insurer shall not be liable for the indemnity to the increased loss or damage attributable to the Insured's failureto fulfill the aforesaid obligations. 3、In case of a change of voyage or any omission or error in the description of the interest, the name of the vesselor voyage, this insurance shall remain in force only upon prompt notice to this Company when the Insurer becomes aware ofthe same and payment of an additional premium if required. 4、The following documents should accompany any claim hereunder made against this Company: Original Policy, Bill of Lading, Invoice, Packing List, Tally Sheet, Weight Memo,Certificate of Loss or Damage and/orShortlanded Memo, Survey Report, Statement of Claim. If any third party is involved, documents relative to pursuing of recovery from such party should also be included. If the Insured fails to provide the aforesaid claim documents, the Insurer shall not be liable for the indemnity to the parts of the loss or damage which can not be verified due to such failure. 5、Immediate notice should be given to the Company when the Cargo Owner's actual responsibility under the contract of affreightment "Both to Blame Collision" Clause becomes known. Otherwise, the Insurer shall not be liable for the indemnityto the loss or damage attributable to such failure. V. Claims Handling The Insurer shall upon receipt of a claim from the Insured, check and ascertain without delay whether this insurance covers the loss or damage ,then notify the Insured of the result.Where in the circumstances of complicated claim the Insurerfails to ascertain the facts within thirty days after receiving the claim and the relevant documents from the Insured, the Insurer shall discuss and agree on a reasonable claim handling period with the Insured according to the actual situation. Then the Insurer shall as certain the facts and notify the insured of the result within this period. Where the loss or damageis covered by the insurance, the Insurer shall fulfil the obligation of indemnity to settle the claim within ten days from reaching an agreement on the amount of indemnity with the Insured. VI. The Time of Validity of a Claim The time of validity of a claim under this insurance shall not exceed a period of two years counting from the day onwhich the peril insured against occurred. English translation is for reference only. For any disputes from policy interpretation Chinese policy will prevail.

PICC PROPERTY AND CASUALTY COMPANY LIMITED
DONGGUAN BRANCH

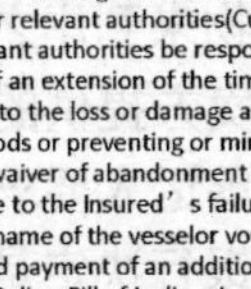

图 5-3 保险单(反面)样例

实操训练（Skill Training）

一、单选题

1. 我国某公司从德国进口一批电冰箱,以 CIF Shanghai（上海）成交,运货船只在途经马六甲海峡附近时遭海盗洗劫,货物尽失,而该批货物只投保了平安险,这种损失的责任方应是（　　）。
　　A. 卖方　　　　B. 买方　　　　C. 保险公司　　　　D. 运输公司
2. 同国际市场的惯例一样,我国海运货物基本险的保险起讫期限一般也采用（　　）的原则。
　　A. "门到门"　　B. "桌到桌"　　C. "仓至仓"　　D. "港到港"
3. 在两伊战争期间,我国 A 公司向伊拉克 B 公司出口一批商品,以 CIF Basra（巴士拉）成交,我国 A 公司按照合同规定加保战争险,货物系租用国外船舶 C 公司的船进行运输。该船于 7 月 10 日抵达巴士拉,但由于港口拥挤未能卸货;7 月 30 日该船遭炮火袭击,货物损失了一半,按照惯例负责赔偿这一半损失的公司是（　　）。
　　A. A 公司　　B. B 公司　　C. C 公司　　D. 保险公司
4. 某公司按 CIF 出口一批货物,但因海轮在运输途中遭遇海啸事故,货物全部灭失,买方（　　）。
　　A. 可借货物未到岸之事实而不予付款
　　B. 应该凭卖方提供的全套单据付款
　　C. 可以向承运人要求赔偿
　　D. 由开证银行决定是否付款
5. 下列危险属于自然灾害的是（　　）。
　　A. 海啸　　　　B. 触礁　　　　C. 失踪　　　　D. 失火
6. 下列风险中属于一般外来风险的是（　　）。
　　A. 战争　　　　B. 没收　　　　C. 罢工　　　　D. 碰撞
7. 共同海损和单独海损都属于（　　）。
　　A. 全部损失　　B. 部分损失　　C. 推定全损　　D. 实际全损
8. 下列险别中保险公司承担责任最多的是（　　）。
　　A. 平安险　　　B. 水渍险　　　C. 一切险　　　D. 特殊附加险
9. 根据中国人保财险公司的规定,保险索赔期限为（　　）。
　　A. 60 天　　　B. 半年　　　C. 一年　　　D. 二年
10. 根据我国"海洋运输货物保险条款"规定,"一切险"包括（　　）。
　　A. 平安险加 11 种一般附加险　　B. 水渍险加 11 种一般附加险
　　C. 水渍险加特殊附加险　　　　　D. 11 种一般附加险加特殊附加险
11. 预约保险以（　　）代替投保单,说明投保的一方已办理了投保手续。
　　A. 提单　　　　　　　　　　　　B. 国外的装运通知
　　C. 大副收据　　　　　　　　　　D. 买卖合同
12. 我国某公司出口稻谷一批,因自然灾害事故被海水浸泡多时而丧失其原有用途,货到目的港后只能低价出售，这种损失属于（　　）。
　　A．单独海损　　B．共同海损　　C．实际全损　　D．推定全损
13．CIC"特殊附加险"是指在特殊情况下要求保险公司承保的险别，特殊附加险（　　）。
　　A．一般可以单独投保
　　B．不能单独投保
　　C．可单独投保两项以上的"特殊附加险"
　　D．在被保险人统一的情况下可以单独投保
14．某批出口货物投保了水渍险，在运输过程中由于雨淋致使货物遭受部分损失，这样的损失保险公司将（　　）。
　　A．负责赔偿整批货物　　　　B．负责赔偿被雨淋湿部分的损失
　　C．不给予任何赔偿　　　　　D．不负责赔偿被雨淋湿部分的损失
15．有一批出口服装，在海上运输途中，因船体触礁导致服装严重受浸。如果将这批服装漂洗后再运至原定目的港所花费的费用已超过服装的保险价值，则这批服装应属于（　　）。
　　A．共同海损　　B．实际全损　　C．推定全损　　D．单独海损
16．平安险（FPA）的英文含意是（　　）。
　　A．单独海损不负责赔偿　　　B．单独海损负责赔偿
　　C．共同海损不负责赔偿　　　D．共同海损负责赔偿
17．使用CFR价格术语成交，若卖方在货物装船之后没有及时发出通知而使买方漏保，如果货物在运输途中遭受损坏或灭失，则责任由（　　）承担。
　　A．买方　　B．卖方　　C．保险公司　　D．运输公司
18．下列危险中属于意外事故的是（　　）。
　　A．火山爆发　　B．爆炸　　C．海啸　　D．地震
19．下列风险中属于特殊外来风险的是（　　）。
　　A．没收　　B．偷窃　　C．碰撞　　D．破碎
20．下列风险中属于一般附加险的承保责任范围的是（　　）。
　　A．船舶触礁造成的损失　　　B．海啸和地震所造成的损失
　　C．受潮、受热造成的损失　　D．原子弹、氢弹等武器所造成的损失

二、判断题
1．上海某公司以CIF条件从国外进口一批货物，货物在运输途中遭遇飓风全部损失。几天后，对方凭包括正本提单在内的全套合格单据要求我方付款，我方以货物灭失为由拒绝付款，这种行为是合理的。（　　）
2．以CIF价格条件成交的合同，当货物在运输途中受损后，卖方仍有权凭符合合同规定的全套单据向买方索取货款，而且事后买方没有索赔权。（　　）
3．由于政府降低利率导致通货膨胀，从而导致原材料价格上涨，这种风险由于有政府行为的介入，应该视为不可抗力事故。（　　）
4．根据我国海洋运输货物保险条款的规定，如投保一切险，保险公司对被保险货物在海运途中由于任何外来原因造成的损坏灭失均应负责赔偿。（　　）

5. 出口的茶叶在装运途中最大的问题是有可能串味。因此在为其投保货运险时，除投保一切险之外，还应加保串味险。   （   ）

三、保险单据的填制

1. 根据信用证条款将正确答案填写在横线上

（1）信用证条款：

Documents Required: INSURANCE POLICY/CERTIFICATE UNTO ORDER AND BLANK ENDORSED COVERING MARINE TRANSPORTATION ALL RISKS, WAR RISKS AS PER INSTITUTE CARGO CLAUSES.

信用证未对保险单抬头做任何其他规定。

则保险单抬头应为：_____

（2）信用证条款：

Documents Required: INSURANCE POLICY COVERING MARINE TRANSPORTATION ALL RISKS, WAR RISKS AS PER INSTITUTE CARGO CLAUSES.

信用证未对投保比例做任何其他规定。

发票显示货物 CIF 总价为"USD 100,000.00"。

则保险单最低投保比例应为：_____

（3）信用证条款：

L/C AMOUNT: USD 550,000.00

Documents Required: INSURANCE POLICY/CERTIFICATE BLANK ENDORSED COVERING MARINE TRANSPORTATION ALL RISKS, WAR RISKS AS PER ICC (A).

信用证未对保险投保金额做任何其他规定。

发票显示：

Total Merchandise Value	USD 1,100,000.00
Less Advance Payment	USD 550,000.00
Net Due under the Letter of Credit	USD 550,000.00

保险单据投保金额最少应为：_____

（4）信用证条款：

Documents Required: INSURANCE POLICY/CERTIFICATE BLANK ENDORSED COVERING MARINE TRANSPORTATION ALL RISKS, WAR RISKS AS PER ICC (A).

信用证未对保险单据份数做任何其他规定。

保险单据上注明：

No. of Originals Issued: THREE

向银行提交的正本保险单据份数最少应为：_____

（5）信用证条款：

Documents Required: INSURANCE POLICY/CERTIFICATE UNTO ORDER AND BLANK ENDORSED COVERING MARINE TRANSPORT ALL RISKS, WAR RISKS AS PER INSTITUTE CARGO CLAUSES FOR 110 PCT OF INVOICE VALUE WITH CLAIMS PAYABLE AT DESTINATION.

信用证未对报销单据投保日期做任何其他规定。
报销单据无任何保险投保日期的相关陈述。
提单显示：
On Board Date: AUGUST 8, 2018
Issuing Date: AUGUST 7, 2018
保险单据的投保日期最迟为：＿＿＿＿＿＿＿＿

2. 根据以下条件填制一份保险单

信用证资料：

L/C No.:	A56439
Applicant:	NEWSTAR COMPANY, NEW YORK
Beneficiary:	ABC COMPANY, SHENZHEN
Loading in Charge:	SHENZHEN
For Transport to:	NEW YORK
Merchandise:	MAN'S T-SHIRT, CIF NEW YORK
Amount:	USD 45,000.00
Packages:	100 CTNS

Documents Required:
FULL SET (2/2) OF INSURANCE POLICY IN DUPLICATE IN NEGOTIABLE FORM BLANK ENDORSED FOR 110 PCT OF INVOICE VALUE COVERING OCEAN TRANSPORTATION CLAUSES ALL RISKS, STRIKES CLAUSES OF PICC, INCL. WAREHOUSE TO WAREHOUSE, I.O.P. CLAIMS PAYABLE AT NEW YORK IN THE CURRENCY OF L/C.

附件信息：

Invoice No.:	SY45/2018

提单显示：

Port of Loading:	SHENZHEN
Port of Discharge:	NEW YORK
Vessel:	GIANTFISH290 ON BOARD
Date:	FEB. 4, 2018
Marks:	T-SHIRTS-NEW YORK

保险单据的投保日期与提单显示的装船日期相同。

四、案例分析

（1）我国某出口公司按 CIF 条件向英国某进口商出口一批草编制品，并向中国人保财险公司投保了一切险，并规定用信用证方式支付。我国出口公司在规定的期限、指定的我国某港口装船完毕后，船公司签发了提单，之后该公司又前往中国银行议付款项。第二天，出口公司接到客户来电，称：装货的海轮在海上失火，草编制品全部烧毁，客户要求我方公司出面向中国人保财险公司提出索赔，否则要求我方公司退回全部货款。

问：该批交易按 CIF 伦敦条件成交，对客户的要求我方公司该如何处理？为什么？

（2）我国某出口公司对日商报出大豆实盘，每吨 CIF 大阪 150 美元，发货港口是大连，现日商要求我方改报 FOB 大连价。

问：我方出口公司对价格应如何调整？如果最后按 FOB 条件签订合同，买卖双方在所承担的责任、费用和风险方面有什么差别？

（3）我国某进口公司以 CFR 上海条件从国外进口一批货物，并据卖方提供的装船通知及时向中国人保财险公司投保水渍险。后来由于国内客户发生变更，进口公司通知承运人货物改卸黄埔港。货物在由黄浦装火车运往南京途中遇到山洪，致使部分货物受损，进口公司据此向保险公司索赔但遭拒绝。

问：保险公司拒赔有无道理？说明理由。

（4）某货轮自天津新港驶往新加坡，在航行途中船舶货舱起火，大火蔓延到机舱，船长为了船、货的共同安全，下令往舱内灌水，火很快被扑灭。但船舶主机受损，无法继续航行，于是船长雇用拖轮将船舶拖回新港修理，修好后重新驶往新加坡。

该起事故造成的损失共有：①1 000 箱货物被火烧毁；②600 箱货物被水浇湿；③船舶主机和部分甲板被烧坏；④拖轮费用；⑤额外增加的燃料费和船上人员的薪酬。

问：从损失的性质看，上述损失各属何种损失？

项目六
Project VI

运输单据
Transport Documents

学习目标（Learning Aims）

- 了解运输单据的概念和作用，熟悉相关规则。
- 熟悉运输单据的内容和填制要求。
- 能够熟练填制与审核运输单据。

情景导入（Lead-in Situation）

在科林国际贸易公司业务员李怡华完成备货以后，公司货运部王立需要向各家船代和货代公司询价，最终确定由中国外运华南有限公司（SINOTRANS South China Co., Ltd）代为订舱，以保证按信用证的规定及时交货。8月2日，王立填制货运托运单并授权货代公司代办货运手续，同时向货代公司提供相关单证，如商业发票、装箱单等。货代公司完成订舱后，王立于8月16日收到货代公司的装货单，要求其在8月25日前将货物送达准备发货的码头仓库。科林国际贸易公司在发货后还须仔细审核海运提单。

一、背景知识（Background Knowledge）

（一）海上运输单据（Marine Transport Documents）

1. 托运单

托运单（Shipping Note，S/N；或 Booking Note，B/N），也称订舱委托书，是出口企业在报关前向船方代理申请租船订舱的一份单据，是日后填制提单的主要依据。托运单一般有12联，每联的作用分别是：第1联，货主留底；第2联，船代留底；第3联，货代留底（1），以向出口单位收取运费；第4联，货代留底（2），由外运（或外代）留存；第5联，装货单（Shipping Order，S/O）；第6联，收货单（Mate's Receipt，M/R）；第7联，外运留底；第8联，配舱回单（1）；第9联，配舱回单（2）；第10联，缴纳港务费申请书；第11、12联，货主机动联。

2. 海运提单

海运提单（Marine / Ocean Bill of Lading，B/L），简称提单，是货物的承运人或其代理人收到托运货物后签发给托运人的一种证明文件，以此说明货物运输有关当事人（即承运人、托运人和收货人）之间的权利与义务。

（1）提单的作用：

1）提单是承运人或其代理人签发的货物收据。

2）提单是货物所有权的凭证。

3）提单是海上货物运输合同的证明。

提单除具有上述的性质与作用外，在业务联系、费用结算、对外索赔等方面也有着重要作用。

（2）提单的种类：

1）根据货物是否已装船可将提单分为已装船提单和备运提单。

已装船提单（On Board B/L）：指由船长或承运人或其代理人在货物装上指定的船舶后签发的提单。已装船提单的正面载有装货船舶的名称和装船日期，表明货物确已装船。这种提单能够在一定程度上保证收货人按时收货，因此，买方在信用证中往往要求卖方提供已装船提单，银行一般也只接受已装船提单。

备运提单（Received for Shipment B/L）：指船方在收到货物后，在货物装船以前签发的提单

2）根据收货人的抬头可将提单分为记名提单、不记名提单和指示提单。

记名提单（Straight B/L）：指提单正面载明收货人名称的提单。在这种情况下，承运人只能向提单上写明的特定收货人，交付货物。记名提单不能背书转让，因此不具备流通性。在国际贸易中，除了某些金银珠宝等贵重物品的运输外，一般不使用记名提单。

不记名提单（Bearer B/L 或 Blank B/L）：指提单正面未载明收货人名称的提单。不记名提单的收货人一栏中空白不填或填写"Bearer"（持有人）的字样。在签发不记名提单的情况下，承运人应向提单的持有人交付货物。这种提单由于未写明收货人的名称，因此转让十分简便，无须背书，只要将提单交给受让人即可。但是这种提单风险也相对较大，因此在实践中也很少使用。

指示提单（Order B/L）：指提单正面载明凭指示交付货物的提单。在收货人一栏中填写"To order"（凭指示）字样的提单称不记名指示提单；在收货人一栏中填写"To order of ××"（凭某某指示）的提单称记名指示提单。指示提单经过背书即可转让，具备良好的流通性，同时又规避了一定的风险，因此在实践中被广泛使用。

3）根据提单有无批注可将提单分为清洁提单和不清洁提单。

清洁提单（Clean B/L）：指提单上没有附加表明货物表面状况有缺陷的批注的提单。承运人如签发了清洁提单，就表明所接收的货物表面或包装完好，承运人事后不得以货物包装不良等为由推卸其运送责任。银行在结汇时一般只接受清洁提单。

不清洁提单（Unclean B/L 或 Foul B/L）：指在提单上批注表明货物表面状况有缺陷的提单。船方在货物装船时，如发现货物的表面状况不良，可以在提单上进行批注，以表明上述不良是在装船以前就存在的，从而减轻船方的货损责任。买方一般不愿接受这种提单，因为包装不良的货物在运输中很容易受损。除非在信用证规定可以接受该类提单，否则银行一般不会接受以不清洁提单办理结汇。

4）根据运输方式可将提单分为直达提单、转船提单和联运提单。

直达提单（Direct B/L）：指表明中途不经转船直接将货物运往目的地的提单。

转船提单（Transshipment B/L）：指当货物的运输不是由一条船直接运到目的港，而是在中途需转换另一船舶运往目的港时，船方签发的包括全程的提单。转船提单往往由第一程船的承运人签发。银行只有在信用证中规定可接受转船提单时，才接受这种提单。

联运提单（Through B/L 或 Combined Transport B/L）：指依联运合同签发的提单。联运提单又分为海上联运提单和多式联运提单。前者指在由一条以上船舶进行海上运输的情况下签发的提单，实际上就是转船提单；后者指以两种以上的运输工具运输时签发的提单。多式联运提单的签发人是多式联运经营人，签发的地点在货物的接收点，而不论该接收点是在装货港还是在发货人仓库。

（二）班轮运输的单据流转（Circulation of Documents in Liner Shipping）

（1）托运人在装货港向船公司或船舶代理人提出货物装运申请，递交托运单（B/N），填写装货联单。

（2）船公司同意承运后，其代理人指定船名，核对装货单（S/O）与托运单（B/N）上的内容无误后，将托运单留底联留下，签发装货单（S/O）给托运人，要求托运人将货物及时送至指定的码头仓库。

（3）托运人持装货单（S/O）及有关单证向海关办理货物出口报关、验货放行手续，海关在装货单（S/O）上加盖放行图章后，货物准予装船出口。

（4）装货港的船舶代理人根据留底联填制装货清单（Loading List, L/L），送船舶及理货公司、装卸公司。

（5）大副根据装货清单（L/L）填制货物积载计划（Stowage Plan），交代理人分送理货公司、装卸公司等，并按计划装船。

（6）托运人将经过检验放行的货物送至指定的码头仓库准备装船。

（7）货物装船后，理货长将装货单（S/O）交大副，大副核实无误后留下装货单（S/O）并签发收货单（M/R）。

（8）理货长将大副签发的收货单（M/R）转交给托运人。

（9）托运人持收货单（M/R）到装货港的船舶代理人处付清运费（预付运费情况下），以换取正本已装船提单（B/L）。

（10）装货港的船舶代理人审核无误后，留下收货单（M/R），签发正本已装船提单（B/L）给托运人。

（三）航空运输单据（Air Transport Documents）

航空货运单（Air Waybill，AWB）是航空运输公司或其代理人签发给发货人，表示已收妥货物并接受托运的货物收据。

航空货运单与海运提单有很大的不同，但与国际铁路运单相似。它是由承运人或其代理人签发的重要的货物运输单据，是承运人出具的货物收据（Cargo Receipt），也是承托双方的运输合同，其内容对双方均具有约束力。但航空货运单不是物权凭证，不能通过背书转让，持有航空货运单也并不能说明可以对货物要求所有权，即不能凭以提货，因而是一种不可议付的单据。

二、认识海上运输单据（Understand the Marine Transport Documents）

（一）托运单的样本与填制要点（Sample and Instructions for B/N）

BOOKING NOTE

(1) Shipper:	(4) No.:
	(17) Date:
	Loading Port:
(2) Consignee:	(5) Destination:
	B/L No.:
	(3) Notify Party:

(6) Shipping Marks	(7) Quantity	(8) Description of Goods	(9a) N.W.	(9b) G.W.	(10) Measurement
Total:					

(14) Partial Shipment:	(18) Original B/L:
(15) Transshipment:	(19) Copy of B/L:
(11) Time of Shipment:	(13) Goods in:
(12) Expiry Date:	Amount:
(16) Freight & Charges:	L/C No.:
Invoice No.:	S/C No.:
Transportation Details:	

| Revenue Tons: | Rate: | Freight Amount: |

(20) Special Conditions

1. **托运人**（Shipper 或 Consignor）

一般情况下，此栏填写出口商的名称和地址。如果是代理货主办理租船订舱的，要列明代理人的名称。例如，若由中国外运华南有限公司代理货主办理租船订舱，则此栏应填写"SINOTRANS South China Co., Ltd"（中国外运华南有限公司）。

2. **收货人**（Consignee）

在信用证支付的条件下，对收货人的规定常有以下两种表示方法。

（1）记名收货人：是指直接将收货人的名称、地址完整地表示出来。这种情况下，收货人即是合同买方。但是记名收货人的单据不能直接转让，这使单据的流通受到了阻碍，故记名收货人的表示方法不常使用。

（2）指示收货人：是指将收货人以广义的形式表示出来。常用空白指示和记名指示两种表达法。指示收货人掩饰了具体的收货人的名称和地址，使单据可以转让。在空白指示的情况下，单据的持有人可以自由转让单据；在记名指示的情况下，记名人有权控制和转让单据。指示收货人的方法补充了记名收货人方法的缺陷，但也给船方通知货方提货带来了麻烦，对此可在被通知人栏做出补充。

3. **被通知人**（Notify Party）

此栏填写信用证中规定的被通知人。被通知人的职责是及时接收船方发出的到货通知并将该通知转告真实收货人，被通知人无权提货。

4. **托运单编号**（No.）

此栏一般填写商业发票的编号。一是为了使发票填写的内容与实际装货的情况完全一致；二是为了便于查寻、核对。在信用证支付的条件下，有时来证规定了发票编号，对此，在填写托运单时就应把来证规定的发票编号填入这一栏。

5. **目的地**（Destination）

此栏按信用证的目的港填写。填写时为避免重名港口产生歧义，一般将目的港所在国家名称也填写在这一栏中。如果目的地是一内陆城市，则此栏应填写卸下最后一艘海轮时的港口名称。

6. **运输标志**（Shipping Marks）

此栏填写信用证或合同中规定的唛头。买卖合同或信用证中没有规定唛头时，可填写"N/M"。

7. **数量**（Quantity）

托运单中的数量是指最大外包装的件数。例如：10 万码（1 码=0.914 4 米）花布，分别用粗坯布捆成 100 捆，则数量栏应填"100 捆"。若出口货物有多件，包装方式和材料都不同，则须分别填写每种货物的最大包装件数及合计总件数，如"10 个托盘，10 个集装袋，125 个捆包布匹，合计 145 件"。

8. **货物描述**（Description of Goods）

对这一栏的内容允许只写大类名称或统称。但是，如果同时出口不同的商品，应分别填写，而不允许只填写其中一种数量较多或金额较大的商品。例如：出口各种用途的化工颜料，无须逐一列出颜料的成分、用途，而只需写"化工颜料"；出口尺寸不一、用途各异的竹制品，只需填写"竹制品"，而无须列出该批货物的明细尺码与品名。但是，如果同时出口化工颜料和竹制品，则应分别填写"化工颜料"和"竹制品"，而不允许只填写其中一种数量较多或金额较大的商品。

9．**重量**（Net Weight / Gross Weight）

重量应分别计算毛重和净重。若一次装运的货物有几种不同的包装材料或者是完全不同的货物，则应分别填写，然后合计。

在计算重量时，要求使用统一的计量单位，常用的计量单位是吨或千克。

10．**尺码**（Measurement）

此栏填写货物的尺码总数，一般单位为立方米。

11．**装运期**（Time of Shipment）

按照信用证中规定的装运期填写。

装运期可以全部使用阿拉伯数字表示，也可以使用英文与阿拉伯数字一起表示。例如：2018 年 5 月 6 日可表示为"6/5/2018"，最好用"MAY 6，2018"表示，但不要写成"5/6、2018"，以免引起混乱。

装运期还可以表示为一段时间。例如：2018 年 9～10 月可以表示为"Not earlier than Sept.1, 2018 and not later than Oct. 31, 2018"（不早于 2018 年 9 月 1 日，不迟于 2018 年 10 月 31 日）；装运期不迟于 2018 年 10 月 31 日表示为"Shipment not later than Oct.31, 2018"，或"The latest date of shipment is Oct. 31, 2018"。

12．**截止日**（Expiry Date）

截止日指信用证的有效期。此栏按信用证的规定填写，一般有效期比装运期晚。

13．**存货地**（Goods in）

此栏用中文填写将货物出口前的最后一个存放仓库的名称与地点。

14．**分批**（Partial Shipment）

按照合同或信用证条款填写，只能在"允许"或"不允许"两者中取其一。如果合同或信用证规定分若干批，或对分批有进一步说明，不要将这些说明填入本栏中，而应填入"特别条款"一栏中。

15．**转船**（Transshipment）

填写要求与分批一致，只能在"允许"或"不允许"两者中取其一。如果合同或信用证对这一内容有其他说明，应在特别条款栏中做出补充说明。

16．**运费**（Freight & Charges）

一般不显示具体运费，只填写"Freight collect"（运费待付）或"Freight prepaid/paid"（运费预付/已付）。

17．**托运单日期**（Date）

此栏可与发票日期一致，即填写开立发票的日期；但也可以早于发票日期，按实际开立托运单的日期填写。

18．**正本提单份数**（Original B/L）

一般一式三份，三份正本提单同时有效（Three Original Bill of Lading 或 Original Bill of Lading in Three），"Full set of Bill of Lading"指全套正本提单，按照习惯，一般是指两份及以上正本提单。

19. 副本提单份数（Copy of B/L）

副本提单份数一般是出口企业留底份数+寄单所需份数+信用证对正本提单要求的份数总和。其中，出口企业留底份数指业务部门留存份数。寄单所需份数一般会在信用证中做出明确规定。

20. 特别条款（Special Conditions）

填写信用证或合同中有关运输方面的特别条款。

（二）海运提单的样本与审核（Sample and Examination of B/L）

(1) Shipper			B/L No.
(2) Consignee			**SINOTRANS**
(3) Notify Party			中国外运华南有限公司 SINOTRANS SOUTH CHINA COMPANY LIMITED
(4) Pre-carriage by	(5) Port of Loading		**OCEAN BILL OF LADING**
(6) Vessel	(7) Port of Transshipment		SHIPPED on board in apparent good order and condition (unless otherwise indicated) the goods or packages specified herein and to be discharged at the mentioned port of discharge or as near thereto as the vessel may safely get and be always afloat. The weight, measure, marks and numbers, quality, contents and value, being particulars furnished by the Shipper, are not checked by the Carrier on loading. The Shipper, Consignee and the Holder of this Bill of Lading hereby expressly accept and agree to all printed, written or stamped provisions, exceptions and conditions of this Bill of Lading, including those on the back hereof. IN WITNESS whereof the number of original Bills of Lading stated below have been signed, one of which being accomplished the other(s) to be void.
(8) Port of Discharge	(9) Final Destination		
(10) Container No./ Seal No. Marks and Nos.	(11) Number and Kind of Package	(12) Description of Goods	(13a) Gross Weight (kgs.)	(13b) Measurement (m^3)
(14) Freight and Charges			REGARDING TRANSSHIPMENT INFORMATION PLEASE CONTACT
Ex. Rate	Prepaid at	Freight Payable at	(15) Place and Date of Issue
	Total Prepaid	(16) Number of Original Bs/L	Signed for or on behalf of the Master As Agent

托运人持大副签发的收货单（M/R）到装货港的船舶代理人处付清运费（预付运费情况下）并换取正本已装船提单（B/L）后，需要参照留底的托运单、合同、信用证对其进行细致审核，以防止海运提单的填制出现问题，进而影响正常收汇。

海运提单的审核主要从以下方面入手。

1．托运人（Shipper）

此栏一般分为下列几种情况：

（1）如果信用证无特殊规定，应以受益人为托运人，注明受益人名称和地址，有的只填受益人名称。

（2）如果受益人是中间商，而货物是从产地直接装运的，这时也可以实际卖方为托运人，因为按《UCP600》规定，如信用证无特殊规定，显示在任何单据中的货物的托运人或发货人不必是信用证的受益人，但也要考虑各方面是否可行。

（3）如果信用证要求提供中性提单（Neutral B/L），即不在提单上显示卖方资料，则可以货运代理等第三方作为托运人。

（4）如果信用证规定以受益人代替某公司（包括某外国公司），例如"China Garment Co. Tianjin on behalf of Rosemac Co., Ltd. Hong Kong"，提单托运人栏应照此规定填写。

2．收货人（Consignee）

收货人即提单抬头人，按信用证规定或根据业务需要，分为下列几种情况：

（1）记名抬头：如果来证提单条款内规定"Consigned to×××""Issued to ×××""Address to×××"或"Issued in name of ×××"等，则意味着提单收货人栏内应直接填写收货人名称。这种提单不能转让，只能由收货人提货。

（2）不记名抬头：如果来证提单条款内未注明收货人，或注有"Made out to bearer"或"Issued to bearer"等，应按来证规定，收货人栏留空不填，或填"To bearer"（货交提单持有人）。

（3）指示抬头：

a．如果来证提单条款内规定"Made out to order"（凭指示），亦称"空白抬头"，则提单收货人栏应打"To order"，这种提单须由发货人背书才能转让。

b．如果来证规定"Made out to order of shipper"或"Made out to shipper's order"（凭发货人指示），提单收货人栏应照打。这种提单也须经发货人背书才可转让。例如：来证要求"B/L issued to order of Applicant"，查Applicant为Big A Co., Ltd，则提单收货人一栏中应填"To order of Big A Co., Ltd"。

3．被通知人（Notify Party）

被通知人即买方的代理人，货到目的港时由承运人通知其办理报关、提货等手续。

（1）如果信用证中有规定，应严格按信用证规定填写，如详细地址、电话、电子邮箱、传真号码等，以使通知顺利。

（2）如果来证中没有具体说明被通知人，则应将开证申请人名称、地址填入提单副本的这一栏中，而正本的这一栏保持空白或填写买方。副本提单必须填写被通知人，以方便目的港代理通知联系收货人提货。

（3）如果来证中规定"Notify … only"，意指仅通知某某，则填写提单被通知人时"only"一词不能漏掉。

（4）如果信用证没有规定被通知人地址，而托运人在提单被通知人后面加注详细地址，银行可以接受，而无须审核。

4．前段运输（Pre-carriage by）

如果货物需转运，则应在此栏中填写第一程船的船名，否则留空。

5．装运港（Port of Loading）

（1）应严格按信用证的规定填写，装运港之前或之后有行政区的，如"Xingang/Tianjin"，应照加。

（2）一些国外开来的信用证会笼统地规定装运港名称，如仅规定为"Chinese ports"（中国港口）或规定"Shipment from China to …"（自中国运至……），这种规定对受益人来说比较灵活，即受益人可根据需要在我国任一港口装运，但在制单时应根据实际情况填写具体港口名称。若信用证规定装运港为"Your port"，则受益人只能在本市港口装运，若本市没有港口，则事先须洽开证人改证。如信用证同时列明几个启运港（地），如"Xingang/Qin-huangdao/Tangshan"，提单应只填一个，即实际装运的港口名称。

6．船名（Vessel）

如果货物需转运，则应在此栏填写第二程船的船名；如果货物不需转运，则应在此栏填写第一程船的船名。

7．转船港（Port of Transshipment）

如果货物需转运，则应在此栏填写中转港口名称，否则留空。

8．卸货港（目的港）（Port of Discharge）

卸货港为海运承运人终止承运责任的港口。如果是联合运输，后面还应有交货地（Place of Delivery）；如果是直达运输，可在此栏填目的港，也可此栏不填而在交货地栏填目的港；如果是转船运输，此栏应填目的港而在转船港栏或在货名下面对转船港另加说明，如"With transshipment at Hong Kong"，也可在此栏填转船港，在交货地栏填目的港。

9．最终目的地（Final Destination）

如果货物的目的地就是目的港，则此栏留空。

填写目的港或目的地应注意下列问题：

（1）除 FOB 价格条件外，目的港不能是笼统的名称（如"European main port"），而必须列出具体的港口名称，如果国际上有重名港口，还应加国名。

（2）如果来证在目的港后注明"In transit to …"，在 CIF 或 CFR 价格条件下不能照加，只能在其他空白处或唛头内加注此段文字，以表示转入内陆运输的费用由买方自理。

（3）有些信用证在目的港后注有"Free Port"（自由港）"Free Zone"（自由区），提单也可照加，例如 Aden（亚丁）、Aqaba（亚喀巴）、Colon（科隆）、Beirut（贝鲁特）、Port Said（塞得港）等，这些目的港后应加"Free Zone"，买方可凭此享受减免关税的优惠。

（4）来证可能注有多个目的港。例如：信用证规定目的港为"Kobe/Nagoya/Yokohama"，此种表示为卖方选港，提单中只填一个即可；而如果信用证规定"Option Kobe/Nagoya/Yokohama"，此种表示为买方选港，提单应按次序全部照填。

（5）如果信用证规定某港口为目的港，同时又规定具体的卸货码头，提单应照填。例如：到槟城目的港有"Penang""Penang/Butterworth""Penang/Georgetown"三种表示，后两种表示并不是选港，Butterworth 和 Georgetown 都是槟城港中的一个具体的卸货码头，如果信用证中规定了具体的卸货码头，提单中应照填。

10. **集装箱号、铅封号与唛头**（Container No. / Seal No., Marks and Nos.）

货物用集装箱装运时，提单上应注明装载货物的集装箱号，通常在集装箱号之后还加注海关查验后作为封箱的铅制关封号。如果是整箱货（Full Container Load，FCL），运到进口国后整箱交给收货人，在提单的集装箱号与铅封号之后加注"（FCL/FCL）"；如果是拼箱货（Less than Container Load，LCL），则应加注"（LCL/LCL）"。

提单上的唛头应与发票等其他单据以及实际货物保持一致，否则会给提货和结算带来困难。

（1）如果信用证上有具体规定，则应以信用证规定的唛头为准；如果信用证上没有具体规定，则以合同规定的唛头为准；如果合同上也没有规定，可按买卖双方私下商订的唛头或由受益人自定。

（2）唛头内的每一个字母、数字、图形以及它们的排列位置等应与信用证规定完全一致，保持原形状，不得随意错位、增减等。

（3）散装货物没有唛头，可以表示为"No mark"或"N/M"。

（4）如果同一发票项下须分制几套提单，而且发票上显示的是综合性大唛头，则提单可将其分解为不同的小唛头，例如发票唛头为：

ROSEMAC
STYLENO.0208/0556/0517
C/NO.1-250
　　251-700
　　701-1000

提单可以分制三套，唛头分别做成：

1) ROSEMAC	2) ROSEMAC	3) ROSEMAC
SIYLENO.0208	STYLENO.0556	STYLENO.0517
C/NO.1-250	C/NO.251-700	C/NO.701-1000

11. **货物包装及件数**（Number and Kind of Package）

如果是集装箱装运，由托运人装箱的整箱货可只注明集装箱数量，如"2 containers"等。只要海关已对集装箱封箱，承运人对箱内的内容和数量不负责任，提单内应加注"Shipper's load & count"（托运人装货并计数）。如需注明集装箱内小件数量，应在其前面加"Said to contain"。

12. **货物描述**（Description of Goods）

货物描述应按信用证规定以及其他单据如发票上的货物描述来填写，应注意避免不必要的描述。

13. **毛重**（千克）**与尺码**（立方米）[Gross Weight (kgs.), Measurement (m^3)]

提单应注明毛重和尺码，且应与发票或包装单据相符。如果是裸装货物没有毛重只有净重，则毛重一栏应按"Net weight"或"N.W."加具体净重数量的形式填写，不得留空。

14. **运费条款**（Freight and Charges）

运费条款应按信用证规定注明。如信用证未明确规定，可根据价格条件是否包含运费决定如何批注。主要有以下几种情况：

（1）如果是 CIF、CFR 等价格条件，运费在提单签发之前支付，提单应注"Freight paid"（运费已付）或"Freight prepaid"（运费预付）。

（2）如果是 FOB、FAS 等价格条件，运费在目的港支付，提单应注明"Freight collect"

"Freight to collect""Freight to be collected"（均表示运费到付或运费待收），或注"Freight payable at destination"（运费目的港支付）。

（3）如果信用证规定"Charter party B/L acceptable"（租船契约提单可以接受），提单内可注明"Freight as per charter party"，表示运费按租船契约支付。

（4）如果卖方知道运费金额或船公司不愿意暴露运费费率，提单可注"Freight paid as arranged"（运费已照约定付讫），或者注"Freight as arranged"或"Freight payable as per arrangement"，表示运费按照约定的时间或办法支付。

（5）对于货物的装船费和装卸费等负担问题，船方往往要求在提单上注明有关条款，如：

F.I.（Free In）：船方不负担装船费。

F.O.（Free Out）：船方不负担卸船费。

F.I.O.（Free In and Out）：船方不负担装船费和卸船费。

F.I.O.S.（Free In, Out and Stowed）：船方不负担装卸费和理舱费。

F.I.O.S.T.（Free In, Out, Stowed and Trimmed）：船方不负担装卸费、理舱费和平舱费。

15．**提单签发地点和日期**（Place and Date of Issue）

提单签发地点通常是承运人收受货物或装船的地址，提单签发日期不得晚于信用证规定的装运期，这对出口商能否安全收汇很重要。

16．**正本提单的份数**（Number of Original Bs/L）

只有正本提单可流通、交单、议付，副本则不行，例如："2/3 original clean on board ocean bills of lading"指制作三份正本提单，其中两份向议付行提交。

17．**已装船批注**（Laden on Board the Vessel）

有些提单正面没有预先印就的类似已装船的条款，这种提单便称为备运提单。备运提单转化为已装船提单的方式有两种：

（1）在提单的空白处加"已装船"批注或加盖类似内容的图章。例如"Shipped on Board"，或只注"On Board"，然后注明装船日期并附加提单签发人的签字或简签。所谓简签，是指签字人以最简单的签字形式，通常只签本人姓名中的一个单词或一个字母，来代替正式签字。

（2）在备运提单下端印有专供填写装船条款的栏目："Laden on Board the Vessel"（已装船标注），也被称为"装船备忘录"。装船后，在此栏内加注必要内容，如船名、装船日期等，并由签字人签字或简签。

（三）信用证中关于海运提单的相关条款（Requirements for B/L in L/C）

（1）Full set clean on board ocean bill of lading issued to order, blank endorsed marked freight payable at destination notifying ABC Company and showing invoice value, unit price, trade terms, contract number and L/C number unacceptable.

整套清洁已装船提单，空白抬头，运费到付，并注明 ABC 公司作为被通知人，且不能将发票总额、单价、价格术语、合同号和信用证号打在提单上。

（2）Full set clean on board port to port bill of lading, made out to order and endorsed to our order, marked freight prepaid dated not later than the latest date of shipment nor prior to the date of this credit. plus three non-negotiable copies.

全套港至港清洁已装船提单，空白抬头并背书给我方（开证行），注明运费预付，日期不得晚于最晚装运日期，也不得早于开证日期，加上三份不议付的副本提单。

(3) Full set of clean on board marine bills of lading, made out to the order of Abc Company, Rotterdam, Netherlands, marked freight prepaid and notify applicant.

整套清洁已装船海运提单，做成凭荷兰鹿特丹 ABC 公司指示的抬头，注明运费预付，通知开证人。

(4) Full set of not less than two clean on board marine bills of lading marked freight prepaid and made out to oder and endorsed to our order showing Blue Bird Trading Company as notify party. Short form bills of lading are not acceptable. Bill of lading to state shipment has been effected in containers and container numbers.

全套不少于两份的清洁已装船海运提单，注明运费预付，空白抬头，背书给我方（开证行），并以蓝鸟贸易公司作为被通知人。简式提单不接受，提单注明集装箱装运及集装箱号码。

(5) Full set of clean on board marine bills of lading consigned to order, blank endorsed marked freight prepaid and claused notify applicant.

整套清洁已装船海运提单，空白抬头，空白背书，注明运费预付，并通知开证人。

（四）情景导入中的运输单据（Transport Documents of the Lead-in Situation）

1. 托运单

BOOKING NOTE

Shipper: KELIN INTERNATIONAL TRADING (HK) CO., LTD RM2403, BLOCK A2, YIHE PLAZA, NO. 413, GUANGZHOU, GHINA		No.: GD57861609		
		Date: 2018/08/02		
		Loading Port: SHEKOU, SHENZHEN		
Consignee: TO ORDER		Destination: NEW YORK		
		B/L No.:		
		Notify Party: GLOBE SOURCING SERVICE CO., LTD 1407, 80TH STREET, S.W., NOVI, MICHIGAN, USA		
Shipping Marks	Quantity	Description of Goods	N.W.	G.W.	Measurement
G.S.S TXT264 NEW YORK C/No. 1-300	300 CARTONS	100% COTTON COLOUR WAVE T-SHIRT	1,500 KGS	1,650 KGS	8.46 CBM
Total:	300CTNS		1,500 KGS	1,650 KGS	8.46 CBM
Partial Shipment: PROHIBITED		Original B/L: 3		
Transshipment: ALLOWED		Copy of B/L: 3		
Time of Shipment: NOT LATER THAN AUG. 30, 2018		Goods in: CARTONS		
Expiry Date: SEPT. 14, 2018		Amount:		
Freight & Charges:		L/C No.: BL170197		
Invoice No.: PI170601		S/C No.: TXT264		
Transportation Details:				
Revenue Tons:	Rate:		Freight Amount:	
Special Conditions				

2. 海运提单

Shipper KELIN INTERNATIONAL TRADING (HK) CO., LTD RM2403, BLOCK A2, YIHE PLAZA, NO. 413, GUANGZHOU, CHINA		B/L No. GD57861609
Consignee TO ORDER		**SINOTRANS** 中国外运华南有限公司 SINOTRANS SOUTH CHINA COMPANY LIMITED **OCEAN BILL OF LADING**
Notify Party GLOBE SOURCING SERVICE CO., LTD 1407, 80TH STREET, S.W., NOVI, MICHIGAN, USA		
Pre-carriage by	Port of Loading SHEKOU, SHENZHEN	SHIPPED on board in apparent good order and condition (unless otherwise indicated) the goods or packages specified herein and to be discharged at the mentioned port of discharge or as near thereto as the vessel may safely get and be always afloat.
Vessel EAST WIND V.23	Port of Transshipment	The weight, measure, marks and numbers, quality, contents and value, being particulars furnished by the Shipper, are not checked by the Carrier on loading. The Shipper, Consignee and the Holder of this Bill of Lading hereby expressly accept and agree to all printed, written or stamped provisions, exceptions and conditions of this Bill of Lading, including those on the back hereof.
Port of Discharge NEW YORK, USA	Final Destination	IN WITNESS whereof the number of original Bills of Lading stated below have been signed, one of which being accomplished the other(s) to be void.

Container No. / Seal No. Marks and Nos.	Number and Kind of Package	Description of Goods	Gross weight (kgs.)	Measurement (m³)
G.S.S TXT264 NEW YORK C/No. 1-300	300 CARTONS	100% COTTON COLOUR WAVE T-SHIRT SHIPPER'S LOAD & COUNT BOARDED ON JUNE 23TH SAY THREE HUNDRED CARTONS ONLY	1,650 KGS	8.46 CBM

Freight and Charges FREIGHT PREPAID			REGARDING TRANSSHIPMENT INFORMATION PLEASE CONTACT
Ex. Rate	Prepaid at SHENZHEN	Freight Payable at	Place and Date of Issue SHENZHEN 23-AUG.-2018
	Total Prepaid	Number of Original Bs/L THREE	Signed for or on behalf of the Master SINOTRANS SOUTH CHINA COMPANY LIMITED As Agent

三、认识航空货运单（Understand the Air Waybill）

（一）航空货运单的样本（A Sample of Air Waybill）

(1)			
Shipper's Name and Address (2)	Shipper's Account Number (3)	NOT NEGOTIABLE **AIR WAYBILL** ISSUED BY	
		Copies 1, 2 and 3 of this Air Waybill are originals and have the same validity.	
Consignee's Name and Address (4)	Consignee's Account Number (5)	It is agreed that the goods described herein are accepted in apparent good order and condition (except as noted) for carriage SUBJECT TO THE CONDITIONS OF CONTRACT ON THE REVERSE HEREOF. ALL GOODS MAY BE CARRIED BY ANY OTHER MEANS INCLUDING ROAD OR ANY OTHER CARRIER UNLESS SPECIFIC CONTRARY INSTRUCTIONS ARE GIVEN HEREON BY THE SHIPPER, AND SHIPPER AGREES THAT THE SHIPMENT MAY BE CARRIED VIA INTERMEDIATE STOPPING PLACES WHICH THE CARRIER DEEMS APPROPRIATE. THE SHIPPER'S ATTENTION IS DRAWN TO THE NOTICE CONCERNING CARRIER'S LIMITATION OF LIABILITY. Shipper may increase such limitation of liability by declaring a higher value for carriage and paying a supplemental charge if required.	
Issuing Carrier's Agent Name and City (6)		Accounting Information (18)	
Agent's IATA Code (7)	Account No. (8)		
Airport of Departure (Addr. of first Carrier) and Requested Routing (9)		Reference Number	Optional Shipping Information

To (10)	By First Carrier (11)	Routing and Destination	to (12)	by (13)	to (14)	by (15)	Currency (19)	CHGS Code (20)	WT/VAL PPD (21a) / COLL (21b)	Other PPD (22a) / COLL (22b)	Declared Value for Carriage (23)	Declared Value for Customs (24)

Airport of Destination (16)	Requested Flight/Date (17a) (17b)	Amount of Insurance (25)	INSURANCE – If Carrier offers insurance, and such insurance is requested in accordance with the conditions thereof, indicate amount to be insured in figures in box marked 'Amount of Insurance'.	TC

Handling Information (26)							SCI
No. of Pieces RCP	Gross Weight	kg/lb	Rate Class (30) / Commodity Item No.	Chargeable Weight	Rate / Charge	Total	Nature and Quantity of Goods (incl. Dimensions or Volume)
(27)	(28)	(29)		(31)	(32)	(33)	(34)

Prepaid	Weight Charge	Collect	Other Charges (46)
	(35a)	(35b)	
	Valuation Charge		
	(36a)	(36b)	
	Tax		
	(37a)	(37b)	
	Total other Charge Due Agent		Shipper certifies that the particulars on the face hereof are correct and that INSOFAR AS ANY PART OF THE CONSIGNMENT CONTAINS DANGEROUS GOODS, SUCH PART IS PROPERLY DESCRIBED BY NAME AND IS IN PROPER CONDITION FOR CARRIAGE BY AIR ACCORDING TO THE APPLICABLE DANGEROUS GOODS REGULATIONS.
	(38a)	(38b)	
	Total other Charge Due Carrier		
	(39a)	(39b)	
			(48)
			Signature of Shipper or his Agent
Total Prepaid		Total Collect	
(40)		(41)	
Currency Conversion Rate		CC Charge in Destination Currency	
(42)		(43)	(49)
			Executed on (date) at (place) Signature of Issuing Carrier or its Agent
For Carrier's Use only at Destination (44)	Charge at Destination (45)	Total Collect Charge (47)	

（二）航空货运单的填制要点（Instructions for Air Waybill）

1．航空货运单号（Air Waybill No.）

运单号通常印在每份运单的左上角和右下角，由 11 位数字构成。前 3 位表示航空公司的数字代号，如我国的国际航空公司的代码就是 999；第 4 位至第 10 位表示货运单序号；最后一位是检验号。

航空货运单分为两种，一种是航空公司的货运单，又称总运单（Master Air Waybill，MAWB）；另一种是航空货运代理公司的货运单，又称分运单（House Air Waybill，HAWB）。

2．托运人姓名、住址（Shipper's Name and Address）

填写托运人的姓名、地址、所在国家及联络方法。

① 托运人可以是货主，也可是货运代理人。如采用的是集中托运，则通常托运人是货运代理人；如采用的是直接托运，则托运人是货主。

② 当托运的是危险货物时，必须由货主直接托运，即托运人栏必须填货主，航空公司不接受货运代理人的托运。

③ 在信用证结汇方式下，托运人一般填受益人的相应信息；在托收方式下，一般填合同中买方的相应信息。

3．托运人账号（Shipper's Account Number）

只在必要时填写，以便承运人在收货人拒付运费时向托运人索偿。

4．收货人姓名、住址（Consignee's Name and Address）

填写收货人的姓名、地址、所在国家及联络方法。

① 与海运提单不同，航空货运单必须是记名抬头，不得填写"To order"或"To order of shipper"字样，因为航空货运单不可转让。

② 收货人可以是实际收货人，也可是货运代理人。集中托运时收货人通常是货运代理人，直接托运时为实际收货人。

③ 承运人一般不接受一票货物有两个或以上的收货人。若在实际业务中确有多个收货人，则在该栏内填写第一收货人，同时在通知栏内填写第二收货人。

5．收货人账号（Consignee's Account Number）

同第 3 栏一样，只在必要时填写。

6．填开货运单的代理人名称和所在城市（Issuing Carrier's Agent Name and City）

例如：该份货运单由航空公司代理人上海 ABC 公司[ABC Co. (Shanghai)]填开，则直接将"ABC Co. (Shanghai)"填在该栏即可。

7．代理人的 IATA 代号（Agent's IATA Code）

填写航空公司代理人的 IATA 代号，具体格式为代理人代码/城市代码，如"ABC/SHA"。

8．代理人账号（Account No.）

同第 3 栏一样，只在必要时填写。

9．始发站机场及所要求的航线（Airport of Departure and Requested Routing）

填写始发站机场的英文全称和所要求的运输路线。实务中一般仅填写启航机场的名称或所在城市的全称。具体填写如下：

① 当始发站机场全称不清楚时，只填始发站所在城市名称。
② 城市重名的不同国家，需填国家名称。
③ 同一城市的不同机场，需填机场名称。

注意： 与前面其他单据的填写一样，当信用证上要求"Any Chinese Airport"时，货运单上不能照填，而必须写具体的机场名称，如"Shanghai Pudong International Airport"，或填其代码"PVG"。

10．**至（由第一承运人）[To (by First Carrier)]**

填写目的站机场或第一个转运点的 IATA 三字代号。

11．**由第一承运人（By First Carrier）**

填写第一承运人的名称或 IATA 两字代号。

12．**至（由第二承运人）[to (by Second Carrier)]**

填写目的站机场或第二个转运点的 IATA 三字代号。

13．**由（第二承运人）[by (Second Carrier)]**

填写第二承运人的名称或 IATA 两字代号。

14．**至（由第三承运人）[to (by Third Carrier)]**

填写目的站机场或第三个转运点的 IATA 三字代号。

15．**由（第三承运人）[by (Third Carrier)]**

填写第三承运人的名称或 IATA 两字代号。

16．**目的港（Airport of Destination）**

填写最终目的站机场的名称或 IATA 三字代码，具体如下：

① 机场的三字代码按 IATA 规范标准填报，如上海浦东国际机场的代码为"PVG"。

② 机场名称不明确时，可填城市名称，当城市与其他国家的城市有重名时，应加上国名。例如悉尼，如果是加拿大悉尼，则填写为"SYD, CA"；如果是澳大利亚悉尼，则填写为"SYD, AU"。

17．**所要求的航班/日期（Requested Flight/Date）**

填写飞机航班号及起飞日期。

18．**财务说明（Accounting Information）**

该栏填写运费缴付方式及其他财务说明事项，具体包括：

① 运费支付方式：Freight Prepaid（运费预付）或 Freight Collect（运费到付）。

② 付款方式：Cash（现金）、Check（支票）或 MCO（旅费证）（用该证付款时，需填写 MCO 号码、旅客客票号码、航班及日期）等。

③ 若承运飞机起飞后需更改运费，则将更改通知单号（CCA No.）填在本栏内。

19．**货币（Currency）**

填入 ISO 货币代码。

20．**收费代号（CHGS Code）**

本栏一般不需填写，仅供电子传送货运单信息时用。

21. **运费及声明价值费**（Weight Charge / Valuation Charge, WT / VAL）

此栏分为两种情况：预付（Prepaid，PPD）或到付（Collect，COLL）。如果是预付则在（21a）中填入"*"，否则填在（21b）中。需要注意的是，航空货物运输中运费与声明价值费的支付方式必须一致，不能分别支付。

22. **其他费用**（Other）

其他费用也分为预付和到付两种支付方式。

23. **运输声明价值**（Declared Value for Carriage）

填写托运人向承运人办理的货物声明价值的金额。当托运人不办理货物声明价值时，此栏必须填写"NVD"（No Value Declaration）。

24. **海关声明价值**（Declared Value for Customs）

填写托运人向海关申报的货物价值，当托运人不办理此项声明，则此栏须填入"NCV"（No Customs Valuation），表明托运人没有向海关声明价值。

25. **保险金额**（Amount of Insurance）

只有在航空公司提供代保险业务而客户也有此需要时才填写此栏。中国民航不代理国际货物运输保险，则该栏须打上"×××"或"NIL"（表示无值）。

26. **操作信息**（Handling Information）

一般填入承运人对货物处理的有关注意事项，具体填写如下：

① 当有两个收货人时，第二收货人的相应信息填写在该栏。

② 若货运单有随附的文件，则该栏需显示文件的名称，如"Attached files including Commercial Invoice, Packing List"。

③ 货物上的标志、号码、包装方法等。

④ 如果货物是危险品，分以下两种情况：需要附托运危险品申报单时，本栏一般填"Dangerous goods as per attached Shipper's Declaration"；不需要附托运危险品申报单时，本栏则填"Shipper's Declaration not required"。

⑤ 填写货物所需的特殊处理，如"DDU"（未完税交付）。

⑥ 其他事项。

27. **货物件数和运价组成点**[No. of Pieces, Rate Combination Point (RCP)]

填入货物包装件数，如 10 包即填"10"。当需要组成比例运价或分段相加运价时，在此栏填入运价组成点机场的 IATA 代码。

28. **毛重**（Gross Weight）

填入货物总毛重，以千克为单位时可保留小数后一位。

29. **重量单位**（kg/lb）

可选择以千克（kg）或磅（lb）为单位。以千克为单位时填入代号"K"，以磅为单位时填入代号"L"。

30. **运价等级**（Rate Class）

依航空公司的资料，按实际填写运价等级的代号，具体代号如表 6-1 所示。

表 6-1　运价等级代号

代码	运价英文名称	运价中文名称
M	Minimum Charge	最低运费
N	Normal Rate	45 千克以下货物适用的普通货物运价
Q	Quantity Rate	45 千克及以上货物适用的普通货物运价
C	Specific Commodity Rate	指定商品运价
S	Surcharged Class Rate	等级货物附加运价
R	Reduced Class Rate	等级货物附减运价
U	Unit Load Device Basic Charge or Rate	集装化设备基本运费或运价
E	Unit Load Device Additional Rate	集装化设备附加运价
X	Unit Load Device Additional Information	集装化设备附加说明
Y	Unit Load Device Discount	集装化设备折扣

31．**计费重量**（Chargeable Weight）

此栏填入航空公司据以计算运费的计费重量，该重量可以与货物毛重相同也可以不同，具体情况如下：

① 当货物是重货时，计费重量可以是货物的实际毛重。

② 当货物是轻泡货时，计费重量可以是货物的体积重量。

③ 计费重量可以是较高重量较低运价的分界点的重量。即按实际计费重量计算出的运费超过较高重量的分界点运费时，航空公司可同意按较低者收取运费。

例如：实际重量为 41 千克的货物运往美国，运价等级为 45 千克以下时 10 美元/千克，45 千克及以上时 8 美元/千克。由于按实际重量计收运费 410 美元（41×10）高于 45 千克分界点运费 360 美元（45×8），则可按分界点重量 45 千克计收运费。

　　从这里我们发现：计费重量=实际毛重（重货）
　　　　　　　　　　　计费重量=体积重量（轻泡货）
　　　　　　　　　　　计费重量=较高重量较低运价的分界点重量

32．**运价/运费**（Rate/Charge）

填入该货物适用的运价或运费：

① 当使用最低运费时，填写与"M"相对应的最低运费。

② 当使用"N""Q""C"运价代号时，填写相对应的运价。

③ 当货物为等级货物时，填写与代号"S""R"对应的附加、附减后的运价。

④ 当货物为集装货物时，填写与代号"U""E"对应的集装货物运费或运价。

33．**运费总额**（Total）

此栏数值应为最低运费值或为适用运价与计费重量两栏数值的乘积。

34．**货物的品名、数量**（含尺码或体积）[Nature and Quantity of Goods (incl. Dimensions or Volume)]

填写合同或信用证中规定的货物品名、数量及尺码时应注意：

① 当托运货物中含有危险货物时，应分别填写，并把危险货物列在第一项。
② 当托运货物为活动物时，应依照 IATA 活动物运输规定填写。
③ 对于集装货物，填写"Consolidation as per attached list"。
④ 货物的体积表示为"长×宽×高"，如"DIMS: 50×30×20"。
⑤ 当合同或信用证要求标明原产地国时，可在此栏标出货物的原产地国。

35．**计重运费**（Weight Charges）

在对应的"预付"或"到付"栏内填入按计费重量计算的运费额，其数值应与上述"运费总额"栏中的金额一致。

36．**声明价值附加费**（Valuation Charge）

如托运人对托运货物声明价值，则在对应的"预付"或"到付"栏内填入声明价值附加费金额，其公式为

$$声明价值附加费金额 = （声明价值 - 实际毛重 \times 最高赔偿额）\times 0.5\%$$

37．**税款**（Tax）

在对应的"预付"或"到付"栏内填入适当的税款。

38．**由代理人收取的其他费用**（Total other Charge Due Agent）

在对应的"预付"或"到付"栏内填入由代理人收取的其他费用，也可填"As arranged"。

39．**由承运人收取的其他费用**（Total other Charge Due Carrier）

在对应的"预付"或"到付"栏内填入由承运人收取的其他费用，也可填"As arranged"。

40．**预付总额**（Total Prepaid）

填写（35a）～（39a）各栏预付款项之和，也可填"As arranged"。

41．**到付总额**（Total Collect）

填写（35b）～（39b）各栏到付款项之和，也可填"As arranged"。

42．**货币兑换比价**（Currency Conversion Rate）

填写目的站国家货币代号及兑换比率。

43．**用目的站国家货币付费**（CC Charge in Destination Currency）

填写换算为目的站国家货币的到付费用总额。

44．**仅供承运人在目的站使用**（For Carrier's Use only at Destination）

此栏不需填写。

45．**在目的站的费用**（Charge at Destination）

填写最后承运人在目的站发生的费用金额，包括利息等。

46．**其他费用**（Other Charges）

填写除运费和声明价值附加费以外的其他费用。根据 IATA 规则，各项费用分别以三个英文字母表示，其中前两个字母是某项费用的代码，如运单费就表示为 AW（Air Waybill Fee），第三个字母是 C 或 A，分别表示费用应支付给承运人（Carrier）或货运代理人（Agent）。

47．**到付费用总额**（Total Collect Charge）

填写到付费用总额。

48．**发货人或其代理人签名**（Signature of Shipper or his Agent）

签名后以示保证本单所填内容正确，且对危险品（如有）已明确表述并已按规定正确处理。

49. 签发运单日期、地点及承运人或其代理人签字[Executed on (date) at (place)，Signature of Issuing Carrier or its Agent]

签单以后正本航空货运单方能生效。本栏所表示的日期为签发日期，也就是本批货物的装运日期。如果信用证规定货运单必须注明实际起飞日期，则以货运单所注的实际起飞日期作为装运日期。本栏的日期不得晚于信用证规定的装运日期。

以代理人身份签章时，同海运提单一样，需在签章处加注"As Agents"；承运人签章则加注"As Carrier"。

实操训练（Skill Training）

一、单选题

1. 下面是四份海运提单的抬头，托运人是 XYZ 公司。根据收货人的不同，（   ）需托运人背书。
   A．To order   B．To ABC Co., Ltd
   C．To order of ABC Co., Ltd   D．To order of ABC Bank

2. CIF 术语中的卖方不愿承担卸货费用，可以选用（   ）。
   A．CIF Liner Terms   B．CIF Landed
   C．CIF Ex Ship's Hold   D．CIF Ex Tackle

3. 国际多式联运的经营人（承运人）（   ）。
   A．对运输全程负责
   B．仅对第一程运输负责
   C．仅对第二程运输负责
   D．接受第二程运输承运人的委托并向原货主负责

4. 国外一张来证的有效期为 2018 年 10 月 30 日，最迟装运期为 10 月 10 日，如果信用证未规定装运日后交单的期限，而实际发运日期是 10 月 1 日，根据《UCP600》的规定，受益人的最迟交单期为（   ）。
   A．2018 年 10 月 10 日   B．2018 年 10 月 22 日
   C．2018 年 10 月 23 日   D．2018 年 10 月 30 日

5. 如果信用证规定"Shipment on or about 15 Oct. 2018"，那么装运期可以是（   ）。
   A．10 月 10 日～10 月 19 日   B．10 月 11 日～10 月 20 日
   C．10 月 10 日～10 月 20 日   D．10 月 11 日～10 月 19 日

6. 提单按收货人分类，可分为记名提单、不记名提单和指示提单。经过背书才能转让的提单是（   ）。
   A．来人抬头提单   B．指示提单
   C．记名提单   D．不记名提单

7. 某外贸公司与国外一进口商订立销售合同，我方出售长毛绒玩具 10 000 个。合同规定，2018 年 5 月 30 日前开出信用证，6 月 20 日前装船。4 月 28 日买方按期来证，有效期至 6 月 30 日。由于卖方按期装船出现困难，故书面向买方申请将装船期延至 7 月 5 日，买方回函表示同意，但未通知开证行。7 月 3 日货物装船后，卖方于 7 月 4 日到银行议付，但遭到

拒绝。对于银行是否有权拒绝议付及其原因，以下说法正确的是（   ）。

    A．银行有权拒绝议付，因为开证申请人没有通过开证行修改信用证

    B．银行无权拒绝议付，因买卖双方只改变约定的装船期，未改变信用证条款

    C．银行无权拒绝议付，因只要买卖双方同意改变装船期，即意味着信用证条款发生改变

    D．银行有权拒绝议付，因为开证行还应接受买卖双方的合同约束

8．关于提单下面说法正确的是（   ）。

    A．提单是代表货物所有权的物权凭证或运输契约

    B．提单辅助发票说明之不足，并详细说明包装内容或货物数量以及标记号

    C．提单是国外卖方或厂商对货物出具的明细账单

    D．提单又称来源证，主要对货物的产地、厂家做佐证，便于海关掌握其国别、地区，以作征税时参考

9．清洁提单是指（   ）。

    A．承运人未加有关货物或包装不良之类批注的提单

    B．不载有任何批注的提单

    C．表面整洁无涂改痕迹的提单

    D．提单收货人栏内没有指明任何收货人的提单

10．某公司先后于 4 月 18 日和 5 月 2 日分别在广州和湛江各装 20 000 吨货物于第 169 航次的"红日"轮运往目的地新加坡，若信用证规定货物禁止分批装运，则下列说法正确的是（   ）。

    A．该公司货物发运日期不同，属于分批装运，违反了信用证的规定

    B．该公司使用同一船只运输，不属于分批装运，没有违反信用证的规定

    C．该公司货物出运时的装运港不同，属于分批装运，违反了信用证的规定

    D．该公司货物分两批出运取得两套单据，属于分批装运，违反了信用证的规定

二、请根据以下信用证中的相关内容填制托运单

……

Doc. Credit Number	*20:	002/0503668
Date of Issue	31C:	180220
Expiry	*31D:	DATE 180515 PLACE CHINA
Applicant	*50:	DE TUINKRAMER B.V.
Beneficiary	*59:	CHINA NATIONAL ARTS & CRAFTS CORPORATION TAIYUAN BRANCH TAIYUAN FOREIGN TRADE BUILDING 85-99, ZHONGSHAN ROAD 7, TAIYUAN, CHINA
Amount	*32B:	CURRENCY USD AMOUNT 16,172.00

……

Partial Shipments	43P:	NOT ALLOWED
Transshipment	43T:	ALLOWED
Loading in Charge	44A:	QINGDAO, CHINA
For Transportation to	44B:	ROTTERDAM

Latest Date of Shipment	44C:	180430
Descript. of Goods	45A:	5,134 UNITS WIRE PRODUCTS CIF ROTTERDAM USD3.15 PER UNIT AS PER CONTRACT NO. 2018KE1985
Documents Required	46A:	* FULL SET OF CLEAN ON BOARD BILL OF LADING MADE OUT TO ORDER BLANK ENDORED, MARKED "FREIGHT PREPAID", NOTIFY THE APPLICANT.

……

其他资料：

Shipping Mark: DE TUINKRAMER B.V.
      C/NOS. 1-171
      ROTTERDAM

Port of Loading: QINGDAO
Port of Discharge: ROTTERDAM W/T HONG KONG
Per Conveyance: S.S QINGYANG V. 126/VINONA
Date of B/L: APRIL 20, 2018
Packing: PACKED IN 171 WOODEN CASES
Invoice No.: 173324009
B/L No.: YSL08487
Case Size: 60cm×40cm×30cm
Gross Weight: 48KGS/CASE
Net Weight: 45KGS/CASE

三、请根据以下信用证中的相关内容填制海运提单

……

Doc. Credit Number	*20:	TT456643132
Date of Issue	31C:	MAR. 5, 2018
Applicant	*50:	DIADORA S.P.A. VIA MAZZINI, 20310310 CAERANO SAN MARCO (TV), ITALY
Beneficiary	*59:	CHINA NATIONAL NATIVE PRODUCT AND ANIMAL BY-PRODUCT IMP. AND EXP. CO. GUANGXI BRANCH XINGHU ROAD, NANNING-GUANGXI-CHINA
Partial Shipments	43P:	NOT ALLOWED
Transshipment	43T:	ALLOWED
Loading in Charge	44A:	ANY PORT IN CHINA
For Transportation to	44B:	VENEZIA, ITALY
Latest Date of Shipment	44C:	JUNE 30, 2018
Descript. of Goods	45A:	

1,110PCS DOWN FILLED JACKET　　MODEL: 20072 AT USD 28.50/PC
1,110PCS DOWN FILLED JACKET　　MODEL: 37408 AT USD 30.00/PC
CIF VENEZIA, ITALY LESS 3% DISCOUNT
PACKED IN CARTONS AS PER S/C NO.00GABP07
MADE IN CHINA

Documents Required　　　46A:
+ 3/3 ORIGINAL BILL OF LADING MADE OUT TO THE ORDER OF DIADORA SPA-VIA MAZZINI 20 310310 CAERANO SAN MARCO (TV), NOTIFY: T.F.F. SRL-VIA VIGONOVEXE 293/I–35020 CAMIN (PD), GENOA, ITALY AND MARKED FREIGHT PREPAID.

Additional Cond.　　　47A:
L/C NO. SHOULD BE INDICATED IN ALL DOCUMENTS PRESENTED FOR NEGOTIATION.

……

其他资料:
Down filled jacket packed in 222 cartons total.
Date of B/L: JUNE 27, 2018
G.W.: 35KGS/CTN　　　N.W.: 33KGS/CTN　　　M.: (40×38×20) CBM/CTN
Port of Loading: SHENZHEN, CHINA
Port of Transshipment: SINGAPORE
Name of Vessel: V.598/CONCORD
B/L No.: DWS84938
Shipping Marks: DIADORA S.P.A./00GABP07/VENEZIA/C.NO.:1-222

项目七
Project VII

原产地证书
Certificate of Origin

学习目标（Learning Aims）

○ 了解原产地证书的作用和种类。
○ 能够独立填制一般原产地证书。
○ 能独立填制普惠制原产地证书。

情景导入（Lead-in Situation）

科林国际贸易公司业务员李怡华根据信用证规定，在中国国际贸易促进委员会（以下简称贸促会）原产地证申报系统（http://www.co.ccpit.org）中填报了申请原产地证书的详细信息。待贸促会审核通过后，李怡华即到贸促会深圳分会领取原产地证书。

一、背景知识（Background Knowledge）

（一）原产地证书的概念（Definition of C/O）

原产地证书（Certificate of Origin，C/O）简称产地证，是由出口国政府主管部门的授权机构、商会或出口商及制造商根据相关的原产地规则签发的，用于证明商品原产地，即货物的生产或制造地的一种证明文件。

（二）原产地证书的作用（Functions of C/O）

在国际贸易中，世界各国根据各自的对外贸易政策，普遍实行进口贸易管制，对进口商品实施差别关税和数量限制，并由海关执行统计。进口国要求出口国出具货物的原产地证明已成为国际惯例，因此，原产地证书是进行国际贸易的一项重要证明文件。总体来说，原产地证书具有以下几方面的作用：

（1）原产地证书是各国海关据以征收关税和实施差别待遇的有效凭证。
（2）原产地证书是进口国海关实行进口限制和不同进口配额的依据文件。
（3）原产地证书有助于各国对进出口货物进行统计。
（4）原产地证书是贸易双方进行交接、结汇的必备单据。

（三）原产地证书的种类（Types of C/O）

1．根据签发者的不同进行分类

（1）海关出具的原产地证书。海关总署公告 2018 年第 106 号《关于中国原产地证书和金伯利进程证书签发有关事宜的公告》指出：根据 2018 年国务院机构改革方案，原国家质量监督检验检疫总局的出入境检验检疫管理职责和队伍划入海关总署。中国原产地证书的签证管理部门由原国家质量监督检验检疫总局变更为海关总署，签证机构中的各地出入境检验检疫机构变更为各直属海关。签发的各类原产地证书具体包括：非优惠原产地证书、普惠制原产地证书、优惠贸易协定原产地证书和输欧盟农产品等专用原产地证书。

（2）商会出具的原产地证书。如：中国国际贸易促进委员会（CCPIT）出具的一般原产地证书，简称贸促会产地证（CCPIT Certificate of Origin）。

（3）制造商或出口商出具的原产地证书。

在国际贸易实务中，应该提供哪种原产地证书，主要依据合同或信用证的要求。一般向对我国实行普惠制的国家出口货物时，都要求出具普惠制原产地证书。如果信用证并未明确规定原产地证书的出具者，那么银行应该接受任何一种原产地证书。现在我国多数出口商习惯使用由贸促会出具的证书。

2．根据使用范围和格式的不同进行分类

（1）一般原产地证书（General Certificate of Origin）。一般原产地证书又称"普通原产地证书"，是证明货物原产于某一特定国家或地区，享受进口国正常关税（最惠国）待遇的证明文件。

(2) 普惠制原产地证书（Generalized System of Preferences Certificate of Origin）。普惠制原产地证书简称"GSP 产地证"，是依据给惠国的要求出具的，证明货物原产自受惠国的，具有法律效力的证明文件，是出口商品在给惠国享受在最惠国税率基础上进一步减免进口关税的官方凭证。

普遍优惠制（Generalized System of Preferences，GSP），简称普惠制，是发达国家给予发展中国家向其出口的制成品或半制成品普遍的、非歧视性的、非互惠的一种关税优惠待遇。目前给予我国普惠制待遇的有澳大利亚、新西兰、日本、挪威、瑞士、俄罗斯等国家，而加拿大和欧盟等国家和地区已相继取消了对我国的普惠制待遇。凡是向给惠国出口受惠商品，均须提供普惠制原产地证书，才能获得关税减免的优惠。

普惠制原产地证书的格式包括格式 A（Form A）、格式 59A（Form 59A）和格式 APR（Form APR），其中格式 A 使用范围最广。出口到新西兰的货物应提供格式 59A，而对澳大利亚不用任何格式，只需在商业发票上加注指定的声明即可。

(3) 优惠贸易协定原产地证书。优惠贸易协定原产地证书是协定成员国之间就特定产品享受互惠减免关税待遇的具有法律效力的官方凭证，是受惠国政府指定部门签发的证明项下货物原产于该国的证明文书。

由海关签发的优惠贸易协定原产地证书包括：
- 中国-东盟自贸协定原产地证书（见图 7-1）。
- 中国-智利自贸协定原产地证书。
- 中国-巴基斯坦自贸协定原产地证书。
- 中国-新西兰自贸协定原产地证书。
- 中国-新加坡自贸协定原产地证书。
- 中国-秘鲁自贸协定原产地证书。
- 中国-哥斯达黎加自贸协定原产地证书。
- 中国-瑞士自贸协定原产地证书。
- 中国-冰岛自贸协定原产地证书。
- 中国-韩国自贸协定原产地证书。
- 中国-澳大利亚自贸协定原产地证书（见图 7-2）。
- 中国-格鲁吉亚自贸协定原产地证书。
- 海峡两岸经济合作框架原产地证书。
- 亚太贸易协定原产地证书。

由贸促会签发的优惠贸易协定原产地证书包括：
- 亚太自由贸易协定原产地证书。
- 中国-新加坡自由贸易协定原产地证书。
- 中国-新西兰自由贸易协定原产地证书。
- 中国-秘鲁自由贸易协定原产地证书。
- 中国-哥斯达黎加自由贸易协定原产地证书。
- ECFA 海峡两岸经济合作框架协议原产地证书。

MXY ZL 3871

Original

1. Products consigned from (Exporter's business name, address, country)	Reference No. E16470ZC3871
SHENZHEN S IMPORT & EXP LTD. SHENZHEN CHINA PH LUOHU DISTRICT,HAI HUAYUAN LONG HORIZON 717 SHENZHEN CHINA	ASEAN-CHINA FREE TRADE AREA PREFERENTIAL TARIFF CERTIFICATE OF ORIGIN (Combined Declaration and Certificate)
2. Products consigned to (Consignee's name, address, country)	FORM E
K N BHD LO NG LAWIN, 33000 KUALA KANGSAR, PERAK, MALAYSIA ATTN:HONG CHOO KHEONG TEL:05-7 47 FAX:05-	Issued in THE PEOPLE'S REPUBLIC OF CHINA (Country) See Overleaf Notes
3. Means of transport and route (as far as known) Departure date Jan. 28, 2018 Vessel's name / Aircraft etc. APL OAKLAND/ W091 Port of Discharge PORT KLANG NORTH	4. For Official Use ☐ Preferential Treatment Given ☐ Preferential Treatment Not Given (Please state reason/s) Signature of Authorised Signatory of the Importing Party

5. Item number	6. Marks and numbers of packages	7. Number and type of packages, description of products (including quantity where appropriate and HS number of the importing Party)	8. Origin criteria (see Overleaf Notes)	9. Gross weight or other quantity and value (FOB)	10. Number and date of invoices
1	KK	SOLAR LED WARNING LIGHT+SOLAR LED WARNING LIGHT ACCESSORY (SCREW) H.S CODE:853080	95%	5350KGS USD:33586.56	BW2018012000 01 JAN.20,2018
2		FLAT CAR H.S CODE: 871639	"WO"	220KGS USD:454.55	
3		LED CONTROL CARD H.S CODE: 854231	98%	25KGS USD:825.67	
4		LED LAMP H.S CODE: 853090	90%	10KGS USD:151.62	
5		LED DISPLAY H.S CODE: 853090	92%	80KGS USD:1818.00	
6		PLASTIC SLICE H.S CODE: 392690 TOTAL: FOUR HUNDRED AND TEN (410) PKGS ONLY. *** *** *** *** *** ***	"WO"	760KGS USD:5440.00	

11. Declaration by the exporter	12. Certification
The undersigned hereby declares that the above details and statement are correct; that all the products were produced in CHINA (Country) and that they comply with the origin requirements specified for these products in the Rules of Origin for the ACFTA for the products exported to MALAYSIA (Importing Country) Shenzhen, China, JAN. 28, 2018 Place and date, signature of authorised signatory	It is hereby certified, on the basis of control carried out, that the declaration by the exporter is correct. Shenzhen, China, JAN. 28, 2018 Place and date, signature and stamp of certifying authority

13. ☐ Issued Retroactively ☐ Exhibition
　　☐ Movement Certificate ☐ Third Party Invoicing

图 7-1　中国-东盟自贸协定原产地证书（FORM E）样例

LJL ZL 4391

CERTIFICATE OF ORIGIN

1. Exporter's name, address and country: SHEN░░░░░░░ IMPORT & EXPORT CO., LTD. SHENZHEN, CHINA 6░░░DEN NO. 1122 SHENNAN EAST ROAD LUOHU DISTRICT SHENZHEN, CHINA	Certificate No.: A164702C43910░░░ **CERTIFICATE OF ORIGIN** Form for China-Australia Free Trade Agreement
2. Producer's name and address (if known): HUIZHOU░░░░░░░ PLASTIC COLOR PRINTING CO., LTD NO 7░░░░░░ROAD, XIAO JIN KOU, HUIZHOU, GUANGDONG PROVINCE, CHINA	Issued in: The People's Republic of China
3. Importer's name, address and country (if known): ROLLSPACK PTY LTD ░░░░░░░░░░DRIVE BRAESIDE ░░░NE, AUSTRALIA CONTACT: NANCY TEL: 61 4░░░░░░	For official use only: ISSUED RETROSPECTIVELY
4. Means of transport and route (if known): Departure date: Oct. 17, 2018 Vessel/Flight/Train/Vehicle No.: XIN CHI WAN/0172S Port of loading: SHENZHEN, CHINA Port of discharge: MELBOURNE, AUSTRALIA	5. Remarks: *******************

6. Item number (max.20)	7. Marks and numbers of packages (optional)	8. Number and kind of packages; description of goods	9. HS code (6-digit code)	10. Origin criterion	11. Gross or net weight or other quantity (e.g. Quantity Unit, litres, m³.)	12. Invoice number and date
1	N/M	PLASTIC BAG TOTAL: FIVE (5) PALLETS ONLY. *** *** *** *** *** ***	3923.21	"WP"	3849.5KGS	FL20181009 OCT. 09, 2018

13. Declaration by the exporter or producer The undersigned hereby declares that the above-stated information is correct and that the goods exported to AUSTRALIA (Importing Party) comply with the origin requirements specified in the China-Australia Free Trade Agreement. Shenzhen, China, OCT. 24, 2018 Place, date and signature of authorised person	14. Certification On the basis of the control carried out, it is hereby certified that the information herein is correct and that the described goods comply with the origin requirements of the China-Australia Free Trade Agreement. Shenzhen, China, OCT. 24, 2018 Place, date, and signature and stamp of the Authorised Body Tel: +86-755-82░░4387 Fax: +86-755-82914106 Address: NO. 1011 FUQIANG ROAD, FU░░░ DISTRICT, SHENZHEN, GUANGDONG, CHINA

图 7-2 中国-澳大利亚自贸协定原产地证书样例

（4）专用原产地证书。专用原产地证书是国际组织或国家根据政策和贸易措施的特殊需要，针对某一特殊行业的特定产品规定的原产地证书。我国海关签发的专用原产地证书主要有输欧盟托考伊葡萄酒原产地证书、输欧盟奶酪制品证书、输欧盟烟草真实性证书等。

二、认识一般原产地证书（Understand the General C/O）

（一）申领要求（Requirement for Application）

出口商申领贸促会原产地证书时各阶段的要求如下：

1. 在贸促会原产地证申报系统提交原产地证书申请

未注册的单位首先根据注册程序申请注册登记，已在贸促会注册登记的申请单位，应在中国国际贸易促进委员会原产地证申报系统中提交原产地证书申请。

2. 审核

签证机构依据中华人民共和国原产地规则、法规和有关规定，通过中国国际贸易促进委员会原产地证申报系统贸促会端对申请单位提交的原产地证书相关数据进行审核，审核通过方可予以签发。

3. 签发

审核通过后，申请单位须持商业发票、装箱单、第 11 栏已盖章签字的空白原产地证书以及签证机构要求的其他文件前往签证机构领取纸质证书。签证机构对申请人提交的文件审核无误后，即在原产地证第 12 栏加盖由贸促会统一刻制的"中国国际贸易促进委员会单据证明专用章"，并由授权签证员签字。

签证机构只签发原产地证正本一份，副本三份，其中一正二副交申请企业。另一副本、商业发票等有关文件，由签证机构存档。

4. 原产地证的更改、补充及重新签发

申请单位要求更改或补充已签发原产地证的内容，必须申明更改理由并提供依据，经签证机构审查符合要求后，重新办理申请手续，收回原发原产地证，换发新证。

如果已签发的原产地证遗失或毁损，从签发之日起半年内，申请单位必须向签证机构说明理由并提供确实的依据，经签证机构审查同意后重新办理申请手续。签证机构在新签证书第 5 栏内加注英文"Certificate No. ×× dated ×× is cancelled"，证书第 11 栏和第 12 栏的日期应为重发证书的实际申请日期和签发日期。

（二）一般原产地证书的样本与填制要点（Sample and Instructions for General C/O）

一般原产地证书共有 12 项内容，除了证书号由签证机构指定、第 5 栏仅供签证机构使用、第 12 栏由签证机构签字盖章外，其余各栏均由出口企业用英文规范填写。

```
                                              ORIGINAL

| (1) Exporter                          | Certificate No.                                                 |
|                                       |                                                                 |
|                                       |              CERTIFICATE OF ORIGIN                              |
| (2) Consignee                         |                      OF                                         |
|                                       |         THE PEOPLE'S REPUBLIC OF CHINA                          |
|                                       |                                                                 |
| (3) Means of Transport and Route      | (5) For Certifying Authority Use Only                           |
|                                       |                                                                 |
| (4) Country / Region of Destination   |                                                                 |
```

| (6) Marks and Numbers | (7) Number and Kind of Packages Description of Goods | (8) H.S. Code | (9) Quantity | (10) Number and Date of Invoice |

(11) Declaration by the Exporter	(12) Certification
The undersigned hereby declares that the above details and statements are correct, that all the goods were produced in China and that they comply with the Rules of Origin of the People's Republic of China.	It is hereby certified that the declaration by the exporter is correct.
Place and date, signature and stamp of authorized signatory	Place and date, signature and stamp of certifying authority

1. **出口商**（Exporter）

填写出口商的全称、详细地址及所在的国家（地区），其中出口商是指具有对外贸易出口经营权的单位，要同出口发票上的公司名称一致。地址部分要填写详细地址，包括街道名称、门牌号码等。应注意的是：此栏不能填境外的中间商，即使信用证有此规定也不可以。

2. **收货人**（Consignee）

填写最终收货方的名称、详细地址及所在的国家（地区）。收货人的名称一般是外贸销售合同中的买方或信用证上规定的运输单据的被通知人。若进口商或信用证要求所有单证收货人一栏留空，在此情况下，此栏可填写"To order"或"To whom it may concerned"，不得留空。

3. **运输方式和路线**（Means of Transport and Route）

此栏填写两项内容：运输路线和运输方式。运输路线以启运地（港）和目的地（港）表示，如果需要转运，还应注明转运地（港）。运输方式填写海运、空运或陆运。例如："From Qingdao to New York by vessel via Hong Kong."（通过海运由青岛港经香港转运至纽约港。）

4. **目的国/地区**（Country/Region of Destination）

此栏填写货物最终运抵的国家或地区的名称，一般与最终收货人或最终目的地（港）所在国家或地区一致，不能填写中间商国家（地区）名称。

5．仅供签证机构使用（For Certifying Authority Use Only）

此栏为签证机构使用栏，签证机构根据需要在此加注。例如：证书更改、证书丢失并重新补发、声明××号证书作废等内容。证书申领单位应将此栏留空。

6．唛头（Marks and Numbers）

此栏填写唛头，应按照出口发票上所列唛头填写完整图案、文字标记及包装号码，不可简单地填写"As per Invoice No."（按照发票）或者"As per B/L No."（按照提单）。唛头内容应与信用证或其他单据中相同栏目的内容完全一致。如无唛头，应填写"No mark"或"N/M"，此栏不得留空。如果内容过长，可续填在第7、8、9、10栏的空白处。

7．包装件数、种类与货物描述（Numbers and Kind of Packages，Description of Goods）

填写货物的件数、包装种类及商品名称。填写此栏时要注意：

① 商品名称要具体详细，应详细到可以准确判定该商品的H.S.编码。例如：睡袋（SLEEPING BAGS）、杯子（CUPS），不得用概括性描述（如"日用品"），否则无法查到商品H.S.编码。

② 包装件数及种类要按具体单位填写，并在包装件数的英文数词描述后用括号加上阿拉伯数字，例如"Four(4) drums of acid green dye stuffs"。

③ 如果货物是散装货，则填写的商品名称后要加注"IN BULK"（散装），所列内容应与信用证或其他单据保持一致。

④ 该栏内容填完后要在其后面加结束符号"**********"，以防伪造。

⑤ 有时信用证要求在原产地证书上加注合同号及信用证号等，可加在此栏。

8．商品编码（H.S. Code）

本栏根据海关发布的《中华人民共和国进出口税则》中规定的商品名称和编码，正确填写货物的H.S.编码。若同一证书包含多种商品，则应将相应的H.S.编码全部填入此栏。填报的商品编码必须与实际货名相符，并与报关单中的商品编码完全一致。

9．数量（Quantity）

依据发票与货运单据中显示的毛重或其他数量填报。若计量单位为重量，则此栏应标明毛重或净重，如："G.W. 400KGS"或"N.W. 3,500KGS"。注意用规范的英文或缩写表示计量单位，如"Kilograms / KGS"（千克）等。

10．发票编号与日期（Number and Date of Invoice）

填写该批申报货物的商业发票的编号和日期，必须与商业发票上标明的内容完全一致。为避免对月份、日期产生误解，月份一律用英文表示，如2018年10月20日，用英文表示为"OCT. 20, 2018"。

11．出口方声明（Declaration by the Exporter）

此栏为出口方声明、签字盖章栏。该栏由出口商法人或法人代表手签，并加盖出口商在签证机构备案的中英文印章，手签人的签字与印章不得重合。此栏还必须填写申报地点和日期，申报日期不得早于发票日期。

12．签证机构证明（Certification）

此栏由签证机构加盖机构印章并由授权人签名，两者不能重叠；并注明签发地点与签发日期，签发日期不能早于发票日期和申请日期。

（三）一般原产地证书实例（Models of General C/O）

1. 情景导入中的一般原产地证书（General C/O of Lead-in Situation）

ORIGINAL

(1) Exporter KELIN INTERNATIONAL TRADING (HK) CO., LTD RM2403, BLOCK A2, YIHE PLAZA, NO. 413, GUANGZHOU, CHINA	Certificate No. CCPIT064814623 CERTIFICATE OF ORIGIN OF THE PEOPLE'S REPUBLIC OF CHINA				
(2) Consignee GLOBE SOURCING SERVICE CO., LTD 1407, 80TH STREET, S.W., NOVI, MICHIGAN, USA					
(3) Means of Transport and Route FROM SHEKOU PORT SHENZHEN TO NEW YORK BY VESSEL	(5) For Certifying Authority Use Only				
(4) Country / Region of Destination USA					
(6) Marks and Numbers	(7) Number and Kind of Packages Description of Goods	(8) H.S. Code	(9) Quantity		(10) Number and Date of Invoice
G.S.S TXT264 NEW YORK C/No. 1-300	100% COTTON COLOUR WAVE T-SHIRT TM111 TM222 TM333 TM444 PACKED IN CARTONS OF 20 PCS EACH *** *** *** ***	61091000	2,000 PCS 2,000 PCS 1,000 PCS 1,000 PCS		PI170601 July 18, 2018
(11) Declaration by the Exporter The undersigned hereby declares that the above details and statements are correct, that all the goods were produced in China and that they comply with the Rules of Origin of the People's Republic of China. *KELIN INTERNATIONAL TRADING (HK) CO., LTD.* GUANGZHOU, CHINA JULY 25, 2018	(12) Certification It is hereby certified that the declaration by the exporter is correct. GUANGZHOU, CHINA JULY 26, 2018				
Place and date, signature and stamp of authorized signatory	Place and date, signature and stamp of certifying authority				

2. 贸易实务中的一般原产地证书

图 7-3 为贸易实务中的一般原产地证书样例。

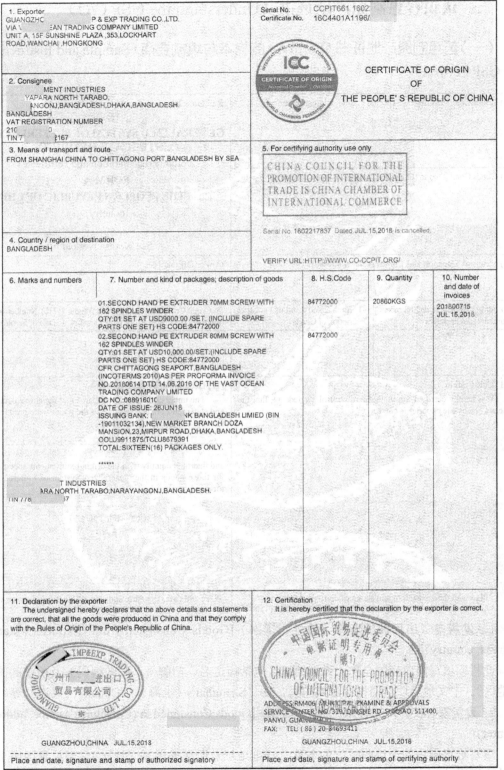

图 7-3 一般原产地证书样例

三、认识普惠制原产地证书（Understand the GSP C/O）

（一）普惠制原产地证书（Form A）的样本与填制要点（Sample and Instructions for GSP Form A）

(1) Goods Consigned from (Exporter's name, address, country)	Reference No.
	GENERALIZED SYSTEM OF PREFERENCES CERTIFICATE OF ORIGIN (combined declaration and certificate) **FORM A** Issued in **THE PEOPLE'S REPUBLIC OF CHINA** (country) See Notes Overleaf
(2) Goods Consigned to (Consignee's name, address, country)	

(3) Means of Transport and Route (as far as known)	(4) For Official Use

(5) Item Number	(6) Marks and Numbers of Packages	(7) Number and Kind of Packages Description of Goods	(8) Origin Criterion (see notes overleaf)	(9) Gross Weight or other Quantity	(10) Number and Date of Invoices

(11) Certification It is hereby certified, on the basis of control carried out, that the declaration by the exporter is correct. Place and date, signature and stamp of certifying authority	(12) Declaration by the Exporter The undersigned hereby declares that the above details and statements are correct; that all the goods were produced in CHINA (country) and that they comply with the origin requirements specified for those goods in the Generalized System of Preferences for goods exported to (importing country) Place and date, signature and stamp of certifying authority

1. **发货自**（出口商的名称、地址、国家）[Goods Consigned from (Exporter's name, address, country)]

此栏须填写出口商的全称、详细地址（包括街道名、门牌号、邮政编码）及所在的国家（地区）。中文地名以汉语拼音形式填写，如"Shanghai"（上海）、"Dalian"（大连）等。

2. **发货至**（收货人的名称、地址、国家）[Goods Consigned to (Consignee's name, address, country)]

填写给惠国内的最终收货方的名称、详细地址及所在的国家（地区）。当给惠国属于某一关税同盟时，以同盟名称代替国家或地区名称。在信用证项下，收货人一般为开证申请人，如果开证申请人不是实际收货人,又不知最终收货人,则可填提单被通知人或发票抬头人。但不可填中间商的名称。

3. 运输工具及航线(据已知)[Means of Transport and Route (as far as known)]

填写本批货物的装运港、目的港或到货地点的名称,以及运输方式(如海运、陆运、空运)。转运商品还应填写转运港,如"Via Hong Kong"。该栏还需填明预定自中国出口的日期,日期必须真实,不得捏造。若货物输往内陆给惠国,如瑞士、奥地利等,由于这些国家没有海岸,因此海运时都须经第三国再转运至该国,填证时应注明。

4. 供官方使用(For Official Use)

此栏由签证部门填写,申请签证的单位应将此栏留空。正常情况下此栏空白。特殊情况下签证部门会在此栏加注,如:

① 货物已出口,签证日期迟于出货日期,签发"后发证书"时,此栏加盖"Issued Retrospectively"红色印章。

② 证书遗失、被盗或损毁,签发"复本证书"时加盖"Duplicate"红色印章,并在此栏注明原证书的编号和签证日期,并声明原发证书作废,其英文表示为"This certificate is in replacement of Certificate of Origin No. … dated … which is cancelled"。

5. 商品顺序号(Item Number)

如果同一批出口货物有不同种类的商品,则各项货物应依次列明,并在此栏填写编号"1""2""3"……"N",只有单项商品时,一般填写"1"或不填写。

6. 唛头及包装号(Marks and Numbers of Packages)

此栏与一般原产地证书中的相应栏目填法相同。

7. 包装件数、种类与货物描述(Number and Kind of Packages, Description of Goods)

此栏与一般原产地证书中的相应栏目填法相同。

8. 原产地标准(见背页注)[Origin Criterion (see notes overleaf)]

此栏是国外海关审核的核心项目。对含有进口成分的商品,因情况复杂,国外要求严格,极易出错而造成退证查询。因此必须严格按各国规定填写,具体要求如表 7-1 所示:

表 7-1 普惠制各国原产地标准

目的国家	填报代码	原产地标准
所有给惠国	"P"	完全原产,不含任何进口成分
挪威、瑞士、土耳其、日本等	"W"+H.S.品目号	非完全原产:满足加工清单要求,未列入的满足品目号改变规则,填写"W"加出口产品HS品目号,例如:"W" 94.05
白俄罗斯、俄罗斯、哈萨克斯坦、乌克兰	"Y"+进口成分百分比	非完全原产:进口成分价值不超过产品离岸价格的50%,填写"Y"加非原产成分价值占产品离岸价的百分比,例如:"Y" 50%
	"PK"	非完全原产:进口成分价值不超过产品离岸价格的50%,在一个受惠国生产而在另一个或数个其他受惠国制造或加工的产品,填写"PK"
澳大利亚、新西兰	空白	非完全原产:本国成分价值不小于产品出厂价的50%,留空

9. 毛重或其他数量(Gross Weight or other Quantity)

此栏与一般原产地证书中的相应栏目填法相同。

10. 发票号和发票日期(Number and Date of Invoices)

此栏与一般原产地证书中相应栏目填法相同。

11. **签证机构证明**（Certification）

此栏由签证机构签字、盖章，并注明签署地点与日期。证明内容已事先印制，签名必须是被授权人手签，签名和公章不得重叠，签署日期不得早于发票日期和申报日期（第12栏），也不能晚于运输单据的日期，除非是"后发证书"。

12. **出口商声明**（Declaration by the Exporter）

生产国横线上填写"CHINA"，进口国横线上填写最终进口国英文名称，进口国必须与第3栏中所填目的港的国别一致。另外，申请单位应授权专人在此栏内手签，注上申报地点、日期，并加盖申请单位中英文印章。盖章时应避免覆盖进口国名称和手签人姓名。本证书一律不得涂改，也不得加盖校对章。

实操训练（Skill Training）

一、单选题

1. 关于中华人民共和国出口货物原产地证明书，下列表述中错误的是（　　）。
   A. 货物确系中华人民共和国原产的证明文件
   B. 进口国海关对该进出口商品适用何种税率的依据
   C. 出口报关的必备证件
   D. 各地直属海关和贸促会均可签发此证

2. 在填制一般原产地证书时，为了防止加填伪造，规定在商品名称填完后紧接下一行加上（　　）符号，以表示结束。
   A. ＊＊＊＊＊＊＊＊＊　　　　　　　B. ＿＿＿＿＿＿＿＿＿
   C. ○○○○○○○　　　　　　　　D. ＋＋＋＋＋＋＋＋＋

3. 普惠制产地证主要有三种形式，其中，（　　）使用范围较广。
   A. 普惠制原产地证书格式A　　　　B. 普惠制原产地证书格式59A
   C. 普惠制原产地证书格式APR　　 D. 一般原产地证书

4. 原产地证书是证明本批出口商品的生产地为我国并符合《中华人民共和国出口货物原产地规则》的一种文件，如果信用证或合同对签证机构未做具体规定，一般由（　　）签发。
   A. 海关　　　　　　　　　　　　 B. 中国国际贸易促进委员会
   C. 商务部　　　　　　　　　　　 D. 出口商

5. 普惠制原产地证书中的"Origin Criterion"（原产地标准）一栏，应根据货物原料中进口成分所占的比例填写，"P"表示（　　）。
   A. 含进口成分　　　　　　　　　 B. 无进口成分
   C. 进口成分占比在40%以下　　　　D. 进口成分占比在20%以下

6. 按我国和东盟之间签署的双边优惠贸易安排提供的原产地证书是（　　）。
   A. FORM A　　B. FORM E　　C. FORM C　　D. FORM F

7. 以下国家未向中国提供普惠制待遇的是（　　）。
   A. 挪威、瑞士、土耳其　　　　　 B. 波兰、韩国、美国
   C. 俄罗斯、哈萨克斯坦、乌克兰　 D. 日本、澳大利亚、新西兰

8. 普惠制原产地证书中的运输方式和路线一栏应按信用证规定填写，如需中途转运，应注明转运地（港），若不知转运地（港），则用（　　）表示。

  A. W/T   B. NO   C. N/M   D. N/N

二、多选题

1. 我国签证机构一般规定，申请一般原产地证书的企业必须提供的文件有（　　）。

  A. 第 11 栏已签字盖章的原产地证明书

  B. 商业发票

  C. 装箱单

  D. 签证机构要求的其他文件

2. 原产地证明书是由出口国政府有关机构签发的一种证明货物原产地或制造地的证明文件，通常多用于不需要提供（　　）的国家或地区。

  A. 海关发票   B. 领事发票   C. 证实发票   D. 联合发票

3. 普惠制原产地证书是指受惠国有关机构就本国出口商向给惠国出口受惠商品而签发的，用以证明原产地的文件，其主要有（　　）三种。

  A. 普惠制原产地证书格式 A   B. 普惠制原产地证书格式 59A

  C. 普惠制原产地证书格式 APR   D. 一般原产地证书

4. 在下列叙述中，符合原产地规则中的实质性改变标准的是（　　）。

  A. 货物经过加工后，在海关《进出口税则》中的四位数一级的税则号列已经改变

  B. 货物经过加工后，增值部分占新产品总值的比例已经达到 30%及以上

  C. 新包装整理后的货物

  D. 经过重新筛选并重新包装的货物

5. 关于原产地证明书，下列说法错误的是（　　）。

  A. 《中国-东盟全面经济合作框架协议》规定的原产地证书应当自东盟国家有关机构签发之日起 6 个月内向我国境内申报地海关提交，经过第三方转运的，提交期限延长为 8 个月

  B. 中国-巴基斯坦自贸协定原产地证书应当自巴基斯坦有关机构签发之日起 4 个月内向我国境内申报地海关提交，经过第三方转运的，提交期限延长为 6 个月

  C. 原产于东盟国家的进口货物，如果产品的 FOB 价不超过 200 美元，无须要求我国的纳税义务人提交原产地证书，但是要提交出口商对有关产品原产于该出口成员国的声明

  D. 亚太贸易协定原产地证书可以重复使用，即一份证书可适用于多批进口货物

三、请根据以下资料填制原产地证书

1. 货物信息：

商品名称：	Lady Shoulder Bag		
商品型号：	PC543212	PC543213	PC543214
商品尺寸：	33cm×28cm×12cm	31cm×28cm×12cm	30cm×25cm×10cm
净重/毛重（个）：	0.70KGS/0.95KGS	0.65KGS/0.78KGS	0.57KGS/0.68KGS
净重/毛重（总）：	700KGS/950KGS	650KGS/780KGS	570KGS/680KGS
数量：	1,000PCS	1,000PCS	1,000PCS

单价：	USD11.00	USD10.00	USD9.50
金额：	USD11,000.00	USD10,000.00	USD9,500.00
集装箱容量：	QTY/40'FCL: 368CTNS	QTY/40'FCL: 383CTNS	QTY/40'FCL: 400CTNS
包装：	1PC in 1 PE Bag	牛皮包商品编码：4202210090	
发票编号：	SJI1801005	发票日期：2018-8-5	授权签字人：李伟
装运船名：	LIANHUA	航次：V. 435	装船日期：2018-8-23
运输标志：	S.I.G TSSC1801005 ZURICH C/NO.1-1151		
原产地标准：	"P"		

2．信用证相关内容：

Sequence of Total	27:	1/1
Form of Doc. Credit	40A:	IRREVOCABLE
Doc. Credit Number	20:	N3423457TH11817
Date of Issue	31C:	180715
Date and Place of Expiry	31D:	180909 CHINA
Applicant Bank	51D:	UNION BANK OF SWITZERLAND BAHNHOFSTRASSE 45, 8098 ZURICH, SWITZERLAND TEL: +41 44 234 11 11
Applicant	50:	AUTHOR CO., LTD LAUFENGASSE 28, 8212 NEUHAUSEN AM RHEINFALL, SWITZERLAND TEL: +41 (52674) 6111 FAX: +41 52 674 65 56
Beneficiary	59:	DALIAN PEACOCK CASE & BAG CO., LTD NANLIAN ROAD DALIAN 116001, CHINA TEL: 0086-0411-78396756
Amount	32B:	USD 30,500.00
Available with/by	41D:	ANY BANK IN CHINA BY NEGOTIATION
Drafts at	42C:	SIGHT
Drawee	42A:	ISSUING BANK
Partial Shipments	43P:	NOT ALLOWED
Transshipment	43T:	NOT ALLOWED
Port of Loading	44E:	DALIAN, CHINA
Port of Discharge	44F:	ZURICH, SWITZERLAND
Latest Date of Shipment	44C:	180825

Descript. of Goods	45A:	CIF ZURICH SHOULDER BAGS, AS PER S/C NO. TSSC1801005
Documents Required	46A:	

+ MANUALLY SIGNED COMMERCIAL INVOICE IN 2 COPIES INDICATING L/C NO. AND CONTRACT NO. CERTIFYING THE CONTENTS IN THIS INVOICE ARE TRUE AND CORRECT.
+ FULL SET OF ORIGINAL CLEAN ON BOARD MARINE BILLS OF LADING MADE OUT TO ORDER, ENDORSED IN BLANK MARKED FREIGHT PREPAID AND NOTIFY APPLICANT.
+ PACKING LIST IN 2 COPIES ISSUED BY THE BENEFICIARY.
+ ORIGINAL GSP FORM A CERTIFICATE OF ORIGIN ON OFFICIAL FORM ISSUED BY A TRADE AUTHORITY.
+ MANUFACTURERS QUALITY CERTIFICATE CERTIFYING THE COMMODITY IS IN GOOD ORDER.
+ BENEFICIARY'S CERTIFICATE CERTIFYING THAT ONE SET OF COPIES OF SHIPPING DOCUMENTS HAS BEEN SENT TO APPLICANT WITHIN 5 DAYS AFTER SHIPMENT.

Additional Conditions   47A:

+ UNLESS OTHERWISE EXPRESSLY STATED, ALL DOCUMENTS MUST BE IN ENGLISH.

项目八
Project VIII

报检与报关单据
Inspection & Customs Declaration Documents

学习目标（Learning Aims）

- 了解进出口货物报检的范围与基本要求。
- 了解进出口货物报关的流程与基本要求。
- 学习与掌握报检报关的基本要领和相关规则。
- 能够准确填制报关单据。

情景导入（Lead-in Situation）

科林国际贸易公司外贸跟单员在货物备好后于2018年8月21日向深圳海关申请报检和报关，随附单据有合同、信用证、发票、装箱单和许可/审批文件（许可证号为7688990）。海关根据国家检验检疫法律法规的要求，依法对货物实施检验检疫。在检验合格后，货物被运至海关监管仓库，之后报关员随附相关单据向深圳海关申报放行，将货装船运送出海。

一、背景知识（Background Knowledge）

（一）报检（Declaration for Inspection and Quarantine）

1. 报检的含义

报检是指有关当事人根据法律、行政法规的规定，以及外贸销售合同的约定或证明履约的需要，向海关申请检验、检疫、鉴定或准出入境，或是取得销售使用的合法凭证及某种公证证明所必须履行的法定程序和手续。

2. 进出口货物的报检范围

根据我国有关检验检疫法律法规的规定，进出口货物的报检范围主要有以下三个方面：
（1）法律、行政法规规定必须由海关实施检验检疫的进出口货物。
（2）有关国际条约或与我国有协议/协定，规定必须经检验检疫的进出口货物。
（3）对外贸易合同约定须凭海关签发的检验检疫证书进行交接、结算的进出口货物。

（二）报关（Declaration for Customs Clearance）

1. 报关的含义

报关是指进出口货物收发货人、进出境运输工具负责人、进出境物品所有人或者他们的代理人向海关办理货物、物品或运输工具进出境手续及相关海关事务的过程，包括向海关申报、交验单据证件，并接受海关的监管和检查等。报关是顺利完成货物进出境的必要环节之一。

2. 进出口货物的通关流程

根据海关监管制度，报关单位在货物进出境时办理通关手续的主要流程如下：

（1）进出口货物的申报（必须由报关员完成）：是指报关单位（报关员）在《海关法》规定的时间内，按照海关规定的形式，向海关报告进出境货物的情况，提请海关按照其申报的内容放行货物的环节。进口货物应在运输工具申报进境之日起 14 日内向海关申报，而出口货物应在其运抵海关监管区后，装货的 24 小时之前，向海关申报。

（2）配合查验（可以由报关员完成）：是指当海关决定查验货物时，报关单位（报关员）应在现场配合海关查验货物，负责搬运、开箱、封箱等，并检查货物是否损坏。

（3）缴纳税费：是指报关单位应根据海关开具的海关税款专用缴款书，向指定银行缴纳货物进出口税费或海关监管费等。

（4）提取或装运货物：是指完成上述环节并在海关决定放行后，凭加盖海关放行章的提货单或装运单提取（进口）或装运（出口）货物的环节。

> **知识链接**
>
> **关于中华人民共和国海关总署"关检合一"的新规定说明**
>
> 2018 年 4 月 16 日，海关总署发布《关于企业报关报检资质合并有关事项的公告》（海关总署公告 2018 年第 28 号），表示关检合一进入实质性的优化整合阶段。同年 5 月 29 日，

海关总署发布《关于全面取消〈入/出境货物通关单〉有关事项的公告》(海关总署公告 2018 年第 50 号),进一步优化营商环境,促进贸易便利化。涉及具有法定检验检疫要求的商品申报时,企业可通过"单一窗口"报关报检合一界面向海关一次申报。同时报关单、报检单合二为一,实现"一张大表"的新版报关单申报。

二、认识报关单(Understand the Customs Declarations)

(一)报关单的样本与填制要点(Samples and Instructions for Customs Declarations)

中华人民共和国海关进口货物报关单

(1)预录入编号:		(2)海关编号:		页码/页数:	
(3)境内收货人	(4)进境关别	(5)进口日期	(6)申报日期	(7)备案号	
(8)境外发货人	(9)运输方式	(10)运输工具名称及航次号	(11)提运单号	(12)货物存放地点	
(13)消费使用单位	(14)监管方式	(15)征免性质	(16)许可证号	(17)启运港	
(18)合同协议号	(19)贸易国(地区)	(20)启运国(地区)	(21)经停港	(22)入境口岸	
(23)包装种类	(24)件数	(25)毛重(千克)	(26)净重(千克)	(27)成交方式	(28)运费	(29)保费	(30)杂费

(31)随附单证及编号
随附单证 1:   随附单证 2:

(32)标记唛码及备注

项号 (33)	商品编号 (34)	商品名称及规格型号 (35)	数量及单位 (36)	单价/总价/币制 (37)(38)(39)	原产国(地区)(40)	最终目的国(地区)(41)	境内目的地 (42)	征免 (43)
01								
02								
03								
04								
05								
06								

(44)特殊关系确认:	(45)价格影响确认:	(46)支付特许权使用费确认:	(47)自报自缴:
(48)申报人员 申报人员证号 电话 兹申明以上内容承担如实申报、依法纳税之法律责任			(50)海关批注及签章
(49)申报单位		申报单位(签章)	

中华人民共和国海关出口货物报关单

(1) 预录入编号：　　　　　　(2) 海关编号：　　　　　　　　　　　　　页码/页数：

(3) 境内发货人	(4) 出境关别	(5) 出口日期	(6) 申报日期	(7) 备案号
(8) 境外收货人	(9) 运输方式	(10) 运输工具名称及航次号	(11) 提运单号	
(13) 生产销售单位	(14) 监管方式	(15) 征免性质	(16) 许可证号	
(18) 合同协议号	(19) 贸易国（地区）	(20) 运抵国（地区）	(21) 指运港	(22) 离境口岸
(23) 包装种类	(24) 件数	(25) 毛重（千克）	(26) 净重（千克）	(27) 成交方式	(28) 运费	(29) 保费	(30) 杂费

(31) 随附单证及编号
随附单证1：　　　　　　　　　　随附单证2：

(32) 标记唛码及备注

项号 (33)	商品编号 (34)	商品名称及规格型号 (35)	数量及单位 (36)	单价/总价/币制 (37)(38)(39)	原产国（地区）(40)	最终目的国（地区）(41)	境内目的地 (42)	征免 (43)
01								
02								
03								
04								
05								
06								
07								

(44) 特殊关系确认：　　　(45) 价格影响确认：　　　(46) 支付特许权使用费确认：　　　(47) 自报自缴：

(48) 申报人员　　　申报人员证号　　　电话　　　　　　　　　　　　　(50) 海关批注及签章
　　　　　　　　　　　兹申明以上内容承担如实申报、依法纳税之法律责任

(49) 申报单位　　　　　　　　　　　　　　　　　申报单位（签章）

1. 预录入编号

预录入编号指预录入报关单的编号，一份报关单对应一个预录入编号，由系统自动生成。

报关单预录入编号为18位，其中第1～4位为接受申报海关的代码（海关规定的《关区代码表》中相应海关代码），第5～8位为录入时的公历年份，第9位为进出口标志（"1"为进口，"0"为出口；集中申报清单"I"为进口，"E"为出口），后9位为顺序编号。

2. 海关编号

海关编号指海关接受申报时给予报关单的编号，一份报关单对应一个海关编号，由系统

自动生成。

报关单海关编号为18位,其中第1~4位为接受申报海关的代码(海关规定的《关区代码表》中相应海关代码),第5~8位为海关接受申报时的公历年份,第9位为进出口标志("1"为进口,"0"为出口;集中申报清单"I"为进口,"E"为出口),后9位为顺序编号。

3．境内收发货人

填报在海关备案的对外签订并执行进出口贸易合同的中国境内法人、其他组织名称及编码。编码填报18位法人和其他组织统一社会信用代码,没有统一社会信用代码的,填报其在海关的备案编码。

特殊情况下填报要求如下:

(1) 进出口货物合同的签订者和执行者非同一企业的,填报执行合同的企业。

(2) 外商投资企业委托进出口企业进口投资设备、物品的,填报外商投资企业,并在标记唛码及备注栏注明"委托某进出口企业进口",同时注明被委托企业的18位法人和其他组织统一社会信用代码。

(3) 有代理报关资格的报关企业代理其他进出口企业办理进出口报关手续时,填报委托的进出口企业。

(4) 海关特殊监管区域收发货人填报该货物的实际经营单位或海关特殊监管区域内经营企业。

4．进出境关别

根据货物实际进出境的口岸海关,填报海关规定的《关区代码表》中相应口岸海关的名称及代码。

特殊情况的填报要求如下:

进口转关运输货物填报货物进境地海关名称及代码,出口转关运输货物填报货物出境地海关名称及代码。按转关运输方式监管的跨关区深加工结转货物,出口报关单填报转出地海关名称及代码,进口报关单填报转入地海关名称及代码。

在不同海关特殊监管区域或保税监管场所之间调拨、转让的货物,填报对方海关特殊监管区域或保税监管场所所在的海关名称及代码。

其他无实际进出境的货物,填报接受申报的海关名称及代码。

5．进出口日期

进口日期填报运载进口货物的运输工具申报进境的日期。出口日期指运载出口货物的运输工具办结出境手续的日期,在申报时免予填报。无实际进出境的货物,填报海关接受申报的日期。

进出口日期为8位数字,顺序为年(4位)、月(2位)、日(2位)。

6．申报日期

申报日期指海关接受进出口货物收发货人、受委托的报关企业申报数据的日期。以电子数据报关单方式申报的,申报日期为海关计算机系统接受申报数据时记录的日期;以纸质报关单方式申报的,申报日期为海关接受纸质报关单并对报关单进行登记处理的日期。本栏目在申报时免予填报。

申报日期为8位数字,顺序为年(4位)、月(2位)、日(2位)。

7. 备案号

填报进出口货物收发货人、消费使用单位、生产销售单位在海关办理加工贸易合同备案或征、减、免税审核确认等手续时，海关核发的加工贸易手册、海关特殊监管区域和保税监管场所保税账册、征免税证明或其他备案审批文件的编号。

一份报关单只允许填报一个备案号。具体填报要求如下：

（1）加工贸易项下货物，除少量低值辅料按规定不使用加工贸易手册及以后续补税监管方式办理内销征税的外，填报加工贸易手册编号。

使用异地直接报关分册和异地深加工结转出口分册在异地口岸报关的，填报分册号；本地直接报关分册和本地深加工结转分册限制在本地报关，填报总册号。

加工贸易成品凭征免税证明转为减免税进口货物的，进口报关单填报征免税证明编号，出口报关单填报加工贸易手册编号。

对加工贸易设备、使用账册管理的海关特殊监管区域内减免税设备之间的结转，转入和转出企业分别填制进、出口报关单，在报关单"备案号"栏目填报加工贸易手册编号。

（2）涉及征、减、免税审核确认的报关单，填报征免税证明编号。

（3）减免税货物退运出口，填报海关进口减免税货物准予退运证明的编号；减免税货物补税进口，填报减免税货物补税通知书的编号；减免税货物进口或结转进口（转入），填报征免税证明的编号；相应的结转出口（转出），填报海关进口减免税货物结转联系函的编号。

8. 境外收发货人

境外收货人通常指签订并执行出口贸易合同的买方或合同指定的收货人，境外发货人通常指签订并执行进口贸易合同的卖方。

此栏填报境外收发货人的名称及编码。名称一般填报英文名称，检验检疫要求填报其他外文名称的，在英文名称后填报，以半角括号分隔；对于 AEO 互认国家（地区）企业的，编码填报 AEO 编码，填报样式按照海关总署发布的相关公告要求填报（如新加坡 AEO 企业填报样式为：SG123456789012，韩国 AEO 企业填报样式为 KR1234567，具体见海关相关公告要求）；非互认国家（地区）AEO 企业等其他情形，编码免予填报。

特殊情况下无境外收发货人的，名称及编码填报"NO"。

9. 运输方式

运输方式包括实际运输方式和海关规定的特殊运输方式，前者指货物实际进出境的运输方式，按进出境所使用的运输工具分类；后者指货物无实际进出境的运输方式，按货物在境内的流向分类。

根据货物实际进出境的运输方式或货物在境内流向的类别，按照海关规定的《运输方式代码表》选择填报相应的运输方式。

10. 运输工具名称及航次号

此栏填报载运货物进出境的运输工具名称或编号及航次号。填报内容应与运输部门向海关申报的舱单（载货清单）所列相应内容一致。

（1）运输工具名称具体填报要求如下：

1）直接在进出境地或采用全国通关一体化通关模式办理报关手续的报关单填报要求如下：

① 水路运输：填报船舶编号（来往港澳小型船舶为监管簿编号）或者船舶英文名称。
② 公路运输：启用公路舱单前，填报该跨境运输车辆的国内行驶车牌号，深圳提前报关模式的报关单填报国内行驶车牌号+"/"+"提前报关"。启用公路舱单后，免予填报。
③ 铁路运输：填报车厢编号或交接单号。
④ 航空运输：填报航班号。
⑤ 邮件运输：填报邮政包裹单号。
⑥ 其他运输：填报具体运输方式名称，如"管道""驮畜"等。
2）转关运输货物的报关单填报要求如下：
A．进口：
① 水路运输：直转、提前报关填报"@"+16位转关申报单预录入号（或13位载货清单号）；中转填报进境英文船名。
② 铁路运输：直转、提前报关填报"@"+16位转关申报单预录入号；中转填报车厢编号。
③ 航空运输：直转、提前报关填报"@"+16位转关申报单预录入号（或13位载货清单号）；中转填报"@"。
④ 公路及其他运输：填报"@"+16位转关申报单预录入号（或13位载货清单号）。
⑤ 以上各种运输方式使用广东地区载货清单转关的提前报关货物填报"@"+13位载货清单号。
B．出口：
① 水路运输：非中转填报"@"+16位转关申报单预录入号（或13位载货清单号）。如多张报关单需要通过一张转关单转关的，运输工具名称字段填报"@"。
中转货物，境内水路运输填报驳船船名；境内铁路运输填报车名（主管海关4位关区代码+"TRAIN"）；境内公路运输填报车名（主管海关4位关区代码+"TRUCK"）。
② 铁路运输：填报"@"+16位转关申报单预录入号（或13位载货清单号），如多张报关单需要通过一张转关单转关的，填报"@"。
③ 航空运输：填报"@"+16位转关申报单预录入号（或13位载货清单号），如多张报关单需要通过一张转关单转关的，填报"@"。
④ 其他运输方式：填报"@"+16位转关申报单预录入号（或13位载货清单号）。
3）采用"集中申报"通关方式办理报关手续的，报关单填报"集中申报"。
4）无实际进出境的货物，免予填报。
(2) 航次号具体填报要求如下：
1）直接在进出境地或采用全国通关一体化通关模式办理报关手续的报关单：
① 水路运输：填报船舶的航次号。
② 公路运输：启用公路舱单前，填报运输车辆的8位进出境日期[顺序为年（4位）、月（2位）、日（2位），下同]。启用公路舱单后，填报货物运输批次号。
③ 铁路运输：填报列车的进出境日期。
④ 航空运输：免予填报。
⑤ 邮件运输：填报运输工具的进出境日期。
⑥ 其他运输方式：免予填报。

2）转关运输货物的报关单：

A．进口：

① 水路运输：中转转关方式填报"@"+进境干线船舶航次。直转、提前报关免予填报。

② 公路运输：免予填报。

③ 铁路运输："@"+8 位进境日期。

④ 航空运输：免予填报。

⑤ 其他运输方式：免予填报。

B．出口：

① 水路运输：非中转货物免予填报。中转货物：境内水路运输填报驳船航次号；境内铁路、公路运输填报 6 位启运日期[顺序为年（2 位）、月（2 位）、日（2 位）]。

② 铁路拼车拼箱捆绑出口：免予填报。

③ 航空运输：免予填报。

④ 其他运输方式：免予填报。

3）无实际进出境的货物，免予填报。

11．提运单号

填报进出口货物提单或运单的编号。一份报关单只允许填报一个提单或运单号，一票货物对应多个提单或运单时，应分单填报。

具体填报要求如下：

（1）直接在进出境地或采用全国通关一体化通关模式办理报关手续的：

① 水路运输：填报进出口提单号。如有分提单的，填报进出口提单号+"*"+分提单号。

② 公路运输：启用公路舱单前，免予填报；启用公路舱单后，填报进出口总运单号。

③ 铁路运输：填报运单号。

④ 航空运输：填报总运单号+"_"+分运单号，无分运单的填报总运单号。

⑤ 邮件运输：填报邮运包裹单号。

（2）转关运输货物的报关单：

A．进口：

① 水路运输：直转、中转填报提单号。提前报关免予填报。

② 铁路运输：直转、中转填报铁路运单号。提前报关免予填报。

③ 航空运输：直转、中转货物填报总运单号+"_"+分运单号。提前报关免予填报。

④ 其他运输方式：免予填报。

⑤ 以上运输方式进境货物，在广东省内用公路运输转关的，填报车牌号。

B．出口：

① 水路运输：中转货物填报提单号；非中转货物免予填报；广东省内汽车运输提前报关的转关货物，填报承运车辆的车牌号。

② 其他运输方式：免予填报。广东省内汽车运输提前报关的转关货物，填报承运车辆的车牌号。

（3）采用"集中申报"通关方式办理报关手续的，报关单填报归并的集中申报清单的进出口起止日期[按年（4 位）月（2 位）日（2 位）年（4 位）月（2 位）日（2 位）]。

（4）无实际进出境的货物，免予填报。

12. 货物存放地点

填报货物进境后存放的场所或地点,包括海关监管作业场所、分拨仓库、定点加工厂、隔离检疫场、企业自有仓库等。

13. 消费使用单位/生产销售单位

(1) 消费使用单位填报已知的进口货物在境内的最终消费、使用单位的名称,包括:
1) 自行进口货物的单位。
2) 委托进出口企业进口货物的单位。

(2) 生产销售单位填报出口货物在境内的生产或销售单位的名称,包括:
1) 自行出口货物的单位。
2) 委托进出口企业出口货物的单位。

(3) 减免税货物报关单的消费使用单位/生产销售单位应与征免税证明中的"减免税申请人"一致;保税监管场所与境外之间的进出境货物,消费使用单位/生产销售单位填报保税监管场所的名称[保税物流中心(B型)填报中心内企业名称]。

(4) 海关特殊监管区域的消费使用单位/生产销售单位填报区域内经营企业("加工单位"或"仓库")。

(5) 编码填报要求:
1) 填报18位法人和其他组织统一社会信用代码。
2) 无18位统一社会信用代码的,填报"NO"。

(6) 进口货物在境内的最终消费或使用以及出口货物在境内的生产或销售的对象为自然人的,填报身份证号、护照号、台胞证号等有效证件号码及姓名。

14. 监管方式

监管方式是以国际贸易中进出口货物的交易方式为基础,结合海关对进出口货物的征税、统计及监管条件综合设定的海关对进出口货物的管理方式。其代码由4位数字构成,前两位是按照海关监管要求和计算机管理需要划分的分类代码,后两位是参照国际标准编制的贸易方式代码。

根据实际对外贸易情况按海关规定的《监管方式代码表》选择填报相应的监管方式简称及代码。一份报关单只允许填报一种监管方式。

特殊情况下加工贸易货物监管方式填报要求如下:

(1) 进口少量低值辅料(即5 000美元以下,78种以内的低值辅料)按规定不使用加工贸易手册的,填报"低值辅料"。使用加工贸易手册的,按加工贸易手册上的监管方式填报。

(2) 加工贸易料件转内销货物以及按料件办理进口手续的转内销制成品、残次品、未完成品,填制进口报关单,填报"来料料件内销"或"进料料件内销";加工贸易成品凭征免税证明转为减免税进口货物的,分别填制进、出口报关单,出口报关单填报"来料成品减免"或"进料成品减免",进口报关单按照实际监管方式填报。

(3) 加工贸易出口成品因故退运进口及复运出口的,填报"来料成品退换"或"进料成品退换";加工贸易进口料件因换料退运出口及复运进口的,填报"来料料件退换"或"进料料件退换";加工贸易过程中产生的剩余料件、边角料退运出口,以及进口料件因品质、规格等原因退运出口且不再更换同类货物进口的,分别填报"来料料件复出""来料边角料复出""进料料件复出""进料边角料复出"。

（4）加工贸易边角料内销和副产品内销，填制进口报关单，填报"来料边角料内销"或"进料边角料内销"。

（5）企业销毁处置加工贸易货物未获得收入，销毁处置货物为料件、残次品的，填报"料件销毁"；销毁处置货物为边角料、副产品的，填报"边角料销毁"。

企业销毁处置加工贸易货物获得收入的，填报为"进料边角料内销"或"来料边角料内销"。

15．征免性质

根据实际情况按海关规定的《征免性质代码表》选择填报相应的征免性质简称及代码，持有海关核发的征免税证明的，按照征免税证明中批注的征免性质填报。一份报关单只允许填报一种征免性质。

加工贸易货物报关单按照海关核发的加工贸易手册中批注的征免性质简称及代码填报。特殊情况填报要求如下：

（1）加工贸易转内销货物，按实际情况填报（如一般征税、科教用品、其他法定等）。

（2）料件退运出口、成品退运进口货物，填报"其他法定"（代码299）。

（3）加工贸易结转货物，免予填报。

16．许可证号

填报进（出）口许可证、两用物项和技术进（出）口许可证、两用物项和技术出口许可证（定向）、纺织品临时出口许可证、出口许可证（加工贸易）、出口许可证（边境小额贸易）的编号。

一份报关单只允许填报一个许可证号。

17．启运港

填报进口货物在运抵我国关境前的第一个境外装运港。

根据实际情况，按海关规定的《港口代码表》填报相应的港口名称及代码；未在《港口代码表》列明的，填报相应的国家名称及代码。货物从海关特殊监管区域或保税监管场所运至境内区外的，填报《港口代码表》中相应海关特殊监管区域或保税监管场所的名称及代码；未在《港口代码表》中列明的，填报"未列出的特殊监管区"及代码。

其他无实际进境的货物，填报"中国境内"及代码。

18．合同协议号

填报进出口货物合同（包括协议或订单）编号。未发生商业性交易的免予填报。

19．贸易国（地区）

发生商业性交易的进口填报购自国（地区），出口填报售予国（地区）；未发生商业性交易的填报货物所有权拥有者所属的国家（地区）。

按海关规定的《国别（地区）代码表》选择填报相应的贸易国（地区）中文名称及代码。

20．启运国（地区）/运抵国（地区）

启运国（地区）填报进口货物启始发出，直接运抵我国或者在运输中转国（地）未发生任何商业性交易的情况下运抵我国的国家（地区）。

运抵国（地区）填报出口货物离开我国关境，直接运抵或者在运输中转国（地区）未发生任何商业性交易的情况下最后运抵的国家（地区）。

不经过第三国（地区）转运的直接运输进出口货物，以进口货物的装货港所在国（地区）为启运国（地区），以出口货物的指运港所在国（地区）为运抵国（地区）；经过第三国（地区）转运的进出口货物，如在中转国（地区）发生商业性交易，则以中转国（地区）作为启运/运抵国（地区）。

按海关规定的《国别（地区）代码表》选择填报相应的启运国（地区）或运抵国（地区）中文名称及代码。

无实际进出境的货物，填报"中国"及代码。

21．经停港/指运港

经停港填报进口货物在运抵我国关境前的最后一个境外装运港。

指运港填报出口货物运往境外的最终目的港；最终目的港不可预知的，按尽可能预知的目的港填报。

根据实际情况，按海关规定的《港口代码表》选择填报相应的港口名称及代码。经停港/指运港在《港口代码表》中无港口名称及代码的，可选择填报相应的国家名称及代码。

无实际进出境的货物，填报"中国境内"及代码。

22．入境口岸/离境口岸

入境口岸填报进境货物从跨境运输工具卸离的第一个境内口岸的中文名称及代码；采取多式联运跨境运输的，填报多式联运货物最终卸离的境内口岸中文名称及代码；过境货物填报货物进入境内的第一个口岸的中文名称及代码；从海关特殊监管区域或保税监管场所进境的，填报海关特殊监管区域或保税监管场所的中文名称及代码。其他无实际进境的货物，填报货物所在地的城市名称及代码。

出境口岸填报装运出境货物的跨境运输工具离境的第一个境内口岸的中文名称及代码；采取多式联运跨境运输的，填报多式联运货物最初离境的境内口岸中文名称及代码；过境货物填报货物离境的第一个境内口岸的中文名称及代码；从海关特殊监管区域或保税监管场所出境的，填报海关特殊监管区域或保税监管场所的中文名称及代码。其他无实际出境的货物，填报货物所在地的城市名称及代码。

入境口岸/离境口岸的类型包括港口、码头、机场、机场货运通道、边境口岸、火车站、车辆装卸点、车检场、陆路港、坐落在口岸的海关特殊监管区域等。按海关规定的《国内口岸编码表》选择填报相应的境内口岸名称及代码。

23．包装种类

填报进出口货物的所有包装材料，包括运输包装和其他包装，按海关规定的《包装种类代码表》选择填报相应的包装种类名称及代码。运输包装指提运单所列货物件数单位对应的包装，其他包装包括货物的各类包装，以及植物性铺垫材料等。

24．件数

填报进出口货物运输包装的件数（按运输包装计）。特殊情况填报要求如下：

（1）舱单件数为集装箱的，填报集装箱个数。

（2）舱单件数为托盘的，填报托盘数。

不得填报为"0"，裸装货物填报为"1"。

25．毛重（千克）

填报进出口货物及其包装材料的重量之和，计量单位为千克，不足1千克的填报为"1"。

26．净重（千克）

填报进出口货物的毛重减去外包装材料后的重量，即货物本身的实际重量，计量单位为千克，不足1千克的填报为"1"。

27．成交方式

根据进出口货物实际成交价格条款，按海关规定的《成交方式代码表》选择填报相应的成交方式代码。

无实际进出境的货物，进口填报"CIF"，出口填报"FOB"。

28．运费

进口货物填报其运抵我国境内输入地点起卸前的运输费用；出口货物填报其运至我国境内输出地点装载后的运输费用。

运费可按运费单价、总价或运费率三种方式之一填报，需注明相应的运费标记（"1"表示运费率，"2"表示每吨货物的运费单价，"3"表示运费总价），并按海关规定的《货币代码表》选择填报相应的币种代码。

29．保费

进口货物填报其运抵我国境内输入地点起卸前的保险费用；出口货物填报其运至我国境内输出地点装载后的保险费用。

保费可按保险费总价或保险费率两种方式之一填报，需注明相应的保险费标记（"1"表示保险费率，"3"表示保险费总价），并按海关规定的《货币代码表》选择填报相应的币种代码。

30．杂费

填报成交价格以外的、按照《中华人民共和国进出口关税条例》相关规定应计入完税价格或应从完税价格中扣除的费用。可按杂费总价或杂费率两种方式之一填报，需注明相应的杂费标记（"1"表示杂费率，"3"表示杂费总价），并按海关规定的《货币代码表》选择填报相应的币种代码。

应计入完税价格的杂费填报为正值或正率，应从完税价格中扣除的杂费填报为负值或负率。

31．随附单证及编号

根据海关规定的《监管证件代码表》和《随附单据代码表》选择填报除第（16）栏规定填报的许可证件以外的其他进出口许可证件或监管证件、随附单据代码及编号。

本栏目分为随附单证代码和随附单证编号两栏，其中代码栏按海关规定的《监管证件代码表》和《随附单据代码表》选择填报相应证件代码；随附单证编号栏填报证件编号。

（1）加工贸易内销征税的货物，随附单证代码填报"c"，随附单证编号填报海关审核通过的内销征税联系单号。

（2）一般贸易进出口货物，只能使用原产地证书申请享受协定税率或者特惠税率（以下统称优惠税率）的（无原产地声明模式），随附单证代码填报原产地证书代码"Y"，随附单证编号填报"<优惠贸易协定代码>"和原产地证书编号。可以使用原产地证书或者原产地声明申请享受优惠税率的（有原产地声明模式），随附单证代码填报"Y"，随附单证编号填报"<优惠贸易协定代码>""C"（凭原产地证书申报）或"D"（凭原产地声明申报），以及原产地证书编号（或者原产地声明序列号）。一份报关单对应一份原产地证书或原产地声明。各优惠贸易协定代码如下：

"01"为"亚太贸易协定"；
"02"为"中国-东盟自贸协定"；
"03"为"内地与香港紧密经贸关系安排"（香港CEPA）；
"04"为"内地与澳门紧密经贸关系安排"（澳门CEPA）；
"06"为"台湾农产品零关税措施"；
"07"为"中国-巴基斯坦自贸协定"；
"08"为"中国-智利自贸协定"；
"10"为"中国-新西兰自贸协定"；
"11"为"中国-新加坡自贸协定"；
"12"为"中国-秘鲁自贸协定"；
"13"为"最不发达国家特别优惠关税待遇"；
"14"为"海峡两岸经济合作框架协议"（ECFA）；
"15"为"中国-哥斯达黎加自贸协定"；
"16"为"中国-冰岛自贸协定"；
"17"为"中国-瑞士自贸协定"；
"18"为"中国-澳大利亚自贸协定"；
"19"为"中国-韩国自贸协定"；
"20"为"中国-格鲁吉亚自贸协定"。

海关特殊监管区域和保税监管场所内销货物申请适用优惠税率的，有关货物进出海关特殊监管区域和保税监管场所以及内销时，已通过原产地电子信息交换系统实现电子联网的优惠贸易协定项下货物的报关单，按照上述一般贸易要求填报；未实现电子联网的优惠贸易协定项下货物的报关单，随附单证代码填报"Y"，随附单证编号填报"<优惠贸易协定代码>"和原产地证据文件备案号。原产地证据文件备案号为进出口货物的收发货人或其代理人录入原产地证明文件电子信息后，系统自动生成的号码。

向我国香港或者澳门特别行政区出口用于生产"香港CEPA"或者"澳门CEPA"项下货物的原材料时，按照上述一般贸易填报要求填制报关单，香港或澳门生产厂商在香港工贸署或者澳门经济局登记备案的有关备案号填报在电子数据报关单中的"关联备案"栏。

电子数据报关单中的"单证对应关系表"中填报报关单上的申报商品项与原产地证书（原产地声明）上的商品项之间的对应关系。报关单上的商品序号与原产地证书（原产地声明）上的项目编号应一一对应，不要求顺序对应。同一批次进口货物可以在同一报关单中申报，不享受优惠税率的货物序号不填报在"单证对应关系表"中。

(3) 各优惠贸易协定项下，免提交原产地证明文件的小金额进口货物的随附单证代码填报"Y"，随附单证编号填报"<协定编号>XJE00000"，"单证对应关系表"享惠报关单项号按实际填报，对应单证项号与享惠报关单项号相同。

32. 标记唛码及备注

主要填报要求如下：

（1）标记唛码中除图形以外的文字、数字，无标记唛码的填报"N/M"。
（2）填报受外商投资企业委托代理其进口投资设备、物品的进出口企业名称。
（3）与本报关单有关联关系的，同时在业务管理规范方面又要求填报的备案号，填报在电子数据报关单中的"关联备案"栏。
（4）与本报关单有关联关系的，同时在业务管理规范方面又要求填报的报关单号，填报在电子数据报关单中的"关联报关单"栏。
（5）申报时其他必须说明的事项。

33．项号

此栏分两行填报：第一行填报所列货物的顺序编号；第二行填报货物的备案序号，专用于加工贸易及保税、减免税等已备案、审批的货物，填报该项货物在加工贸易手册或征免税证明等备案、审批单证中的顺序编号。有关优惠贸易协定项下货物的报关单填制要求按照海关总署相关规定执行。

34．商品编号

填报由 13 位数字组成的商品编号。前 8 位为《中华人民共和国进出口税则》和《中华人民共和国海关统计商品目录》确定的 H.S.编码，第 9、10 位为监管附加编号，第 11～13 位为检验检疫附加编号。

35．商品名称及规格型号

此栏分两行填报：第一行填报进出口货物规范的中文商品名称；第二行填报规格型号。

36．数量及单位

此栏分三行填报：

（1）第一行按进出口货物的法定第一计量单位填报数量及单位，法定计量单位以《中华人民共和国海关统计商品目录》中的计量单位为准。
（2）凡列明有法定第二计量单位的，在第二行按照法定第二计量单位填报数量及单位；无法定第二计量单位的，第二行为空。
（3）成交计量单位及数量填报在第三行。

37．单价

填报同一项号下进出口货物实际成交的商品单位价格；无实际成交价格的，填报单位货值。

38．总价

填报同一项号下进出口货物实际成交的商品总价格；无实际成交价格的，填报总货值。

39．币制

按海关规定的《货币代码表》选择填报相应的货币名称及代码，若《货币代码表》中无实际成交币种，需将实际成交货币按申报日外汇折算率折算成《货币代码表》列明的货币填报。

40．原产国（地区）

原产国（地区）依据《中华人民共和国进出口货物原产地条例》、海关总署令第 122 号《关于非优惠原产地规则中实质性改变标准的规定》以及海关总署关于各项优惠贸易协定原产地管理规章规定的原产地确定标准填报。同一批进出口货物的原产地不同的，分别填报原产国（地区）。进出口货物原产国（地区）无法确定的，填报"国别不详"。

按海关规定的《国别（地区）代码表》选择填报相应的国家（地区）名称及代码。

41. 最终目的国（地区）

填报已知的进出口货物的最终实际消费、使用或进一步加工制造国家（地区）。不经过第三国（地区）转运的直接运输货物，以运抵国（地区）为最终目的国（地区）；经过第三国（地区）转运的货物，以最后运往国（地区）为最终目的国（地区）。同一批进出口货物的最终目的国（地区）不同的，分别填报最终目的国（地区）。进出口货物不能确定最终目的国（地区）时，以尽可能预知的最后运往国（地区）为最终目的国（地区）。

按海关规定的《国别（地区）代码表》选择填报相应的国家（地区）名称及代码。

42. 境内目的地/境内货源地

境内目的地填报已知的进口货物在国内的消费、使用地或最终运抵地，其中最终运抵地为最终使用单位所在的地区。最终使用单位难以确定的，填报货物进口时预知的最终收货单位所在地。

境内货源地填报出口货物在国内的产地或原始发货地。出口货物产地难以确定的，填报最早发运该出口货物的单位所在地。

海关特殊监管区域、保税物流中心（B型）与境外之间的进出境货物，境内目的地/境内货源地填报本海关特殊监管区域、保税物流中心（B型）所对应的国内地区名称及代码。

按海关规定的《国内地区代码表》选择填报相应的国内地区名称及代码，并根据《中华人民共和国行政区划代码表》选择填报境内目的地对应的县级行政区名称及代码。无下属区县级行政区的，可选择填报地市级行政区。

43. 征免

按照海关核发的征免税证明或有关政策规定，对报关单所列每项商品选择海关规定的《征减免税方式代码表》中相应的征减免税方式填报。

加工贸易货物报关单根据加工贸易手册中备案的征免规定填报；加工贸易手册中备案的征免规定为"保金"或"保函"的，填报"全免"。

44. 特殊关系确认

根据《中华人民共和国海关审定进出口货物完税价格办法》（以下简称《审价办法》）第十六条规定，确认进出口行为中买卖双方是否存在特殊关系，有下列情形之一的，应当认为买卖双方存在特殊关系，此栏填报"是"，反之则填报"否"：

（1）买卖双方为同一家族成员的。
（2）买卖双方互为商业上的高级职员或董事的。
（3）一方直接或者间接地受另一方控制的。
（4）买卖双方都直接或间接受第三方控制的。
（5）买卖双方共同直接或间接地控制第三方的。
（6）一方直接或者间接地拥有、控制或持有对方5%以上（含5%）公开发行的有表决权的股票或股份的。
（7）一方是另一方的雇员、高级职员或董事的。
（8）买卖双方是同一合伙的成员。

买卖双方在经营上相互有联系，一方是另一方的独家代理、独家经销或者独家受让人，如果符合上述条件，也应当视为存在特殊关系。

出口货物免予填报，加工贸易及保税监管货物（内销保税货物除外）免予填报。

45．价格影响确认

根据《审价办法》第十七条规定，确认纳税义务人是否可以证明特殊关系未对进口货物的成交价格产生影响，纳税义务人能证明其成交价格与同时或者大约同时发生的下列任何一款价格相近的，应视为特殊关系未对成交价格产生影响，此栏填报"否"，反之则填报"是"：

（1）向境内无特殊关系的买方出售的相同或者类似进口货物的成交价格。

（2）按照《审价办法》第二十三条的规定所确定的相同或者类似进口货物的完税价格。

（3）按照《审价办法》第二十五条的规定所确定的相同或者类似进口货物的完税价格。

出口货物免予填报，加工贸易及保税监管货物（内销保税货物除外）免予填报。

46．支付特许权使用费确认

根据《审价办法》第十一条和第十三条规定，填报确认买方是否存在向卖方或者有关方直接或者间接支付与进口货物有关的特许权使用费，且未包括在进口货物的实付、应付价格中。

买方存在需向卖方或有关方直接或间接支付特许权使用费，且未包含在进口货物实付、应付价格中，并且符合《审价办法》第十三条规定的，此栏填报"是"。

买方存在需向卖方或有关方直接或间接支付特许权使用费，且未包含在进口货物实付、应付价格中，但纳税义务人无法确认是否符合《审价办法》第十三条规定的，此栏填报"是"。

买方存在需向卖方或有关方直接或间接支付特许权使用费，且未包含在进口货物实付、应付价格中，纳税义务人根据《审价办法》第十三条规定，可以确认需支付的特许权使用费与进口货物无关的，此栏填报"否"。

买方不存在向卖方或有关方直接或间接支付特许权使用费的，或者特许权使用费已经包含在进口货物实付、应付价格中的，此栏填报"否"。

出口货物免予填报，加工贸易及保税监管货物（内销保税货物除外）免予填报。

47．自报自缴

进出口企业、单位采用"自主申报、自行缴税"（自报自缴）模式向海关申报时，此栏填报"是"；反之则填报"否"。

48．申报人员/证号/电话

报关人员填报在海关备案的姓名、编码和电话号码。

49．申报单位

自理报关的，填报进出口企业的名称及编码；委托代理报关的，填报报关企业名称及编码（18位法人和其他组织统一社会信用代码），并加盖申报单位印章。

50．海关批注及签章

供海关作业时签注。

（二）情景导入中的报关单（Customs Declaration of the Lead-in Situation）

中华人民共和国海关出口货物报关单

预录入编号：		海关编号：		页码/页数：	
境内发货人 科林国际贸易（香港）有限公司 （18位统一社会信用代码）	出境关别 深圳蛇口（5304）	出口日期	申报日期 2018.08.23	备案号	
境外收货人 环球采购服务有限公司 （18位统一社会信用代码）	运输方式 水路运输	运输工具名称及航次号 EAST WIND V.23	提运单号 GD57861609		
生产销售单位 科林国际贸易（香港）有限公司 （18位统一社会信用代码）	监管方式 一般贸易（0110）	征免性质 一般征税（101）	许可证号 7688990		
合同协议号 TXT264	贸易国（地区） 美国（502）	运抵国（地区） 美国（502）	指运港 纽约	离境口岸	
包装种类 纸箱	件数 300	毛重（千克） 1650	净重（千克） 1500	成交方式 CIF	运费 502/800/3	保费 502/330/3	杂费
随附单证及编号 随附单证1：B/4400010510			随附单证2：		
标记唛码及备注 G.S.S TXT264 NEW YORK C/NO.1-300					

项号	商品编号	商品名称及规格型号	数量及单位	单价/总价/币制			原产国（地区）	最终目的国（地区）	境内货源地	征免
01	61091000	全棉彩色波纹T恤 TM111	2000 件	11	22000	美元	中国（142）	美国（502）	惠州	照章征税
02	61091000	全棉彩色波纹T恤 TM222	2000 件	10	20000	美元	中国（142）	美国（502）	惠州	照章征税
03	61091000	全棉彩色波纹T恤 TM333	1000 件	9.5	9500	美元	中国（142）	美国（502）	惠州	照章征税
04	61091000	全棉彩色波纹T恤 TM444	1000 件	8.5	8500	美元	中国（142）	美国（502）	惠州	照章征税

特殊关系确认：否	价格影响确认：否	支付特许权使用费确认：否	自报自缴：是
申报人员	申报人员证号	电话 兹申明以上内容承担如实申报、依法纳税之法律责任	海关批注及签章
申报单位 科林国际贸易（香港）有限公司		申报单位（签章）	

实操训练（Skill Training）

一、单选题

1. 日本商人从北京购买一批地毯，陆路运至我国香港，再空运经日本到英国伦敦，其运抵国（地区）应为（　　）。
  A. 香港　　　　　B. 伦敦　　　　　C. 英国　　　　　D. 日本

2. 大连某中日合资企业在投资总额内委托辽宁省机械设备进出口公司与日本三菱重工公司签约进口工程机械，并委托大连外运公司代理报关，在填制进口报关单时，"境内收货人"一栏应填报（　　）。
  A. 大连外运公司　　　　　　　　　B. 该中日合资企业
  C. 辽宁省机械设备进出口公司　　　D. 日本三菱重工公司

3. 根据《海关法》规定，进口货物的报关期限为：自运输工具申报进境之日起（　　）日内申报，若进口货物的收货人或其代理人逾期申报，海关将征收滞报金，滞报金的日征收金额为进口货物到岸价的（　　）。
  A. 14，0.05%　　B. 14，0.5%　　C. 15，0.05%　　D. 15，0.5%

4. 出口报关单上对于货物出口海运费总价为 5 000 美元的正确填报应是（　　）。
  A. 110/5 000/2　　B. 502/5 000/1　　C. 110/5 000/1　　D. 502/5 000/3

二、多选题

1. 申报人必须按照海关规定，对于同一批货物中不同的（　　）应分单申报。
  A. 运输工具名称　　　　B. 提运单号
  C. 征免性质　　　　　　D. 许可证号

2. 按海关规定，每项申报货物的（　　）栏目应分行填报。
  A. 项号　　　　　　　　B. 商品名称、规格型号
  C. 单价　　　　　　　　D. 数量及单位

3. 按海关规定，以下（　　）的编号应填报在报关单的"备案号"栏目内。
  A. 加工贸易手册　　　　B. 征免税证明
  C. 出口货物通关单　　　D. 加工贸易低值小量辅料

4. 按海关规定，进出口货物报关单中"境内收发货人"栏目可以填报（　　）。
  A. 执行外贸合同的企业
  B. 签订外贸合同但不执行外贸合同的企业
  C. 有报关权但无进出口经营权的企业
  D. 进出口企业之间相互代理进出口情况下的代理方企业

三、请根据以下信用证和补充资料填制报关单（条件未给出的可免填）

……

Doc. Credit Number	*20:	6764/07/12345B
Date of Issue	31C:	180516
Expiry	*31D:	DATE 180831 PLACE CHINA
Applicant	*50:	THOMAS INTERNATIONAL COMPANY LIMITED 1/F WINFUL CENTRE, SHING YIP STREET, KOWLOON, HONG KONG, CHINA
Beneficiary	*59:	FENGYUAN LIGHT INDUSTRIAL PRODUCTS IMP. AND EXP. CORP. P. O. BOX 789, SHANGHAI, CHINA
Amount	*32B:	CURRENCY USD AMOUNT 10,560.00

......

Partial Shipments	43P:	NOT ALLOWED
Transshipment	43T:	ALLOWED
Loading in Charge	44A:	CHINA PORT
For Transport to…	44B:	ANTWERP
Latest Date of Ship.	44C:	180815
Descript. of Goods	45A:	

APPLICANT'S ITEM NO. HW—045 WOODEN HANGER, 66,000 PCS, THE PACKING IS 100PCS PER STRONG EXPORT CARTON OF 3.00 CUFT @USD16.00 PER CARTON CIF ANTWERP INCLUDING 3 PCT COMMISSION AS PER SALES CONFIRMATION NO. 484LFVS15783

补充资料：

Port of Loading: SHANGHAI　　　Port of Transshipment: HONG KONG
S.S.: TONGMEI V.155/FARROR　　Date of B/L: AUG. 2, 2018
B/L No.: KEY48609
G. W. = 52.6KGS/CTN×660　　　　N.W. = 50.4KGS/CTN×660
Tariff No. 4421.1000.90　　　　　 Legal Unit: KG
Container No. CBHU9755587/40'/K444924
Freight: USD 2,600/FCL　　　　　 Insurance Fee: USD625.35
Shipping Marks:　　　　　TIC
　　　　　　　　　　484LFVS15783
　　　　　　　　　　 ANTWERP

卖方中文名称：丰原轻工产品进出口公司。

项目九
Project IX

汇票
Bill of Exchange

学习目标（Learning Aims）

- 了解票据的含义和特性。
- 熟悉汇票的种类和票据行为。
- 掌握填制汇票的要点。
- 能够依据所给出的资料正确填制汇票。

情景导入（Lead-in Situation）

科林国际贸易公司第 TXT264 号合同项下货物已装船并获得海运提单，按照国际惯例，公司必须在信用证有效期内，且提单签发日后的 21 日内到信用证指定的银行交单议付，业务员李怡华开始着手填制汇票。

一、背景知识（Background Knowledge）

国际贸易的开展离不开国际结算，而现代国际结算的主要工具是票据。票据在结算中起着流通手段和支付手段的作用，远期票据还能发挥信用工具的作用。国际结算中的票据主要包括汇票、本票和支票，它们也被称为国际结算的支付工具。

（一）票据及其特性（Negotiable Instruments and Characteristics）

票据是指出票人依法签发的由自己或指示他人无条件支付一定金额给收款人或持票人的有价证券，即可以代替现金流通的有价证券。广义的票据包括所有在商业活动中作为权利凭证的单据，即包括各种有价证券和凭证，如商业发票、仓单、提单、资金票据等；狭义的票据则仅指我国《票据法》中规定的票据，即仅指以支付一定金额为目的的有价证券，包括汇票、本票和支票。

狭义的票据主要具有以下特性。

（1）流通性：多数国家的票据法中规定票据仅凭交付或适当背书即可转让，无须通知债务人。流通转让是票据的基本特性，一张票据即便经过多次转让，但最后的持票人仍有权要求票据上的债务人向其清偿，票据债务人不得以没有接到转让通知为理由而拒绝偿付。

（2）无因性：票据的受让人无须调查出票、转让原因，只要票据记载合格，受让人即可取得票据文义载明的权利，即票据本身与其基础关系相分离。各国票据法均认为，票据上的权利义务关系一经成立，即与原因关系相脱离，不论其原因关系是否有效或存在，都不影响票据的效力。票据的无因性使票据得以流通。

（3）要式性：票据的做成必须符合法定的形式要求，即其格式和内容必须完全符合我国《票据法》。票据上规定记载的必要记载项目必须齐全，各项必要项目以及票据形式必须符合规定，否则就不能产生票据的效力。各国法律对于票据所必须具备的形式条件都做了具体的规定，当事人不能随意加以变更。

（4）文义性：票据当事人的权利和责任须完全根据票据上记载的文义来解释。票据的债权人可依据票据文义行使权利，票据债务人也仅对文义负责。任何人不得以票据文义以外的事情改变票据权利和义务。

（5）提示性：票据上指明的债权人请求债务人履行票据义务时，必须向付款人提示票据。如果持票人不提示票据，付款人就没有履行付款的义务。《票据法》还规定了票据的提示期限，若超过期限则丧失票据权利。

（6）返还性：票据的持票人领到付款人支付的票款时，应将签收的票据交还给付款人，从而结束票据的流通。

（二）汇票的种类和票据行为（Types and Actions of B/E）

汇票（Bill of Exchange，B/E）是最常见的票据类型之一，我国《票据法》第十九条规定："汇票是出票人签发的，委托付款人在见票时或者在指定日期无条件支付确定的金额给收款人或者持票人的票据。"汇票是国际结算中广泛使用的一种信用工具，是一种委付证券，其基本的法律关系至少包括三方当事人，即出票人、受票人和收款人。

1．汇票的种类

（1）根据是否附有运输单据，可将汇票分为光票（Clean Bill）和跟单汇票（Documentary Bill）。

（2）根据付款时间的不同，可将汇票分为即期汇票（Sight Bill）和远期汇票（Time Bill）。

（3）根据出票人的不同，可将汇票分为商业汇票（Commercial Bill）和银行汇票（Banker's Bill）。

（4）根据付款人的不同，可将汇票分为商业承兑汇票（Commercial Acceptance Bill）和银行承兑汇票（Banker's Acceptance Bill）。

2．汇票的票据行为

一张汇票从开立、流通直至付款，是通过一系列的行为来实现其功能的，这一系列的行为就是票据行为。狭义的票据行为是以承担票据上的债务为目的所做的必要形式的法律行为，包括出票、背书、承兑、参加承兑和保证；广义的票据行为还包括提示、付款、参加付款、拒付和追索等。

（1）出票（Issue）：即出票人签发汇票并将其交付给收款人的行为。汇票的出票行为是各项票据行为的开端，是基本的汇票行为。出票后，出票人即承担保证汇票得到承兑和付款的责任。

（2）背书（Endorsement）：即汇票的抬头人在汇票背面签上自己的名字，或再加注受让人（即被背书人）的名字，并把汇票交受让人的行为。背书是转让汇票的一种法定手续，背书后汇票的收款权利便转移给受让人。

（3）提示（Presentation）：即持票人向付款人出示票据，要求其承兑或付款的行为。付款人见到汇票称为见票。提示分为提示承兑和提示付款两种。汇票、本票和支票都需要提示付款，且必须在规定的时限或规定的地点进行。

（4）承兑（Acceptance）：即汇票付款人承诺在汇票到期时支付汇票金额的票据行为。汇票一经承兑，付款人即成为承兑人，并成为汇票的主债务人，而出票人则成为汇票的从债务人。"参加承兑"是指票据提示后遭到付款人拒绝承兑，或因付款人死亡、逃避等原因而无法获得承兑时，由第三者（即参加承兑人）对汇票承兑的行为。

（5）付款（Payment）：即持票人在规定的时间内和规定的地点向付款人做出付款提示，付款人支付票据以消除票据关系的行为。汇票记载的付款人完成正当付款后，不仅解除了付款人的付款义务，而且票据所有债务人的债务也因此解除。所以付款人付款后，一般要求收款人在汇票背面签字作为收款证明并收回汇票，注上"付讫"字样，汇票就可以注销了。"参加付款"是指当票据的付款人拒绝付款时，由第三者（即参加付款人）对票据进行付款的行为。

（6）拒付（Dishonor）：或称退票。无论是提示付款时遭到拒绝付款的行为，或是提示承兑时遭到拒绝承兑的行为，均称为拒付。付款人逃匿、死亡或宣告破产，以致持票人无法实现提示的情况，也属于拒付。

（7）追索（Right of Recourse）：即汇票遭到拒付时，持票人有权向其前手要求偿付汇票金额、利息和其他费用的权利。

二、认识汇票 (Understand the B/E)

(一) 汇票的记载事项 (Items of B/E)

1. 汇票的绝对应记载事项

按照《日内瓦统一汇票和本票法公约》(以下简称《日内瓦统一票据法》) 规定, 汇票必须具备必要项目才能发生票据效力。我国《票据法》第二十二条规定汇票必须记载下列事项 (汇票上未记载以下规定事项之一的, 汇票无效)。

(1) 标明"汇票"(Draft or Bill of Exchange) 字样。目的在于与其他票据加以区别。根据《日内瓦统一票据法》的规定, 汇票应有记载其为汇票的词句, 否则汇票无效。

(2) 无条件支付的委托。汇票的出票人在签发汇票时须委托付款人无条件支付一定金额, 即为收款人的一项付款委托。因此, 汇票必须同时满足以下两个条件:

① 汇票是一项支付命令, 必须使用英语的祈使句作为命令式语句, 例如 "Pay to ABC Company or order the sum of five thousand pounds", 而不能用表示请求的虚拟句。

② 汇票的支付命令必须是无条件的, 凡是附有条件的支付命令的汇票均为无效。例如 "Pay to ABC Company or order the sum of five thousand pounds within six days after receipt of the goods" 或 "Pay to ABC Company or order the sum of five thousand pounds from our account No. 1 with you", 均为错误表述。

(3) 确定的金额。汇票的金额包括两部分: 货币名称和金额数值。汇票的权利必须以一定数额的货币来表示, 否则汇票无效。

① 汇票的支付标的必须是金钱, 其金额必须是可以确定的。任何选择性的、浮动的或未定的记载, 都使汇票无效。例如 "The sum of about one thousand USD" 即为错误表述。

汇票上注明一定的利率或某一日市场利率加付利息是允许的, 但利息条款须注明利率、起算日和终止日。例如 "Pay to ABC Company or order the sum of five thousand pounds plus interest calculated at the rate of 6% per annum from the date hereof to the date of payment"。

② 汇票金额须以大写和小写两种形式同时记载。其中, 小写金额由货币符号和阿拉伯数字组成; 大写金额由货币全称和表述相应金额的大写数目文字组成。例如, 小写金额为 "Exchange for GBP 5,000", 则对应的大写金额为 "THE SUM OF FIVE THOUSAND POUNDS ONLY"。如果两种方式间记载出现差错, 各国对此的处理方式有所不同: 我国《票据法》规定, 大小写金额必须一致, 否则汇票无效;《英国票据法》和《日内瓦统一票据法》则规定, 按大写文字来支付。

(4) 付款人名称。付款人 (Payer) 又称受票人 (Drawee), 是接受命令的人, 并不一定付款, 他也可以拒付。付款人的名称、地址必须写清楚, 以便持票人向他提示要求承兑或付款。我国汇票的付款人和出票人通常为两个不同当事人。但《日内瓦统一票据法》和《英国票据法》都规定, 汇票的付款人可以是出票人自己。受票人只有对汇票做出承兑或付款, 才成为承兑人或付款人。

(5) 收款人名称。汇票的收款人就是汇票的记名债权人, 实务中又称为"抬头"。抬头的不同写法直接影响汇票的流通与否, 其具体内容如下:

① 空白抬头：即不指定收款人名称，持票人或来人即为收款人。这种汇票无须背书，仅凭交付就可转让。例如"Pay to bearer"或"Pay to ABC Co. or bearer"。但是，《日内瓦统一票据法》和我国《票据法》均不允许汇票做成空白抬头。我国《票据法》第二十二条明确规定，汇票必须记载收款人名称，否则汇票无效。

② 限制性抬头：即抬头是唯一限定的，仅限于交付款项给收款人。这种汇票只能由特定的人去提示并收款，不能转让。例如"Pay to John Smith only"或"Pay to John Smith not transferable"。

③ 指示性抬头：即抬头不是唯一限定的，而是凭指示支付。这种汇票的出票人要求付款人支付款项给某人或其指定人，持票人可以通过背书的方式将汇票转让给他人。这类汇票通常在收款人一栏里注有"Order"字样。例如"Pay to the order of ABC Co."或"Pay to ABC Co. or order"。

(6) 出票日期。汇票的出票日期即签发汇票的日期，具有以下作用：

① 决定汇票的有效期。按各国票据法的一般规定，票据均应注有一定的有效期，持票人须在有效期内向付款人提示要求其付款或承兑。《日内瓦统一票据法》规定，见票后定期付款的汇票，或见票即付的汇票必须在出票日起一年内提示要求承兑或提示要求付款，出票日期即为有效期的起始日期。

② 决定付款的到期日。出票后定期付款的汇票，其付款到期日须从出票日算起。

③ 决定出票人的行为能力。若出票人在出票时已宣告破产或清理，则表明出票人已丧失行为能力，该汇票应为无效。

(7) 出票人签章。出票人出具的汇票必须要有自己的签字，汇票方能生效。出票人签字以示承认自己的债务和承担汇票的责任，收款人因此享有债权，票据也因此成为债权凭证。如果汇票上的签字是伪造的，或是未经授权的人签字，则汇票无效。

出票人如果是受公司或单位委托而签字的，需在签名之前做出说明，并在公司或单位名称前加上"For"或"Per pro."或"On behalf of"字样，同时在个人签名后写明职务。例如"For ABC Co. Ltd., London … Peter Manager"。这样，ABC 公司受到 Peter 签字的约束，而 Peter 不是以个人名义开出汇票，而是代表 ABC 公司开出汇票。

2. 汇票的其他记载事项

汇票除了上述必要记载事项外，还可以列有《票据法》允许的其他记载事项。其中，有些事项虽应在汇票上记载，但如果当事人没有记载，汇票并不因此失效，而是由法律另行规定，对这些事项加以补充，这类事项称为相对应记载事项。另外，汇票上可以记载《票据法》规定以外的其他出票事项，但该记载事项不具有汇票上的效力。

(1) 付款期限。付款期限又称付款到期日，是汇票所记载金额的支付日期，即付款人履行付款义务的日期。我国《票据法》规定，汇票上记载付款日期的，应当清楚、明确；未记载付款日期的，为见票即付。付款期限可以按照下列形式之一记载：

① 即期付款（At sight / on demand / on presentation）。即期付款也称见票即付，提示汇票的当天即为付款日，无须承兑。例如"At sight pay to …"。

② 见票后定期（若干天/月）付款（Bills payable at … days/months after sight）。这种汇票必须由持票人向受票人提示要求承兑并从承兑日起算和确定付款到期日。这样，出票人就不可能自行确定付款日，付款日期取决于受票人承兑汇票的日期。例如"At 15 days after sight"。

③ 出票后定期（若干天/月）付款（Bills payable at … days/months after dated）。这种汇票直接根据汇票记载的出票日期计算出付款到期日，持票人应在到期日前向受票人提示要求承兑。例如"At 15 days after dated"。

在实务中，对于见票后定期付款和出票后定期付款的汇票的付款到期日，通常按照以下原则计算：

A．对于见票或出票后若干天付款的汇票，采取"算尾不算头"的原则。也就是说，付款期限不包括见票日或出票日，但必须包括付款日。若到期日为节假日，则顺延至节假日后第一个工作日。

B．对于见票或出票后一个月或数个月付款的汇票，其到期日是见票日或出票日在应该付款的那个月中的相应日期，避免了一个月是 30 天或 31 天的计算。若没有相应日期，则以该月的最后一天为到期日。

（2）出票地点。我国《票据法》规定，汇票上记载出票地点的，应当清楚、明确；未记载出票地点的，出票人的营业场所、住所或经常居住地为出票地。出票地点事关汇票的法律适用问题，即判定汇票（票据）是否完善有效，应采用哪国法律。

（3）付款地点。我国《票据法》规定，汇票上记载付款地点的，应当清楚、明确；未记载付款地点的，付款人的营业场所、住所或经常居住地为付款地。付款地点应该清楚写明付款人的具体地址，以便持票人向其提示要求承兑或付款。

（4）成套汇票。成套汇票中各联汇票的面额和内容必须是完全一致的，且每联必须有编号。为避免重复付款，各联必须交叉注明在成套汇票中，其中任何一联兑付后，其余各联将不再兑付，即一套汇票只做一次兑付。例如"Pay this first bill of exchange (second of the same tenor and dated being unpaid)"。

（二）汇票的样本和填制要点（Sample and Instructions of B/E）

```
                          BILL OF EXCHANGE
凭                                          信用证
Drawn under _____(1a)_____          L/C No. _____(1b)_____
日期
Dated _____(1c)_____     支取 Payable with interest @ _(2)_ %  按  息  付款
号码                          汇票金额
No. ___(3)___                Exchange for _____(4)_____(5)_____
                             见票           日后（本汇票之副本未付）付交
                             At ____(6)____ sight of this FIRST of Exchange (Second of Exchange being unpaid)
Pay to the order of _____(7)_____
金额
The sum of _____(8)_____
此致
To _____(9)_____
                                                      _____(10)_____
                                                              (Signature)
```

1. **出票条款**(Drawn Clause)

即开具汇票的依据。信用证项下,(1a)栏填写开证行名称,(1b)栏填写信用证号,(1c)栏填写开证日期。托收汇票此项填写合同号、货物名称和件数,也可以不填。

2. **年息条款**(Payable with interest @ …%)

这一栏由结汇银行填写,用以清算企业与银行间的利息费用,出口公司不必填写。

3. **汇票号码**(No.)

一般填写商业发票号码(Invoice No.),以便与发票核对相关内容及整套单证的查阅和引用。汇票号码有两种编制方法,一是按汇票的顺序编号,二是按发票号码编号。因发票是全套单据的中心,我国出口贸易多采用后者,即按发票号码编号,说明该汇票是某一发票项下的。

4. **汇票金额**(小写)(Exchange for)

此栏填写由支付货币和数字构成的小写汇票金额。填写时,先写货币名称缩写,再写用阿拉伯数字表示的汇票金额,金额数保留到小数点后两位。例如"USD 20,000.00"。

5. **出票地点与日期**(Place, Date)

我国出口贸易中,汇票的出票地点一般都已印好,无须填。出票地点后的横线填写出票日期,信用证方式下,一般以议付日期作为出票日期;托收方式下的出票日期按托收行寄单日期填写(该日期不得早于各种单据的出单期,也不得迟于信用证的交单/有效日期)。实际业务中,出票日期一栏多留空白,由银行代为填写。

6. **付款期限**(At … sight)

采用即期付款时,在本栏"At"与"Sight"之间的横线上填写符号"****",不得留空;采用远期付款时,在横线上填写日数(或月数)。例如,见票60日付款的汇票,付款期限即可表示为"At 60 days sight"。采用托收方式时,一般在"At"前注明交单方式,如"D/P at sight"或"D/A at 30 days"。

7. **付款给**(Pay to the order of)

此栏填写收款人名称。目前,在我国出口合同履行中,无论是信用证支付还是托收支付,均以议付行或托收行(多为中国银行)为汇票的收款人。一般在汇票"Pay to the order of"后的空白处填写议付银行或者托收银行的名称,如"Bank of China"。

8. **金额**(大写)(The sum of)

大写金额应与小写金额一致(不超过信用证金额),一般顶格填写在此栏虚线内,货币名称写在数额之前,应写全称,大写金额后加"ONLY"。例如,"USD 20,000.00"对应的大写金额即可表述为"U.S. DOLLARS TWENTY THOUSAND ONLY"。

9. **开票给**(To)

此栏填写付款人(即受票人)名称。按《UCP600》规定,议付信用证项下汇票的受票人是开证行,证内一般会有"Available by drafts on us"或"Drawn on us"的词句,此时,汇票付款人栏应填写开证行名称(和地址)。托收条件下,填写买卖合同中的买方。

10. **出票人签章**(Signature)

出票时,汇票右下角须有出票人(即出口企业法人代表)的签字及印有企业全称的图章。在信用证业务中,出票人通常是卖方(即信用证的受益人)。换句话说,此栏包括两项内容:一是出口公司名称,通常以盖章表示;二是公司法人代表签字。

(三) 汇票实例（Models of B/E）

1. 情景导入中的汇票

```
                           BILL OF EXCHANGE

凭                                              信用证
Drawn under   HSBC BANK (CHINA) COMPANY LIMITED    L/C No.    BL 170197

日期
Dated         AUGUST 29, 2018           支取 Payable with interest @    %    按    息    付款

号码                  汇票金额                        深圳
No.   PI170601        Exchange for    USD 60,000.00   SHENZHEN

                      见票             日后（本汇票之副本未付）付交
                      At      ****    sight of this FIRST of Exchange (Second of Exchange being unpaid)

Pay to the order of   BANK OF CHINA, SHENZHEN BRANCH
金额
The sum of            U.S. DOLLARS SIXTY THOUSAND ONLY

此致
To                    HSBC BANK (CHINA) COMPANY LIMITED

                                        KELIN INTERNATIONAL TRADING (HK) CO., LTD.
                                                                (Signature)
```

2. 贸易实务中的汇票

图 9-1 为贸易实务中的汇票样例。

```
                           BILL OF EXCHANGE

凭                                                    不可撤销信用证
Drawn Under  CATHAY BANK LOS ANGELES, CALIFORNIA, USA  Irrevocable  L/C No. 93/U125-FTC

日期        Feb. 11 2018                              @    %    按    息    付款
Date                         支取 Payable With interest   上海
号码                  汇票金额                          shanghai  Mar. 28, 2018, Shanghai, CHINA
No.                  Exchange for   USD 20,880.00
                     见票                              日后（本汇票之副本未付）付交
                      at    ******   sight of this FIRST of Exchange (Second of Exchange being unpaid)

Pay to the order of
金额
the sum of           U. S. DOLLARS TWENTY THOUSAND AND EIGHT HUNDRED AND EIGHTY ONLY

此致
To          CATHAY BANK LOS ANGELES, CALIFORNIA, USA
                                                   Shanghai Stationery&Sporting Goods
                                                   Imp.&Exp. Corp.
                                                              (Authorized Signature)
```

图 9-1 汇票样例

实操训练（Skill Training）

一、请根据以下提供的信息填制英文汇票

1. Draft for USD 100,000.00 is drawn by the American Exporter Co. Inc. Tampa, Florida, USA on the French Issuing Bank, Paris on 9 May, 2018, payable at 60 days after sight to the order of themselves marked "Drawn under the French Issuing Bank, Paris L/C No. 154 dated 25 Feb, 2018".

2. 2018年5月3日，B公司（Garments Singapore Co., Ltd.）出具了一张以A公司（Import and Export Corp.）为付款人，收款人凭C公司（Office Products Co.）指示，见票后90日付款的远期汇票，票面金额为1万美元，并将汇票交给了C公司。请填制一张远期汇票。

3. 美国纽约A公司向法国巴黎B公司采购一批商品，签约日期为2018年5月13日，订单（P/O）编号为95E03LC001，金额为10 000.00美元，约定装运后30日付款，货物装运日期为2018年7月10日。而巴黎B公司又向巴黎C公司采购了一批商品，价值也为10 000.00美元。于是巴黎B公司于7月13日开出一张汇票，收款人是巴黎C公司，受票人是纽约A公司。请为其填制此汇票。

二、汇票的改错

1. 广东省华达食品有限公司按期收到香港ABC公司的信用证，请根据以下信用证内容审核并修改汇票。

信用证内容：

From:	KWANGTUNG PROVINCIAL BANK, HK
To:	BANK OF CHINA, GUANGZHOU BRANCH,
	HONG KONG NOV. 13, 2018

Irrevocable Documentary Credit No.: 002-10358
Advising Bank: BANK OF CHINA, GUANGZHOU BRANCH

Beneficiary:	GUANGDONG HUADA FOOD CO., LTD.
	58 BEIJING ROAD, GUANGZHOU, CHINA
Applicant:	HONG KONG ABC CO.
	3/F GUANGTEX BUILDING TALKOKTSUI KOWLOON, HONG KONG
Amount:	USD 14,200.00
Expiry Date:	JAN. 15, 2018

Dear Sirs:

WE HEREBY ISSUE AN IRREVOCABLE DOCUMENT CREDIT IN YOUR FAVOR WHICH IS AVAILABLE BY NEGOTIATION OF YOUR DRAFTS AT SIGHT DRAWN ON APPLICANT, FOR 100% INVOICE VALUE MARKED AS DRAWN UNDER THIS CREDIT ACCOMPANIED BY THE FOLLOWING DOCUMENTS: …

Special Conditions:

ALL DOCUMENTS MENTIONING THIS CREDIT NUMBER, DOCUMENTS TO BE PRESENTED WITHIN 15 DAYS AFTER DATE OF ISSUANCE OF THE TRANSPORT DOCUMENTS BUT WITHIN THE VALIDITY OF CREDIT.

……

汇票：

```
                        BILL OF EXCHANGE
NO. 002-10358                              DATE: JAN. 10, 2018
EXCHANGE FOR USD 14,200.00
AT 15 DAYS AFTER SIGHT OF THIS FIRST OF EXCHANGE (SECOND OF EXCHANGE BEING UNPAID)
PAY TO THE ORDER OF KWANGTUNG PROVINCIAL BANK, HK
THE SUM OF US DOLLARS FOUTTEEN THOUSAND TWO HUNDRED,
DRAWN UNDER THIS CREDIT
TO KWANGTUNG PROVINCIAL BANK, HK
                                            HONG KONG ABC, CO.
```

2. 广东省五矿进出口公司收到沙特阿拉伯 MIGHWLLI STEEL PRODUCTS CO. 公司开来的信用证后，如期交货，请按信用证内容审核并修改该公司制单员填制的汇票。

信用证内容：

TO:　　　　BANK OF CHINA, GUANGDONG
FM:　　　　ARAB NATIONAL BANK
　　　　　　P.O. BOX 18745 JEDDAH SAUDI ARABIA

DEAR SIRS:

　　KINDLY ADVISE BENEFICIARY'S M/S GUANGDONG METALS AND MINERALS I/E CORP. 5 TIANHE ROAD, GUANGZHOU, CHINA OF OUR OPENING WITH YOU AN IRREVOCABLE DOCUMENTARY CREDIT DATED 10 MARCH, 2018 IN THEIR FAVOR ON BEHALF OF M/S MIGHWLLI STEEL PRODUCTS CO. P.O. BOX 18741 JEDDAH SAUDI ARABIA FOR AMOUNT ABOUT USD 75,683.00 VALID IN CHINA UNTIL 20 MAY 2018, AVAILABLE WITH YOU BY PAYMENT AGAINST PRESENTATION OF BENEFICIARY'S DRAFT AT 30 DAYS AFTER B/L DATE DRAWN ON OURSELVES AND MARKED DRAWN UNDER ARAB NATIONAL BANK CREDIT NO. 254LK254 5% COMMISSION MUST BE DEDUCTED FROM DRAWINGS UNDER THIS CREDIT.

汇票：

```
                        BILL OF EXCHANGE
凭                                          信用证
Drawn under    ARAB NATIONAL BANK           L/C No. _____
日期
Dated        10 ,MARCH, 2018          支取 Payable with interest @    %   按    息    付款
号码                  汇票金额                         中国广州
No. _____       Exchange for   USD75,683.00      GUANGZHOU CHINA
                      见票        日后（本汇票之副本未付）付交
                      At    30 DAYS     sight of this FIRST of Exchange (Second of Exchange being unpaid)
Pay to the order of   BANK OF CHINA, GUANGDONG
金额
The sum of     US DOLLARS SEVENTY FIVE THOUSAND SIX HUNDRED AND EIGHT THREE
此致
To       MIGHWLLI STEEL PRODUCTS CO. P.O. BOX 18742 JEDDAH, SAUDI ARABIA
                           GUANGDONG METALS AND MINERALS I/E CORP.
                                      ( Signature )
```

项目十 Project X

其他单据（装运通知书、受益人证明、船公司证明等）
Other Documents (Shipping Advice, Beneficiary's Certificate and Carrier's Certificate)

学习目标（Learning Aims）

- 了解装运通知书、受益人证明和船龄证明等单据的作用和格式。
- 能够依据信用证或合同的规定正确填制装运通知书和受益人证明。
- 能够按照合同或信用证的规定要求向相关部门申请出具相关单据如船公司证明等。

情景导入（Lead-in Situation）

科林国际贸易公司与美国环球采购公司达成的 TXT264 号合同项下的货物已经安排装船并启运后，业务员李怡华在备好前述主要单据的情况下，还需要按信用证要求填制装运通知书和受益人证明等相关证明文件。

一、背景知识（Background Knowledge）

除前述各类主要单据外，对外贸易所涉及的其他单据主要包括有关运输方面的装运通知书、受益人证明（或声明）以及船公司证明等相关证明文件。在信用证支付方式下，有的信用证会规定卖方必须提供这类单据，此时该单据就成为卖方议付结汇的单证之一，卖方必须认真对待，否则买方就有可能因单证不符而拒付货款。

（一）装运通知书（Shipping Advice / Shipping Note）

装运通知书亦称为装船通知书，是出口商在货物装船后发给进口方的已装船通知。其目的是让进口商了解货物已经装船发运，可准备付款接货了。在 FOB、CFR 等条件下成交的合同，需由进口方自行办理货物保险的凭证，因此装运通知书应在装船后立即发出，以便进口商办理投保手续。

装运通知书没有固定的格式，每个公司可以自行设计，主要内容包括：收件人名称和地址、合同号或信用证号、货物名称、数量、总值、唛头、装运口岸、装运日期、船名、开船日期、提单号码、预计到达目的港时间和发电日期等。

装运通知必须在信用证或合同规定的时限内发出，如果没有规定具体时间，应在提单日期后 3 日内发出。可采用电报、电传、传真及 E-mail 等各种形式发送装运通知。

（二）受益人证明（Beneficiary's Certificate / Beneficiary's Statement）

受益人证明亦称为出口商证明，是由受益人签发的以证实某件事实的单据。常见的受益人证明有：寄单证明、寄样证明、产品补充说明、借记通知（俗称收款单）和贷记通知（俗称借款单）等。在信用证项下，出口商用以说明已按开证申请人要求办理某项工作或证实某件事，以达到进口商的要求和其所在进口国的有关规定。

受益人证明的内容一般包括：单据名称、出证日期与地点、抬头、事由、证明文句、受益人名称及签章。

（三）船公司证明（Carrier's / Shipping Company's Certificate）

船公司证明是船公司或其代理人（在我国一般为中国外轮代理有限公司或中国外运股份有限公司）说明所载船舶某些特定事项的证明文件，是进口商为了解货物运输情况或为满足进口国当局的规定而要求出口商提供的单据。如：船籍证明、航程证明、船龄证明和船级证明等。

二、认识其他单据（Understand the Other Documents）

（一）装运通知书的样本、填制要点和实例（Sample, Instructions and Models of Shipping Advice）

1. 公司名称和地址（Seller's Name & Address）

此栏填制出口公司的中英文名称和详细地址、电话号码、传真号码、电子邮箱等。

		(1) ×××COMPANY	
		(Address)	
		(2) SHIPPING ADVICE	
(3) To:		(4) Issue Date:	
		S/C No.	
		L/C No.	

Dear Sir or Madam:
We are pleased to advice you that the following mentioned goods have been shipped out, full details were shown as follows:

(5) Name of Commodity:	
(6) Invoice Number:	
(7) Bill of Loading Number:	
(8) Name of Vessel:	
(9) Port of Loading:	
(10) Date of Shipment:	
(11) Port of Destination:	
(12) Containers/Seals Number:	
(13) Description of Goods:	
(14) Shipping Marks:	
(15) Quantity/Packages:	
(16) Total Value:	

Thank you for your patronage. We look forward to the pleasure of receiving your valuable repeat orders.

Sincerely yours,

(17) Signature

2．**单据名称**（Name of the Document）

装运通知书的单据名称一般为"Shipping Advice"，也可表示为"Advice of Shipment"或"Shipping Note"。

3．**抬头人**（To）

此处填写收件人的名称和地址。抬头人可以是买方，也可以是买方指定的代理人或保险公司。若抬头为买方指定的保险公司，则应同时注明预保险单合同号（Cover Note）。当保险人直接收到装船通知后，可以将预约保单及时转成一份正式保险单。

4．**日期**（Issue Date）

填写发出装运通知书的实际日期。这个日期非常重要，能反映卖方是否按照有关规定及时发出了装运通知书。

5．**货物名称**（Name of Commodity）

填写该批货物的名称，应与提单上的相同栏目内容一致。

6．**发票号**（Invoice Number）

填写该批货物的发票号码。

7．**提单号**（Bill of Lading Number）

填写运输该批货物的提单号码。

8．**船名**（Name of Vessel）

填写运输该批货物的轮船的名称。需要转船时，必须填写第一程和第二程的船名。

9．**装运港**（Port of Loading）

填写货物装运港的名称，与提单所载装运港一致。

10．**启运日期**（Date of Shipment）

按实际填写，与提单所载启运日期一致。

11．**目的港**（Port of Destination）

填写目的港的名称，与提单所载目的港一致。

12．**集装箱号/铅封号**（Containers/Seals Number）

分别填写装载该批货物的集装箱号和铅封号。

13．**货物描述**（Description of Goods）

详细描述货物的规格型号及包装。

14．**唛头**（Shipping Marks）

按发票中的唛头填写。

15．**数量/包装件数**（Quantity/Packages）

数量按发票填写，外包装件数按装箱单和提单的件数填写。

16．**总金额**（Total Value）

填写该批货物的总金额，用数字表示即可，并写明货币种类。

17．**签名**（Signature）

此栏由发出装运通知书的经办人员签名。

情景导入中的装运通知书：

科林国际贸易（香港）有限公司
KELIN INTERNATIONAL TRADING (HK) CO., LTD

SHIPPING ADVICE

To:	GLOBE SOURCING SERVICE CO., LTD 1407, 80th Street, S.W., Novi, Michigan, USA	Issue Date:	Aug. 23, 2018
		S/C No.	TXT264
		L/C No.	BL 170197

Dear Sir or Madam:

We are pleased to advice you that the following mentioned goods have been shipped out, full details were shown as follows:

Name of Commodity:	100% COTTON COLOUR WAVE T-SHIRT
Invoice Number:	PI170601
Bill of Loading Number:	GD57861609
Name of Vessel:	EAST WIND V. 23
Port of Loading:	SHEKOU PORT, SHENZHEN
Date of Shipment:	AUG. 23, 2018 SHEKOU, SHENZHEN
Port of Destination:	NEW YORK
Description of Goods:	100% COTTON COLOUR WAVE T-SHIRT MODEL NO.: TM111, TM222, TM333, TM444
Shipping Marks:	G.S.S/TXT264/NEW YORK/C/No. 1-300
Quantity/Packages:	TOTAL OF 6,000PCS PACKED TO 300 CARTONS
Total Value:	USD60,000.00 (SAY U.S. DOLLARS SIXTY THOUSAND ONLY)

Thank you for your patronage. We look forward to the pleasure of receiving your valuable repeat orders.

Sincerely yours,

李怡华 （LIYIHUA）（公司签章）

贸易实务中的装运通知书样例（见图10-1）：

```
                    VAS     AN TRADING COMPANY LIMITED
              UN        , SUNSHINE PLAZA 353, LOCKHART ROAD, WANCHAI, HONGKONG
                           TEL:008         0

                              ADVICE OF SHIPMENT

    TO: I     BANK BANGLADESH LIMIED , NEW MARKET BRANCH, DHAKA. BANGLADESH    DATE:15-JULY-2018

    (B          34)


    APPLICANT:          AMENT INDUSTRIES
              TH TARABO,NARAYANGONJ,BANGLADESH AND ISLAMI BANK BANGLADESH LTD.,
         N   RKET BRANCH,DHAKA,BANGLADESH.
    VAT REGISTRATION NUMBER 2105-
    DC NUMBER: 0   9160102    , DATE OF ISSUE:26JUN18
    DC ISSUING BANK:IBBLBDDH129
         WE INFORM THAT WE HAD ONE SHIPMENT(B/L NO.: C    U257521    )FROM SHANGHAI TO CHITTAGONG SEAPORT,
    THE COMMODITY IS 1SET.SECOND HAND PE EXTRUDER 70MM SCREW WITH 162 SPINDLES WINDER
    AND 1SET.SECOND HAND PE EXTRUDER 80MM SCREW WITH 162 SPINDLES WINDER,CFR AMOUNT:USD19,000.00.
    SHIPMENT DETAIL AS BELOW
    CONTAINER NUMBER:TC U8679391/40HQ &  O    9911875/40HQ
    1. :PORT OF LOADING:SHANGHAI, CHINA
    2. :PORT OF DISCHARGE:CHITTAGONG SEAPORT, BANGLADESH
    3. :PORT OF DESTINATION:CHITTAGONG SEAPORT, BANGLADESH
    4. :NAME OF OCEAN VESSEL :YM ORCHID 131W
    4. :ETD:14-JULY-2018
    5. :ETA:5-AUG-2018
    AIRWAY BILL NUMBER (DHL.): 566 3410 690
```

图10-1　装运通知书样例

（二）受益人证明的填制要点和实例（Instructions and Models of Beneficiary's Certificate）

1．公司名称和地址（Seller's Name & Address）

此栏填制出口公司的中英文名称和详细地址、电话号码、传真号码、电子邮箱等。

2．单据名称（Name of the Document）

按照来证的要求填制。

3．出证日期（Date of Issue）

按照实际日期填写，并与所证明内容的时间相匹配。

4．抬头（To）

可以填写买方公司名称，也可以笼统地写成"To whom it may concern"。

5．事由（Refer to）

一般填写合同号、发票号或信用证号。

6．证明文句（Body）

此项内容必须按信用证的要求填写。

7．受益人名称及签章（Name, Stamp and Signature）

情景导入中的受益人证明：

信用证中的单据要求：Beneficiary's certificate that one set of shipping documents has been faxed to applicant within one day after shipment.

```
科林国际贸易（香港）有限公司    (1)
KELIN INTERNATIONAL TRADING (HK) CO., LTD
RM2403, BLOCK A2, YIHE PLAZA, NO. 413, SHOUGOU ROAD,
GUANGZHOU, CHINA


BENEFICIARY'S CERTIFICATE    (2)

                                        DATE: AUG. 25, 2018   (3)
L/C NO.:BL 170197   (5)
INVOICE NO.: PI170601                        S/C NO.:  TXT264
To: GLOBE SOURCING SERVICE CO., LTD   (4)
    WE HEREBY CERTIFY THAT ONE COPY EACH OF INVOICE, N/N B/L HAVE BEEN FAXED TO BUYER WITHIN 3
DAYS AFTER SHIPMENT.    (6)

                                KELIN INTERNATIONAL TRADING (HK) CO., LTD
                                        GUANGZHOU, CHINA
                                            (SEAL)
                                          李怡华     (7)
```

贸易实务中的受益人证明样例（见图 10-2）：

```
                    VAS    AN TRADING COMPANY LIMITED
                        NSHINE PLAZA 353, LOCKHART ROAD, WANCHAI, HONGKONG
                            TEL:       1110

                            CERTIFICATE

        TO: I        BANGLADESH LIMIED , NEW MARKET BRANCH, DHAKA. BANGLADESH

        (BIN-1         )

        ATTN:         AMENT INDUSTRIES
        9        TARABO,NARAYANGONJ,BANGLADESH AND ISLAMI BANK BANGLADESH LTD.,
        NEW MARKET BRANCH,DHAKA,BANGLADESH.

        VAT REGISTRATION NUMBER 2
        DC NUMBER: 0889160010        , DATE OF ISSUE:26JUN18
        DC ISSUING BANK: IBBLBDDH129

                HEREBY, WE , VAS     AN TRADING COMPANY LIMITED CERTIFY THAT

        1. :WE DISPTACHED ONE SET OF NON-NEGOTIABLE DOCUMENTS INCLUDING DETAILED PACKING LIST TO APPLICANT WITHIN FIVE WORKING
           DAYS AFTER SHIPMENT BY COURIER, THE AIRWAY BILL NUMBER:
        2. :THE QUANTITY , QUALITY, CLASSIFICATION, DESCRIPTION , SPECIFICATION AND WEIGHT OF THE GOODS ARE FULLY  AS PER L/C TERMS
        3. :IMPORTERS NAME, ADDRESS AND TIN 7787-8627-2167 HAD BEEN INSCRIBED ON EACH PACKAGES CONTAINING THE IMPORTED GOODS.
        4. :COUNTRY OF ORIGIN HAD BEEN MENTIONED CLEARLY ON  THE FACE OF GOODS/PACKAGES OF GOODS/CONTAINER ETC.
        5. :THE ADVICE OF SHIPMENT TO ISSUING BANK BY FAX (FAX NO.880-2-8627045)  WITHIN 5 WORKING DAYS AFTER SHIPMENT.
        6. :THE ADVICE OF INSURANCE TO PROVATI INSURANCE CO. LTD. BY FAX (FAX NO.:880-2-9564455) WITHIN 5 WORKING
                                                            For and on behalf of
                                                            Authorized Signature(s)
```

图10-2 受益人证明样例

（三）船公司证明的填制要点和实例（Instructions and Models of Carrier's Certificate）

1. 单据名称（Name of the Document）
2. 出证地点和时间（Place and Date of Issue）

3．抬头（To）
4．发票与相关单据号码（Invoice No., S/C No., L/C No.）
5．证明内容（Content）
6．公司名称及负责人签名（Authority's Seal and Representative's Signature）

情景导入中的船公司证明：

CERTIFICATE   (1)

DATE: AUG. 27, 2018   (2)

INVOICE NO.: PI170601   (4)
B/L NO.: GD57861609
VESSEL NAME: EAST WIND V. 23

TO WHOM IT MAY CONCERN: (3)
　　WE HEREBY CERTIFY THAT THE CARRYING VESSEL IS NOT A BLACK LISTED SHIP NOR OF ISRAELI NATIONALITY AND SHE IS NOT SCHEDULED TO CALL AT ANY ISRAELI PORTS.   (5)

SINOTRANS SOUTH CHINA CO., LTD

李 三   (6)

贸易实务中的船公司证明样例（见图10-3）：

CERTIFICATE

VSL: YM ORCHID 131W
B/L: OOLU257521
Container/SEAL:
TCL 579391/OOLEEC4814
OOL 1875/OOLEEC6791
ETD:2018-7-15

THIS SHIPMENT /TRANSSHIPMENT OF GOODS DESTINED FOR BANGLADESH NOT BY ISREALI FLAG VESSEL.
DC NO.:08891601   DATE OF ISSUE:26JUN18
APPLICANT:/   AMENT INDUSTRIES
　　　　　　RA NORTH TARABO,NARAYANGONJ,BANGLADESH.
VAT NUMBER:2105-1008-610
ISSUING BANK: BANGLADESH LIMITED NEW MARKET BRANCH DOZA MANSION,23,MIRPUR ROAD,DHAKA,BANGLADESH(BIN:-19011032134)

Signed for the Carrier
Orient Overseas Container Line
2018-7-15

图10-3　船公司证明样例

实操训练（Skill Training）

一、单项选择题

1. 近年来进口贸易的结算方式日益呈现多样化，但最常用的还是（　　）。
   A. 信用证方式和进口代收
   B. 货到付款和进口代收
   C. 信用证方式和预付货款
   D. 信用证方式和货到付款

2. 对于（　　）术语，装运通知书具有特别意义。
   A. CIP
   B. CIF
   C. DDP
   D. CFR

3. 原产国的基本含义是出口产品的（　　）。
   A. 启运国
   B. 制造国
   C. 出口国
   D. 消费国

4. GSP Form A 是一种（　　）。
   A. 品质证明书
   B. 普惠制原产地证明书
   C. 重量证明书
   D. 动植物检疫证明书

5. 关于结汇单证，以下说法正确的是（　　）。
   A. 结汇单证是指国际贸易中，为解决货币收付问题所使用的单据、证明和文件
   B. 结汇单证就是商业单证，以商业发票、包装单据、运输单据、保险单等为主
   C. 仅指国家外汇管理需要的单证，主要指出口收汇核销单
   D. 结汇单证就是金融单证，主要指汇票

6. 出口商应在（　　）通过传真、邮寄等方式，向进口商发出装运通知书。
   A. 装运前
   B. 装船完毕
   C. 交单后
   D. 收款后

7. 信用证规定贸易术语为 CIF New York，海洋运输，提单上运费栏目应作（　　）表示。
   A. Freight Prepaid
   B. Freight Prepayable
   C. Freight Collect
   D. Freight to be Prepaid

案例（习题 8~10）：

某外贸企业出口货物一批，重量为 1 000 吨，价格为每吨 65 美元（CIF Rotterdam），国外买方通过开证行按时开来信用证，该证规定：总金额不得超过 65 000 美元，有效期为 7 月 31 日。证内注明按《UCP600》办理。该外贸企业于 7 月 4 日将货物装船完毕，取得提单，签发日期为 7 月 4 日。

8. 该外贸企业最迟应在（　　）将单据送交银行议付。
   A. 7 月 4 日
   B. 7 月 14 日
   C. 7 月 25 日
   D. 7 月 31 日

9. 本批货物最多能交（　　）吨。
   A. 1 100
   B. 1 075
   C. 1 050
   D. 1 000

10. 本批货物最少需交（　　）吨。
    A. 1 000
    B. 975
    C. 950
    D. 900

二、多选题

1. 填制受益人证明时，必须注意（　　）。
   A. 单据名称和出具人签章符合信用证要求
   B. 单据内容应符合信用证要求，并与其他单据相关内容不矛盾

C. 应该至少提供一份正本
D. 应注明出单日期

2. 信用证项下，只要同时符合下述（　　）条件，对货物数量的容差允许有 5%的增减幅度。
A. 信用证未规定货物数量不得增减
B. 信用证已有条款规定数量增减幅度
C. 支取金额不超过信用证金额
D. 货物数量不是按包装单位或个数计数的，如长度（米、码）；体积（立方米）；容量（升、加仑）；重量（吨、磅）等

3. 以下单据中，对发票起补充作用的有（　　）。
A. 装箱单　　　B. 运输单据　　　C. 重量单　　　D. 保险单

4. 海运提单中对于货物描述说法正确的是（　　）。
A. 和信用证对于货物的描述不抵触
B. 必须要使用货物的全称
C. 必须要和信用证中对于货物的描述完全一致
D. 可以使用货物的统称

5. 信用证做出的如下规定中，属于"非单据条件"的有（　　）。
A. 载货船舶的船龄不超过 15 年
B. 载货船舶挂巴拿马国旗
C. 装船后立即通知申请人装货细节并提交传真副本
D. 提供原产地证明书

三、判断题

1. 有一笔托收出口交易，价格条件是 CFR TOKYO，合同规定出口商装运后须向进口商发送装运通知书。因为是采用托收方式收款，对此装运通知的发送日期没有限制。（　　）

2. 船公司证明的签署需与提单中承运人或其代理人的签署相一致。（　　）

3. 贸易术语的变化只涉及买卖双方费用的划分，不涉及风险划分。（　　）

4. 汇付是付款人主动通过银行或其他途径将款项交收款人的一种支付方式，所以属于商业信用，而托收通常称为银行托收，因而它属于银行信用。（　　）

5. 一张汇票的收款人写成"Pay to John Stone only"或者"Pay to order"，都可以经过背书转让。（　　）

四、单据的填制

1. 根据下列资料填制受益人证明
Doc. Credit No.: 63211020049
Sales Contract No.: F09LCB0912
Applicant: FASHION FORCE CO., LTD
P.O.BOX 8935 NEW TERMINAL, ALTA, VISTA OTTAWA, CANADA
Beneficiary: NANJING TANG TEXTILE GARMENT CO., LTD.
HUARONG MANSION RM2901 NO.85 GUANJIAQIAO,
NANJING 210005, CHINA

Documents Required:
……
+BENEFICIARY'S LETTER STATING THAT ORIGINAL CERTIFICATE OF ORIGIN FORM A, ORIGINAL EXPORT LICENCE, COPY OF COMMERCIAL INVOICE, DETAILED PACKING LISTS AND A COPY OF BILL OF LADING WERE SENT DIRECTLY TO APPLICANT BY COURIER WITHIN 5 DAYS AFTER SHIPMENT. THE RELATIVE COURIER RECEIPT IS ALSO REQUIRED FOR PRESENTATION.

DATE OF SHIPMENT: OCT. 30, 2018

2. 根据下列资料填制装运通知书
……

Doc. Credit Number	*20:	M0756510NS0023000
Date of Issue	31C:	SEPT.08, 2018
Expiry	*31D:	DATE NOV.30, 2018 PLACE CHINA
Applicant	*50:	CHANG JI TRADING CO.,
		305, SEONG CHANG BLDG.,
		2972 SEOKCHON DONG, SEOUL, KOREA
Beneficiary	*59:	HUAYUE MEDICINE & HEALTH PRODUCTS IMP. AND EXP. CORP.
		196 TIANHE ROAD, GUANGZHOU, CHINA
Amount	*32B:	Currency USD Amount 45,600.00

……

Partial Shipments	43P:	ALLOWED
Transshipment	43T:	PROHIBITED
Loading in Charge	44A:	CHINA PORT
For Transport to…	44B:	INCHON, KOREA
Latest Date of Ship.	44C:	NOV. 15, 2018
Descript. of Goods	45A:	

CINNAMON WHOLE 8.64M/T @ USD2,250.00/MT AS PER INDENT NO.57152
CINNAMON BROKEN 12 M/T @ USD2,180.00/MT AS PER INDENT NO.57151
CFR INCHON

Additional Cond.   47A:

*SHIPPING MARK   ‾‾CHANGJI‾‾‾
                    INCHON

SHOULD BE INDICATED ON BOTH SIDES OF PACKING CARTONS.

*BENEFICIARY'S FAX SENT TO APPLICANT WITHIN 48 HOURS AFTER SHIPMENT INDICATING CONTRACT NO., L/C NO., GOODS NAME, QUANTITY, INVOICE VALUE, VESSEL'S NAME, LOADING PORT, SHIPPING DATE AND ETA. COPY OF WHICH SHOULD BE PRESENTED AS ONE OF THE NEGOTIATION DOC.

Some useful information:

Cinnamon whole: 216 cartons of 40kgs net each, Gross Weight: 42.5KGS/CTN
Cinnamon broken: 300 cartons of 40kgs net each, Gross Weight: 42.5KGS/CTN
M: 45CM×30CM×20CM/Carton

Port of Loading: Yantian   Port of Discharge: Inchon
S.S. : CHANGYUN V. 356   B/L Date: Nov. 8, 2018
Sales Confirmation No. 05MHS14655 ETA: ×××

附　录

综合实训一　CIF 信用证项下整套单据的填制

请根据提供的信用证的内容制作信用证指定的议付单证，包括：商业发票、装箱单、海运提单、普惠制产地证、保险单、汇票。要求格式清楚、内容完整。

1. 信用证

LETTER OF CREDIT

Sequence of Total	27:	1 / 1
Form of Doc. Credit	40A:	NON-TRANSFERABLE
Doc. Credit Number	20:	TDA-HE12
Date of Issue	31C:	20180405
Applicable Rules	40E:	UCP LATEST VERSION
Expiry	31D:	DATE 20180615 PLACE CHINA
Applicant Bank	51D:	BANK OF SCOTLAND
Applicant	50:	ALICE TRADING CO., LTD
		PO BOX 23581, EDINBURGH, SCOTLAND
Beneficiary	59:	GRACY COSMETIC TRADING CO., LTD
		356 ZHONGSHAN ROAD, NANJING, CHINA
Amount	32B:	CURRENCY USD AMOUNT 17,400,00
Available with/by	41D:	BANK OF CHINA BY NEGOTIATION
Drafts at ...	42C:	DRAFTS AT SIGHT FOR FULL INVOICE VALUE
Drawee	42D:	BANK OF SCOTLAND
Partial Shipments	43P:	ALLOWED
Transshipment	43T:	ALLOWED
Loading in Charge	44A:	NANJING PORT
For Transport to ...	44B:	EDINBURGH
Latest Date of Ship.	44C:	20180531
Descript. of Goods	45A:	LADIES GARMENTS AS PER S/C NO. NJL435
		PACKING: 10PCS/CTN
		ART NO.　　　　　QUANTITY　　UNIT PRICE
		STYLE NO. LUX1201　2,000 PCS　USD 4.5
		STYLE NO. ROM1001　2,000 PCS　USD 4.2
		CIF EDINBURGH
		SHIPPING MARK: GRACY/EDINBURGH/NO, 2-300
Docs. Required	46A:	*3/3 SET OF ORIGINAL CLEAN ON BOARD OCEAN BILLS OF LADING MADE OUT TO ORDER OF SHIPPER AND BLANK ENDORSED AND MARKED "FREIGHT PREPAID" NOTIFY APPLICANT (WITH FULL NAME AND ADDRESS).
		*ORIGINAL SIGNED COMMERCIAL INVOICE IN 5 FOLDS.
		*INSURANCE POLICY OR CERTIFICATE IN 2 FOLDS ENDORSED IN BLANK, FOR 110 PCT OF THE INVOICE VALUE COVERING THE INSTITUTE CARGO CLAUSES (A), THE INSTITUTE WAR CLAUSES, INSURANCE CLAIMS TO BE PAYABLE IN JAPAN IN THE CURRENCY OF THE DRAFTS.
		*CERTIFICATE OF ORIGIN GSP FORM A IN 1 ORIGINAL AND 1 COPY.
		*PACKING LIST IN 5 FOLDS.

Additional Cond.	47A:	1. T.T. REIMBURSEMENT IS PROHIBITED
		2. THE GOODS TO BE PACKED IN EXPORT STRONG COLORED CARTONS.
Charges	71B:	ALL BANKING CHARGES OUTSIDE JAPAN INCLUDING REIMBURSEMENT COMMISSION, ARE FOR ACCOUNT OF BENEFICIARY.
Period for Presentation	48:	DOCUMENTS TO BE PRESENTED WITHIN 10 DAYS AFTER THE DATE OF SHIPMENT, BUT WITHIN THE VALIDITY OF THE CREDIT.
Confirmation	49:	WITHOUT
Instructions to Bank	78:	THE NEGOTIATION BANK MUST FORWARD THE DRAFTS AND ALL DOCUMENTS BY REGISTERED AIRMAIL DIRECT TO U.S. IN TWO CONSECUTIVE LOTS, UPON RECEIPT OF THE DRAFTS AND DOCUMENTS IN ORDER, WE WILL REMIT THE PROCEEDS AS INSTRUCTED BY THE NEGOTIATING BANK.

2．商品补充资料

包装：10PCS PER CARTON
单位毛重：15.00KGS/CTN
单位净重：13.50KGS/CTN
单位尺码：60CM×40CM×50CM/CTN
发票号码：CSA345，汇票号同发票号
发票日期：2018-4-20
船名：DAPENG VI666
提单号码：DP227526
提单日期：2018-5-15
汇票出票日期：2018-5-20
产地证日期地点：NANJING APR. 20, 2018
卖方：歌力思美妆贸易有限公司
GRACY COSMETIC TRADING CO., LTD.
356 ZHONGSHAN ROAD, NANJING, CHINA
TEL:025-8887788 025-8887789 FAX:567834

综合实训二 CFR 信用证项下整套单据的填制

请根据信用证及所提供的资料,制作商业发票、装箱单、原产地证书、汇票和装运通知书,要求格式清楚、内容完整。

1. 信用证

LETTER OF CREDIT

Sequence of Total	27:	1 / 1
Form of Doc. Credit	40A:	NON-TRANSFERABLE
Doc. Credit Number	20:	372623
Date of Issue	31C:	180514
Applicable Rules	40E:	UCP LATEST VERSION
Expiry	31D:	DATE 180705 PLACE LINZ
Applicant	50:	BELLAFLORA GARTENCENTER GESELLSCHAFT M.B.H. FRANZOSENH-AUSWEG 50 A-2040 LINZ
Beneficiary	59:	DALIAN ARTS & CRAFTS IMPORT & EXPORT CORP NO. 23 FUGUI STR. DALIAN, CHINA
Amount	32B:	CURRENCY USD AMOUNT 22,509.40
Pos. /Neg. Tol. (%)	39A:	10/10
Available with/by	41D:	OBKLAT2L *BANK FUER OBEROEATERREICH UND *SALZBURG (OBERBANK) *LINZ BY NEGOTIATION
Partial Shipments	43P:	ALLOWED
Transshipment	43T:	ALLOWED
Port of Loading	44E:	CHINA PORT
Port of Discharge	44F:	VIENNA
Latest Date of Ship.	44C:	180620
Descript. of Goods	45A:	CHRISTMAS GIFTS AS PER SALES CONFIRMATION NO. 205001 OF MAY. 9TH 2018 CFR VIENNA
Documents Required	46A:	1. COMMERCIAL INVOICE, 5 FOLDS, ALL DULY SIGNED CERTIFYING THAT THE GOODS HAVE BEEN PACKED AND MARKED SEPARATELY FOR EACH BELLAFLORA BRANCH. 2. FULL SET OF CLEAN ON BOARD ORIGINAL MARINE BILL OF LADING, MADE OUT TO ORDER, BLANK ENDORSED NOTIFY THE APPLICANT. 3. CERTIFICATE OF P. R. CHINA ORIGIN GSP FORM A. ISSUED AND MANUALLY SIGNED BY AN AUTHORITY ALSO MANUALLY SIGNED BY EXPORTER, BEARING A REFERENCE NUMBER AND SHOWING AUSTRIA AS IMPORTING COUNTRY. 4. PACKING LIST, 5 FOLDS. 5. SHIPPING ADVICE
Additional Cond.	47A:	UPON RECEIPT OF DOCUMENTS STRICTLY COMPLYING WITH CREDIT TERM, WE SHALL REMIT FUNDS.
Charges	71B:	BANKING CHARGES, EXCEPT CHARGES OF ISSUING BANK, ARE FOR ACCOUNT OF BENEFICIARY. IF DOCUMENTS ARE PRESENTED WITH DISCREPANCY, WE SHALL DEDUCT COUNTER VALUE OF USD 50.00
Period for Presentation	48:	21 DAYS
Confirmation	49:	WITHOUT
Send. to Rec. Info.	72:	L/C IS SUBJECT TO UCP DC ICC IN USE PLEASE ADVISE URGENTLY TO BEN.

2. 补充资料

合同号：No. 205001　　　　　　合同日期：2018-05-09
发票号码：2018AC031　　　　　发票日期：2018-06-02
信用证如未规定唛头，可自行填制或填写"N/M"。
提单号：COSCO1806088　　　　提单日期：2018-06-18
启运港：大连　　　　　　　　　目的港：维也纳
船名航次：Hongyuan, V. 023
商品编码：95051000.10
商品名称、规格、数量、价格如下：

品名及规格 NAME OF COMMODITY & SPECIFICATION	单价 UNIT PRICE	数量 QUAN	金额及术语 AMOUNT & PRICE TERMS
CHRISTMAS GIFTS	CFR VIENNA	(SETS)	CFR VIENNA
AG-1355	USD 0.66	768	USD 506.88
AG-1409A	0.46	1,600	736.00
AG-1409B	1.01	600	606.00
AG-1429	0.78	768	599.04
AG-1434	0.50	1,600	800.00
AG-1451	0.50	600	300.00
AG-1455	0.52	672	349.44
AG-1473	0.76	420	319.20
AG-1476	0.90	382	343.80
AG-1410	0.95	240	228.00
AG-1501	0.52	900	468.00
AG-1502	0.68	648	440.64
AG-1503	0.58	840	487.20
AG-1505	0.52	960	499.20
PACKAGE: 200SETS TO A CARTON			
DL- (EACH 400 DOZ)		(DOZ)	
1556B, 1568B, 1571B, 1603B, 1637B,	2.15	4,000	8,600.00
1679B, 1691B, 1768B, 1770B, 1771B	4.10	400	1,640.00
DL-1734B	3.96	800	3,168.00
(EACH 400 DOZ) DL-1846B, DL-1889B	0.54	750 PCS	405.00
PACKAGE: 200DOZ TO A CARTON	1.54	750 PCS	1,155.00
AM-648	1.43	600 PCS	858.00
AM-3			
C-32			
PACKAGE: 100PCS TO A CARTON			
		TOTAL	USD 22,509.40

数量及总值均允许增减 _____ %。
With ___10___ percent more or less both in the amount and quantity of the S/C allowed.
总金额：
Total Value：U.S. DOLLARS TWENTY TWO THOUSAND FIVE HUNDRED AND NINE POINT FORTY.

包装：　　　　　　　　　　　　　　纸箱规格：
Packing：TOTAL IN 102 CARTONS,　CARTON SIZE：（45cm×60cm×45cm）
毛重　　　　　　　　　　　　　　　净重
Gross weight: 24kgs　　　　　　　　Net weight: 23kgs

综合实训三　CIF 信用证项下整套单据的填制（全英文）

Make out the relevant documents with the following information from the L/C.

1. Letter of Credit

LETTER OF CREDIT

From:		STANDARD AND CHARTERED BANK LTD. COPENHAGEN
To:		BANK OF CHINA, TAIYUAN BRANCH
Sequence of Total	27:	1 / 1
Form of Doc. Credit	40A:	NON-TRANSFERABLE
Doc. Credit Number	20:	002/0503668
Date of Issue	31C:	180320
Applicable Rules	40E:	UCP LATEST VERSION
Expiry	31D:	DATE 180615 PLACE CHINA
Applicant	50:	DE TUINKRAMER B.V.
Beneficiary	59:	CHINA NATIONAL ARTS & CRAFTS CORPORATION TAIYUAN BRANCH TAIYUAN FOREIGN TRADE BUILDING 85-99, ZHONGSHAN ROAD 7, TAIYUAN, CHINA
Amount	32B:	CURRENCY USD AMOUNT 16,172.10
Available with/by	41D:	ANY BANK FOR NEGOTIATION
Draft at …	42C:	DRAFTS AT 30 DAYS SIGHT FOR FULL INVOICE VALUE
Drawee	42A:	DONTUSU COMMERCIAL BANK, HONG KONG
Partial Shipments	43P:	NOT ALLOWED
Transshipment	43T:	ALLOWED
Loading in Charge	44A:	QINGDAO, CHINA
For Transport to …	44B:	ROTTERDAM
Latest Date of Ship.	44C:	180530
Descript. of Goods	45A:	5134 UNITS WIRE PRODUCTS CIF ROTTERDAM USD 3.15 PER UNIT AS PER CONTRACT NO. 2018KE1985
Documents Required	46A:	*SIGNED COMMERCIAL INVOICE IN FIVE COPIES CERTIFYING THAT GOODS ARE AS PER INDENT NO. ABC567 OF 2018.02,25 QUOTING L/C NO. *FULL SET OF CLEAN OCEAN BILL OF LADING MADE OUT TO OUR ORDER QUOTING L/C NO. AND NOTIFY BUYER, MARKED FREIGHT PAID. *PACKING LIST IN FIVE COPIES * CERTIFICATE OF ORIGIN *INSURANCE POLICY COVERING ALL RISKS AND WAR RISK AND SRCC AS PER CIC FOR 110 PCT OF INVOICE VALUE, CLAIMS, IF ANY, PAYABLE AT THE PORT OF DESTINATION IN CURRENCY OF DRAFT. *BENEFICIARY'S DECLARATION DECLARING THAT SHIPPING MARK "DE TUINKRAMER B.V. / ROTTERDAM / C/NOS …" WILL BE MARKED ON BOTH SIDES OF EACH OF THE CASES, AND THIS L/C NO. WILL BE MENTIONED ON ALL DOCUMENTS PRESENTED FOR NEGOTIATION.

2. Some messages from the Shipping Order

Shipping Mark:　　DE TUINKRAMER B.V.
　　　　　　　　　ROTTERDAM
　　　　　　　　　C/NOS. 1—171

Port of Loading: QINGDAO　　　　Port of Discharge: ROTTERDAM

Port of Transshipment: HONG KONG
Invoice No. 173324009　　　　　　Date: May 18, 2018
Goods packed in wooden cases, 171 CASES TOTAL
G.W.: 97KG/CASE　　　N.W.: 94KG/CASE　　　M.: 50CM×45CM×45CM/CASE
Date of Shipment: MAY 20, 2018　　　　B/L No. KJ0293485
Container No. 467934587M48　　(20'×1)
Name of Vessel: QINGYANG V. 126/VINONA
H.S.Code/Tariff No.: 4602.1010
Freight: USD2,130/FCL　　　　　　Insurance Fee: USD347.10
Insurance Policy No.: DR57513567865365　　Insurance Policy Date：MAY 20, 2018

综合实训四　托收项下全套出口单据的填制

依据《托收统一规则》(国际商会第 522 号出版物)第二条的规定：托收(Collection)是指由接到委托指示的银行处理金融单据和/或商业单据以便取得承兑或付款，或凭承兑或付款交出商业单据，或凭其他条件交出单据。

一、托收流程

1．即期付款交单流程

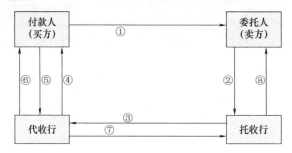

① 买卖双方签订贸易合同。

② 卖方按照合同规定装运货物，填写托收申请书，开立即期汇票，连同货运单据交托收行，委托其代收货款；或不开立汇票，仅将货运单据交给托收行，委托其代收货款。

③ 托收行根据托收申请书填制托收委托书，连同汇票和货运单据交进口地代收行委托其代收货款。

④ 代收行按托收委托书的指示向买方提示跟单汇票和货运单据。

⑤ 买方见票，审单无误后立即付款。

⑥ 代收行交单。

⑦ 代收行办理货款的转账手续，并通知托收行已收妥货款。

⑧ 托收行向卖方交款。

2．远期付款交单流程

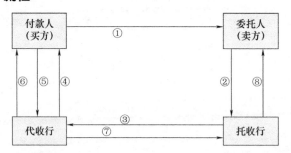

① 买卖双方签订贸易合同。

② 卖方按照合同规定装运货物，填写托收申请书，开立远期汇票，连同货运单据交托收行，委托其代收货款。

③ 托收行根据托收申请书填制托收委托书，连同汇票和货运单据交进口地代收行委托其代收货款。

④ 代收行按托收委托书的指示向买方提示跟单汇票和货运单据。买方审单无误后，在汇票上做出承兑，代收行收回汇票与单据。

⑤ 买方到期付款。

⑥ 代收行交单。

⑦ 代收行办理货款的转账手续，并通知托收行已收妥货款。

⑧ 托收行向卖方交款。

3．承兑交单流程

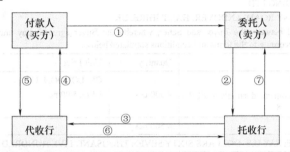

① 买卖双方签订贸易合同。

② 卖方按照合同规定装运货物，填写托收申请书，开立远期汇票，连同货运单据交托收行，委托其代收货款。

③ 托收行根据托收申请书填制托收委托书，连同汇票和货运单据交进口地代收行委托其代收货款。

④ 代收行按托收委托书的指示向买方提示跟单汇票和货运单据。买方审单无误后，在汇票上做出承兑，代收行收回汇票，将货运单据交给买方。

⑤ 买方凭货运单据办理提货事项，到期后支付货款。

⑥ 代收行办理货款的转账手续，并通知托收行已收妥货款。

⑦ 托收行向卖方交款。

二、托收方式下填制全套单据

1．需提交的单据

① 托收委托书/托收申请书。

② 常用结汇单据。

③ 报关单据。

2．填制要点

① 在填写托收委托书/托收申请书时，代收行（Collecting Bank）一栏内最好填写国外进口商的开户银行的名称和地址，这样有利于国外银行直接向付款方递交单据，有利于早收到钱。

② 在填制汇票的时候要注意和信用证项下的汇票填制方法的区别。

③ 托收项下的提单要做成指示性抬头。

3．制单训练

2018 年 3 月 15 日，科林国际贸易（香港）有限公司与英国太平洋贸易有限公司签订了一份全棉女式夹克出口的销售合同。本次采用托收方式收款。请依据合同填制商业发票、装箱单、提单、原产地证书、保险单和汇票。合同内容如下：

SALES CONTRACT

NO.: SJZHY0739　　　　　　　　　　　　　　　　　　　DATE: MAR. 15, 2018

THE SELLER: 科林国际贸易（香港）有限公司
　　　　　　　KELIN INTERNATIONAL TRADING (HK) CO., LTD
　　　　　　　RM2403, BLOCK A2, YIHE PLAZA, NO. 413, GUANGZHOU, CHINA

THE BUYER: PACIFIC TRADING LTD
　　　　　　UNIT 5, ALBANY ROAD, ANDOVER, HAMPSHIRE, UK

This Contract is made by and between the Buyer and Seller, whereby the Buyer agree to buy and the Seller agree to sell the under-mentioned commodity according to the terms and conditions stipulated below:

Commodity & Specification	Quantity	Unit Price	Amount
Ladies Jacket（6204320090） 100% COTTON, As per the confirmed sample of FEB. 10, 2018 and Order No. SKY888	4,500 pcs	CIF LONDON, U.K. USD15.00/pc	USD 67,500.00
TOTAL	4,500 pcs		USD 67,500.00

TOTAL CONTRACT VALUE: SAY U.S. DOLLARS SIXTY SEVEN THOUSAND FIVE HUNDRED ONLY.

Size/color assortment　　　　　　**Unit: piece**

Size	S	M	L	XL	Total
White	250	500	1,000	500	2,250
Red	250	500	1,000	500	2,250
Total	500	1,000	2,000	1,000	4,500

More or less 5% of the quantity and the amount are allowed.

PACKING: 10 pieces of ladies jackets are packed in one export standard carton, solid color and solid size in the same carton.
MARKS: Shipping mark includes PT, S/C no., port of destination and carton no.
Side mark must show the color, the size of carton and pieces per carton.

TIME OF SHIPMENT:
Within 60 days after this Contract.

PORT OF LOADING AND DESTINATION:
From HUANGPU, GUANGZHOU, CHINA to LONDON, U.K.
Transshipment is allowed, and partial shipment is prohibited.

INSURANCE: To be effected by the seller for 110% of invoice value covering All Risks as per CIC of PICC.

TERMS OF PAYMENT: By D/P after 30 days sight.

DOCUMENTS:
+ Signed Commercial Invoice in triplicate.
+ Full set of clean on board ocean Bill of Lading marked "freight prepaid" made out to order of shipper blank endorsed notifying the applicant.
+ Insurance Policy in duplicate endorsed in blank.
+ Packing List in triplicate.
+ Certificate of Origin certified by Chamber of Commerce or CCPIT.

INSPECTION:
The certificate of Quality issued by China Customs shall be taken as the basis of delivery.

CLAIMS:
In case discrepancy on the quality or quantity (weight) of the goods is found by the buyer, after arrival of the goods at the port of destination, the buyer may, within 30 days and 15 days respectively after arrival of the goods at the port of destination, lodge with the seller a claim which should be supported by an Inspection Certificate issued by a public surveyor approved by the seller. The seller shall, on the merits of the claim, either make good the loss sustained by the buyer or reject their claim, it being agreed that the seller shall not be held responsible for any loss or losses due to natural cause failing within the responsibility of Ship-owners of the Underwriters. The seller shall reply to the buyer within 30 days after receipt of the claim.

LATE DELIVERY AND PENALTY:
In case of late delivery, the Buyer shall have the right to cancel this contract, reject the goods and lodge a claim against the Seller. Except for Force Majeure, if late delivery occurs, the Seller must pay a penalty, and the Buyer shall have the right to lodge a claim against the Seller. The rate of penalty is charged at 0.5% for every 7 days, odd days less than 7 days should be counted as 7 days. The total penalty amount will not exceed 5% of the shipment value. The penalty shall be deducted by the paying bank or the Buyer from the payment.

FORCE MAJEURE:
The seller shall not be held responsible if they, owing to Force Majeure cause or causes, fail to make delivery within the time stipulated in the Contract or cannot deliver the goods. However, in such a case, the seller shall inform the buyer immediately by cable and if it is requested by the buyer, the seller shall also deliver to buyer by registered letter, a certificate attesting the existence of such a cause or causes.

ARBITRATION:
All disputes in connection with this contract or the execution thereof shall be settled amicably by negotiation. In case no settlement can be reached, the case shall then be submitted to the China International Economic Trade Arbitration Commission for settlement by arbitration in accordance with the Commission's arbitration rules. The award rendered by the commission shall be final and binding on both parties. The fees for arbitration shall be borne by the losing party unless otherwise awarded.

This contract is made in two original copies and becomes valid after signature, one copy to be held by each party.

Signed by:

THE SELLER:　　　　　　　　　　　　　　　　　　　　**THE BUYER:**
Kelin International Trading (HK) Co., Ltd　　　　　　　　　Pacific Trading Ltd

刘燕　　　　　　　　　　　　　　　　　　　　　　　　*Johnson Black*

补充资料：

商业发票号码：PIT160789

发票日期：May 1, 2018

唛头：P.T./SJZHY0739/LONDON/CT.NO.1-UP

商品编码：6204320090

托收银行：BANK OF CHINA

提单号码：EN356789000

船名与航次:HUALIN STEAMER　V.N. 221

装运期：MAY, 10, 2018

可否分批：NOT ALLOWED

可否转运：ALLOWED

收货人：Pacific Trading Ltd

Unit 5, Albany Road, Andover, Hampshire, UK

保险单号：GD06991705399　　　保险单日期：MAY, 7, 2018

商品包装详情：Packed in export standard carton，450 cartons in total

毛重：17 千克/箱　　净重：15 千克/箱　　体积：0.07 立方米/箱

参 考 文 献

[1] 许德金. 单证[M]. 北京：首都经济贸易大学出版社，2010.
[2] 田运银. 国际贸易单证精讲[M]. 北京：中国海关出版社，2010.
[3] 王胜华. 国际商务单证操作实训教程[M]. 重庆：重庆大学出版社，2008.
[4] 王佳. 外贸单证制作实操教程[M]. 上海：上海财经大学出版社，2009.
[5] 童宏祥. 外贸单证实务[M]. 3版. 上海：上海财经大学出版社，2016.
[6] 夏新燕，刘迎春. 国际商务单证实务[M]. 北京：北京理工大学出版社，2010.
[7] 孔灵灵，曲继武. 外贸单证实战技巧[M]. 广州：广东经济出版社，2010.
[8] 谢桂梅. 国际贸易实务：英文版[M]. 北京：清华大学出版社，2010.
[9] 田运银. 国际贸易实务精讲[M]. 北京：中国海关出版社，2007.
[10] 刘杰英. 世纪商务英语：函电与单证[M]. 4版. 大连：大连理工大学出版社，2014.
[11] Mark Ellis，Christine Johnson. 商务英语教学[M]. 上海：上海外语教育出版社，2002.
[12] 吴百福，徐小薇，聂清. 进出口贸易实务教程[M]. 7版. 上海：格致出版社，上海人民出版社，2015.
[13] 严新党，刘红. 1+1实操商务英语教程：函电[M]. 北京：首都经济贸易大学出版社，2009.
[14] 王俐俐. 外贸英语函电与单证[M]. 北京：机械工业出版社，2010.